General Editors: *Malcolm Bradbury and David Palmer*

For a long time, the postwar English novel has been
associated with 'realism' and 'anger'. It has been viewed
as a fiction out of touch with contemporary
developments in the novel in other countries. But the
English novel has changed radically during the 1960s
and 1970s, though little has been written about the shift
in manner and mood. This volume emphasizes the
recent achievements of the contemporary English novel:
its technical experiments, its relation to modern fiction
in other countries, and its distinctive attempts to
preserve a measure of realism in a more experimental
climate.

Writers considered include John Fowles, Muriel Spark,
Iris Murdoch, Doris Lessing, B. S. Johnson, Alan
Burns, Angus Wilson, Anthony Burgess, Beryl
Bainbridge, David Caute, Margaret Drabble and J. G.
Farrell.

Mr and Mrs Clark and Percy by David Hockney is
reproduced by permission of the Knoedler Galley and
the Tate Gallery, London.

ISBN 0-8419-0571-1

Holmes & Meier Publishers, Inc.
IUB Building
30 Irving Place
New York, N.Y. 10003

STRATFORD-UPON-AVON STUDIES 18

General Editors

MALCOLM BRADBURY
& DAVID PALMER

Also available in this series

3 EARLY SHAKESPEARE

5 HAMLET

6 RESTORATION THEATRE

7 AMERICAN POETRY

8 LATER SHAKESPEARE

9 ELIZABETHAN THEATRE

Under the General Editorship of Malcolm Bradbury and David Palmer

11 METAPHYSICAL POETRY

12 CONTEMPORARY CRITICISM

13 THE AMERICAN NOVEL AND THE NINETEEN TWENTIES

15 VICTORIAN POETRY

16 MEDIEVAL DRAMA

17 DECADENCE AND THE 1890S

STRATFORD-UPON-AVON STUDIES 18

THE CONTEMPORARY ENGLISH NOVEL

HOLMES & MEIER PUBLISHERS, INC.
New York

© EDWARD ARNOLD (PUBLISHERS) LTD 1979

First published in the
United States of America 1980 by
HOLMES & MEIER PUBLISHERS, INC.
30 Irving Place, New York
N.Y. 10003

Library of Congress Cataloging Publication Data
Main entry under title
The Contemporary English Novel.
(Stratford-upon-Avon Studies; 18)
Bibliography: P.
Includes Index.
 1. English Fiction—20th Century—History and
Criticism—Addresses, Essays, Lectures.
I. Bradbury, Malcolm, 1932–   II. Palmer, David John.
III. Series.
PR883.C6 1979   823′.03   79-20447

ISBN 0-8419-0570-3 (Cloth)
ISBN 0-8419-0571-1 (Paper)

Printed in Great Britain

Contents

		PAGE
	Preface	7
I	People in Paper Houses: Attitudes to 'Realism' and 'Experiment' in English Postwar Fiction A. S. BYATT	19
II	Fictions of History BERNARD BERGONZI	43
III	Female Fictions: The Women Novelists LORNA SAGE	67
IV	Beckett, Lowry and the Anti-Novel RONALD BINNS	89
V	Reflections on 'Fictionality' N. H. REEVE	113
VI	The Novel Interrogates Itself: Parody as Self-Consciousness In Contemporary English Fiction ROBERT BURDEN	133
VII	'Angels Dining at the Ritz': The Faith and Fiction of Muriel Spark RUTH WHITTAKER	157
VIII	Putting in the Person: Character and Abstraction in Current Writing and Painting MALCOLM BRADBURY	181
	INDEX	211

Preface

THE ENGLISH NOVEL in the period since the Second World War—a point at which we may see distinct signs of a break or a change in the fictional tradition—has not generally received a very enthusiastic press. The writing of this period has been reported, by those who have considered it, as a late, lowered and unambitious phase in the long history of the English novel. When critics write about 'modern English fiction', they write usually about a season of achievement which remains in one sense ours, but in another sense is evidently over: they write about that period from around the turn of the century to about 1940 or 1941, when Virginia Woolf and James Joyce died, and a whole creative phase in the remaking of the novel into an instrument of modern expression seemed to come to an end. That period is, of course, outstanding, extraordinary, and genuinely modern. It is dense with major achievements and major figures; it remains in a real way a contemporary fiction, retaining its significance and relevance for our lives now. But time passes, and increasingly that fiction becomes an historical fiction. Major novels have lasting values, but they are also made out of the cultural, stylistic and linguistic opportunities of a particular era, a particular aesthetic synthesis. This is one reason why the novel changes, one reason why we no longer think of ourselves as in a 'modernist' universe. And if we still live within the power of and the sphere of that 'modern' novel, we also need, or merit, a novel for our present times, for the end-of-the-century season in which we live. Yet it is not widely thought that in England we have one, of any great significance.

One essential purpose of this book is to challenge that judgement, that neglect, and some of the folklore behind it. For there are growing grounds for disputing the judgements and challenging the neglect of a fiction that, while it has certainly not been driven by the same sense of radical historical and formal transformation that shaped the early twentieth-century novel in England, and has not generated talents of the same scale and confidence, has nonetheless been complex, significant, highly interesting, highly various, and has also been 'ours' in the most immediate sense—for it has sought to find language, structure, meaning and style for the kind of world in which we now live. Of course the relative neglect of contemporary English fiction is in many ways understandable; and there are good and bad reasons for it. Criticism has grown accustomed to let time do its sifting for it; the great fictional reputations of the early century were, after all, not readily granted by their contemporaries, and the names we support with confidence now—Henry James, Joseph Conrad, D. H. Lawrence, E. M. Forster, James Joyce, Virginia Woolf—have really become the significant canon only relatively recently. One notable event of the postwar period has, in fact, been the increased attention that has been given to the novel, which has come to be regarded as a central form in the way, once, that poetry was. There has been catching up to do. In any case, contemporary writing is notoriously hard to assess. The institutionalization of writing as 'literature' is a slow process, and a way of gradually giving ourselves a significant past. Yet that slow sifting process is not the only reason for the relative neglect of contemporary English fiction. For there has also grown up a folklore of justification for it. And we now have a version of the contemporary English novel, compounded in humility (a sensibility perhaps appropriate to a once powerful nation come down in the world), which proposes that these are diminished times, that significant talents have fled the novel for other areas, notably the theatre, and that in any case the significant developments now taking place in fiction are taking place elsewhere—in French fiction, American fiction, Commonwealth or South American fiction—while in England, as Bernard Bergonzi once put it, the novel is 'no longer novel'.

There is both justice and virtue in some of these judgements. Certainly they have helped break the containing provincialism that has always been dangerous to the reading and the writing of English fiction. The novel has always been an international form, hard to contain within convenient territorial boundaries. In the modern world, it has become increasingly a medium of global expression, and many of its most significant achievements do now have to be looked for outside any narrowly conceived British or European tradition. One profitable consequence has been that young English critics concerned with contemporary fiction have turned their eyes elsewhere. Three of the best books on the modern novel in recent years by English critics have been by Tony Tanner, John Sturrock and Stephen Heath; Tanner's *City of Words* (1971) is on the postwar American novel, Sturrock's and Heath's books on the French *nouveau roman*. But

there has been little attention of equivalent quality given to contemporary English fiction by English critics; with a few notable
exceptions—Frank Kermode, Bernard Bergonzi, David Lodge,
Antonia Byatt—the record has been depressing. The new attention
being given by English critics to the novel is being given very largely
to the novel of the past. Such significant criticism as *has* been given to
current English fiction has come very largely from European or
American critics; indeed the three main general surveys of postwar
English fiction—Frederick R. Karl's *A Reader's Guide to the Contemporary English Novel* (London, 1959; rev. ed., 1963), James Gindin's
Postwar British Fiction: New Accents and Attitudes (London, 1962) and
Rubin Rabinowitz's *The Reaction Against Experiment in the English
Novel: 1950–1960* (New York, 1967)—are all by Americans. However,
these books, partly because of the dates at which they were written,
partly because they were concerned to see the postwar novel in relation
to the general lineage of English fiction, tend to compound a prevailing folklore, summed up in the title of Rabinowitz's book: a
folklore which assumes the isolation of contemporary English fiction
from the main developments of the novel elsewhere, and hence its
relative stagnation.

One of the aims of this book is to challenge that folklore, so it is
worth elaborating it further. The lore runs something like this: there
was, from the beginning of this century, when what Alan Friedman
has termed 'the turn of the novel' occurred, until the outbreak of the
Second World War, a high season of English fiction; here we find the
great modern reputations. The war broke the sequence; the modernist
experiment faded; the distinct new generation of writers who emerged
after the war were radically different in temper and commitment
from their predecessors. They dismissed the largest achievements of
the modern novel, reached back to nineteenth- or eighteenth-century
sources, through Bennett and Dickens and George Eliot to Fielding,
sought to reinstate 'realism' and the social novel, but sought all this in
a minor key, so making the novel not a mode of formal or imaginative
experiment but a practical instrument for expression. The old preoccupations of the English novel, with class and custom and morality,
reasserted themselves, partly as a result of the need to document and
interpret the social changes that had come about as a result of the
welfare state—so that the characteristic English novel became a
contemplation of a working-class or lower-middle-class youth wandering in a state of solemn but remediable social anguish along a canal

bank near Wakefield—and partly as a consequence of a new mood of provincialism that seemed to have entered English culture, separating it from developments elsewhere. There was thus a cult of formal modesty and of Little Englandism, and Kingsley Amis's *I Like It Here* (1958)—which devoted itself to mocking the experimental and expatriate tradition in the novel, blamed on Henry James, and celebrating the common-sensical, realist, English virtues of Henry Fielding, while also indicating how much better England was than anywhere fancy abroad—could hence be an exemplary text for the prevailing mood. In Karl's, Gindin's and Rabinowitz's books, then, the mainstream of the postwar English novel is represented by the 'provincial' or 'angry' novel of the 1950s; the return to realism and to formal modesty is emphasized; the main theme of the English novel is the representation of English society. Thus, says Karl, postwar English fiction is a fiction with 'far less grandiose plans' than the fiction of its antecedents; moreover, writers were disposed to the assumption that 'the experimental novel—especially its treatment of plot—is no longer viable and that retreat is perhaps expedient'. So, if contemporary fiction in other countries was concerned with formal or fictional crisis, or the philosophical dilemmas of existentialism and absurdism, English novelists were not. They felt capable of being renewed by tradition; an inherited pre-modernist lore of plot and character served them; this was both their strength and their weakness.

Versions of such views have continued, and of course there is a weight of justification for the case. Quite the best general book on the postwar English novel is Bernard Bergonzi's *The Situation of the Novel* (London, 1970); it has the benefits of a later date, a longer view, a wider reading, and a more varied sense of the novel as a form. It is also an anxious text, emphasizing the persistence of the lineage of liberal realism in contemporary English fiction, while noting that a more experimental but also more totalitarian formalism is growing evident in fiction elsewhere. Where, then, Bergonzi proposes, an existential or post-modernist regimen in the novel was evolving in other countries, involving the defeat of the traditional liberal idea of character as a free and growing agent, or of plot as a significant ordering of experience, and so an emphasis on lexicality or on the victimization of the individual, the English novel was, either out of traditionalism or philosophical conviction, seeking to retain those attributes of character, plot and realism that had long been associated with the novel. But this was happening at a price, and resulting in a tendency toward the simpler pleasures of genre fiction; for many modern readers, it was not answering to the modern experience. Bergonzi's book, in its mixture of moral approval and technical scepticism, in fact seemed to mirror an anxiety that could be observed in many contemporary English novels; one reviewer aptly saw it as a typical novel itself. Bergonzi fills out the case with profit, and takes it further in this book. And it is indeed true, as several of the following essays suggest, that the attempt to mediate between the traditional realism and humanism of the nineteenth-century novel and the epistemological problems of fiction in our time has been of considerable importance in English fiction, and given it something of a distinctive character. In fact, however, the anxiety or dilemma seems very characteristic of many novelists of the postwar period, in a variety of countries. And one danger of the entire argument has been that it has led to the view that the English novel since the war has followed a course quite distinct from developments in other countries —developments that are then seen as more 'modern' or 'experimental'. In practice this seems far from true, and the comparisons and discriminations need to be a good deal more subtle than they have been. And one of the problems is that discussion of English fiction has worked on a canon far too narrow; indeed the desire to suggest a broader canon, a greater variety of approaches, and above all a more serious status for the achievement of the very varied writers who have emerged in England since the war is the essential motive behind this book.

It is, of course, true that a distinctive new generation did emerge in the English novel after 1945, though we must not forget those writers who had begun their writing careers before the war but significantly extended them afterwards: Lawrence Durrell, Malcolm Lowry, Samuel Beckett, Graham Greene, Evelyn Waugh, Ivy Compton-Burnett, George Orwell, William Cooper. The new generation was undoubtedly influenced by a changed social climate, which bred a new aesthetic climate; for the postwar period was an era of revived liberalism, a tone appropriate to a political time when totalitarianism had been a national enemy, and when, in another form, its threat continued, a time when democratic institutions needed to be remade, and when liberal anxiety and uncertainty about human nature itself was a logical consequence of the impact of the revelations of Buchenwald and Auschwitz. The preoccupations of the existential novel in France, or the Jewish-American novel in America, are part of this mood; so was the renewed liberalism of the English novel. With the postwar emergence of a novelist like Angus Wilson, and the appearance of George Orwell's late novels, English fiction began to find a voice that expressed its sense of liberal ambiguity and its consciousness of the social and moral change the postwar world had brought. Wilson's early stories, *The Wrong Set* (1949) and *Such Darling Dodos* (1950), are partly portraits of a new, welfare-state world in which a once domin-ant bourgeoisie finds itself displaced, made dodo-like, by social change, in the form of increased democracy and increased bureaucracy, partly an ironic expression of a liberalism forced into self-doubt, and manifested not as certainty but anxiety; this has led to an extremely complex pattern of social realism and extreme irrealism in his later work. But it was also in the late 1940s that Samuel Beckett was completing his central trilogy, an enterprise that would have a quiet effect on the 1950s, influencing, for example, Iris Murdoch's first novel, *Under the Net* (1954). And it was also in the late 1940s that another work of late modernism, from another expatriate writer, appeared: Malcolm Lowry's *Under the Volcano* (1947), encyclopedic, mythological, massively conceived, a work of internationalist am-bitions. There were, as Ronald Binns emphasizes in his essay on Beckett and Lowry in this book, really two lineages, rather than one, feeding the postwar novel.

Indeed it is appropriate to see the novel in the 1950s, even, in this light. There was indeed a revival of the social and liberal novel, following on from Wilson's *Hemlock and After* (1952) and William Cooper's *Scenes from Provincial Life* (1950); the moral urgencies of postwar English culture indeed seemed to generate a new use and value for the novel in this function. Fiction also became the voice for times when new social groups and classes were seeking articulacy, and this was part of the cultural power of early novels by Kingsley Amis, John Braine, Alan Sillitoe, John Wain, David Storey and others. It was these books that, for many observers, came to represent the novel in the 1950s, but in practice the scene was vastly more various, and writers of a quite different temper, some of them writers of very great importance, were bringing a much more fabulous and specu-lative mode into postwar English fiction: Muriel Spark, William Golding, Iris Murdoch, Doris Lessing, Anthony Burgess. Many of the most interesting writers to emerge in what now seems, in retro-spect, a good decade for the English novel—Wilson, Murdoch, Storey, Golding, Lessing, Burgess, Spark and, a little later, B. S.

Johnson—were, in short, very doubtful members of any realist first eleven, and in the best of them we may see an extraordinary extension and alteration of their talents. In many cases their best work was to come after the 1950s, and some of it has been their most recent. It is a writing, increasingly self-aware, much concerned with the nature of fictions, and the freedom of the imagination, which requires a quite different reading from that generally canvassed in the 1950s, when, it should be remembered, the temper of criticism, influenced especially by Leavis and Trilling, was much devoted to interpreting the novel as a socio-moral form. And so Muriel Spark's more recent novels are concerned with elaborate speculation about the nature of a fictional text and the God-like power of a plotter; Iris Murdoch's become thoughtful considerations of the nature of character and myth in fictions; Angus Wilson's more recent novels, *No Laughing Matter* (1967) and *As If By Magic* (1973), though working from the base of the panoramic social novel, subvert it, in the first case through establishing (as Robert Burden argues in his essay here) a parodic mode of narrative, in the second by undertaking to violate the provincialism of the form by producing a global, multi-perspectivized novel.

By the 1960s, in fact, it was coming to seem, in England as elsewhere, that the tradition of what Robert Scholes usefully called 'fabulation' was beginning to become very powerful in the English novel; this was evident in perhaps the most interesting and important talent to emerge in the 1960s, John Fowles. We may try to trace cultural causes for all this; there can be no doubt that the realistic mode was becoming harder to negotiate in a world of hard materialism and liberal disorientation. The confident provincialism of some writers in the 1950s began to collapse in an era of uneasy internationalism, a world of new politics and new styles; and if, as some contributors to this volume argue, the English novelists sought to protect a degree of realism and liberal humanism in their fictions, they often did so in a context in which the waves of fictional revisionism emanating from the French *nouveau roman* and from American exponents of that plural cause labelled 'post-modernism' did not pass them by. Perhaps John Fowles's attempt, in *The French Lieutenant's Woman* (1969), to reconcile a modern, self-sceptical, post-existential modern text with a traditional one makes it thus an exemplary book of the 1960s. What, in the 1960s, did become evident was the coming into English fiction of a new internationalism of form and perspective; we can discern a distinct change of emphasis and mood. A. S. Byatt's essay in this

volume notes the way in which 'experimentalist' arguments began to
strengthen during the 1960s, and the direction of a number of important careers began to change; at the same time younger writers like
B. S. Johnson, Alan Burns, Christine Brooke-Rose and Gabriel
Josipovici were coming to serious notice. What was becoming clear
was that the criticism which read the contemporary English novel
according to the lore of socio-moral realism was insufficient to deal
with contemporary developments. It remains to be added that the
English reveiwers, and so presumably the readers they represented,
tended to maintain their realist preferences and to avoid the new
developments. One disturbing consequence was that many of the
best English novelists found their reputations advancing, and their
critical understanding emerging, better abroad than at home. Indeed
a number of the important figures—John Fowles, Muriel Spark,
Doris Lessing, Anthony Burgess—have made their main audiences
outside Britain; only slowly have their reputations been seriously
accepted here, and this often by a grudging process. In short, one of the
disturbing features of the novel in England now is the absence of a
criticism responsive to its character and direction; this, surely, is one of
the reasons for its relative neglect.

Today, in fact, the English fictional scene looks very different
from that established in the earlier histories. There are now, in England,
a group of novelists who would seem major figures in any international
account of the contemporary novel: Graham Greene, Samuel Beckett,
Anthony Powell, Angus Wilson, Iris Murdoch, Muriel Spark, Doris
Lessing, Anthony Burgess and John Fowles are surely writers of this
order. We have come to see the increased importance of certain
writers who were pushed out to the eccentric fringes: Malcolm
Lowry especially, William Golding, perhaps Lawrence Durrell. Of
the writers who established themselves in the 1950s, many have greatly
strengthened their hand in recent years: David Storey, B. S. Johnson,
Margaret Drabble. Then we must add Christine Brooke-Rose, Dan
Jacobson, A. S. Byatt, David Lodge, Ann Quin, J. G. Farrell, Paul
Scott, Robert Nye, Alan Burns, Michael Moorcock, J. G. Ballard,
Nicholas Moseley, and beyond them Angela Carter, Beryl Bainbridge,
Martin Amis, Ian McEwan. These are writers of varied quality and
of various achievement; some have sustained their careers with more
splendour and energy than others. Doubtless there are names that
have been missed; still many of these writers are discussed in this
book. The value of such lists is that they indicate not only a degree of

activity and liveliness in the novel now which has, in general, been
insufficiently recognized, but also a great eclecticism in fiction now;
there is no convenient single label to describe what these writers are
doing, no single enterprise or tradition to which they can be held to
contribute to. The point is that they change the emphasis; and what
certainly is clear is that the one approach *least* likely to elicit their
value is one that insists on the dominant realism of the English novel.
There are, as Robert Burden suggests in his essay, distinct 'national'
qualities to be found in their work. There is indeed something guarded
and something uncertain in our younger writers now, and, as several
essays here show, they have not gone generally to the extremes of
anti-anthropomorphic or anti-representational form that we may
find in contemporary fiction elsewhere. But they have considerably
re-synthesized our idea of the English novel, and this calls for attention.

Today, as A. S. Byatt suggests in her article, we may well be past
the point where it is useful to think in terms of the antitheses of
'realism' and 'experiment' which have often served as the debating
ground for the discussion of current English fiction. When, recently,
The New Review encouraged fifty-six novelists or critics of fiction to
reflect on the state of the novel, most noted the way in which a new
flexibility and use of fantasy had entered the novel. Most noted, too,
the poor recognition given to the novel in England, by publishers,
by reviewers, by critics, by readers. The essays in this book were
collected in the conviction that we are, indeed, in a period of significant achievement in English fiction now—an achievement quite as
relevant as that in theatre, and comparable to that in other countries—
and that it was criticism's business to pay attention. Like any such
book, this one has its own biases and selectivities, some regrettable—
for space has confined the range of the essays and, in particular,
prevented as many essays on single authors as we would have wished—
and some intentional. There are significant writers who have gone
shamefully unattended to; moreover, for convenience's sake, there
has been a narrowly 'English' concentration inappropriate to the
spirit of contemporary developments. But the bias away from the
fiction of the 1950s, covered in other studies, has been deliberate.
The essays here have, of course, their own distinct and different
assumptions and emphases, and the organization has not been prescriptive. But we have attempted to draw a map of general signifi-
cances and at the same time to indicate a variety of critical approaches.
One aim was to have a novelist commenting on contemporary fiction

and on his own work; in the absence of other takers, one of the editors finally contributed. But the main aim of this collection is to extend discussion of the contemporary novel in Britain, and draw attention to its interest. In this, at least, we greatly hope it succeeds.

MALCOLM BRADBURY

DAVID PALMER

Note

The chief general studies of contemporary English fiction are: Bernard Bergonzi, *The Situation of the Novel* (London, 1970); Malcolm Bradbury, *Possibilities: Essays on the State of the Novel* (London/New York, 1973); James Gindin, *Post-War British Fiction: New Accents and Attitudes* (London, 1962); Gabriel Josipovici, *The World and the Book* (London, 1971); Frederick R. Karl, *A Reader's Guide to the Contemporary English Novel* (London, 1963; New York, 1959); Frank Kermode, *Puzzles and Epiphanies: Essays and Reviews 1958-1961* (London, 1962), *Continuities* (London, 1968) and *Modern Essays* (London, 1971); David Lodge, *Language of Fiction* (London, 1966), *The Novelist at the Crossroads* (London, 1971) and *The Modes of Modern Writing* (London, 1977); Rubin Rabinowitz, *The Reaction Against Experiment in the English Novel, 1950-1960* (New York, 1967) and Patrick Swinden, *Unofficial Selves* (London, 1973). There is a general survey of the postwar novel by Malcolm Bradbury in C. B. Cox and A. E. Dyson (eds.), *The Twentieth Century Mind, Vol. 3, 1945-65* (London, 1972) with a useful bibliography. For a survey of more recent English fiction, see Ronald Hayman, *The Novel Today: 1967-1975* (London, 1976). Malcolm Bradbury (ed.), *The Novel Today* (London/Manchester, 1977) is a collection of useful literary statements, mostly by novelists, about the form and intention of the postwar novel; also see Giles Gordon, *Beyond the Words: Eleven Writers in Search of a New Fiction* (London, 1975).

Iris Murdoch (b. 1919).

    Novels: *Under the Net* (1954); *The Flight from the Enchanter* (1956); *The Sandcastle* (1957); *The Bell* (1958); *A Severed Head* (1961); *An Unofficial Rose* (1962); *The Unicorn* (1963); *The Italian Girl* (1964); *The Red and the Green* (1965); *The Time of the Angels* (1966); *The Nice and the Good* (1968); *Bruno's Dream* (1969); *A Fairly Honourable Defeat* (1970); *An Accidental Man* (1971); *The Black Prince* (1973); *The Sacred and Profane Love Machine* (1974); *A Word Child* (1975); *Henry and Cato* (1976); *The Sea, The Sea* (1978).

    Philosophy: *Sartre, Romantic Rationalist* (1953); *The Sovereignty of Good* (1970).

    Criticism: A good bibliography is Anne Culley with John Feaster, 'Criticism of Iris Murdoch: A Selected Checklist', *Modern Fiction Studies* XV, iii (Autumn 1969), 449–57. The main studies are A. S. Byatt, *Degrees of Freedom* (London, 1965) and *Iris Murdoch* (Writers and Their Work, London, 1976); Peter Wolfe, *The Disciplined Heart* (London, 1966); and Frank Baldanza, *Iris Murdoch* (New York, 1974). Also see W. K. Rose, 'An Interview with Iris Murdoch', *London Magazine* VIII (June 1968), 59–73.

(Details for Angus Wilson, Doris Lessing, J. G. Farrell, John Fowles, etc., may be found in the notes to other essays in this volume.)

People in Paper Houses:
Attitudes to 'Realism' and 'Experiment' in English Postwar Fiction

A. S. BYATT

I

MUCH of the debate about appropriate form in the English novel since the war has been concerned with the acceptance or rejection of appropriate or inappropriate models. Thus what has been called the 'reaction against experiment' of the 1950s was much preoccupied with rejecting the model of James Joyce and Virginia Woolf. We had C. P. Snow's reductive description of the innovations of these two writers as 'a method, the essence of which was to represent brute experience through moments of sensation';[1] we had the linked complaints of Kingsley Amis: 'The idea about experiment being the life-blood of the English novel is one that dies hard. "Experiment" in this context boils down pretty regularly to "obtruded oddity", whether in construction . . . or in style; it is not felt that adventurousness in subject matter or attitude or tone really counts.'[2] The 'avant garde' of the 1960s and 1970s have now rejected this rejection, declaring that the 'nineteenth-century novel', with which many novelists of the 1950s felt a continuity, is the convention now leading novelists into bad faith, and a perverse ignorance of the revolution that was effected once and for all by Joyce, the 'Einstein of the novel'. Thus we have the desperately hectoring voice of B. S. Johnson, berating writers who do not realize that 'literary forms do become exhausted, clapped out . . .', and that 'the nineteenth-century novel' was finished by the outbreak of the First World War: 'No matter how good the writers are who now attempt it, it cannot be made to work for our

[1] See Rubin Rabinowitz, *The Reaction Against Experiment in the English Novel 1950–1960* (New York & London, 1967), p. 98.
[2] *Ibid.*, p. 40

time, and the writing of it is anachronistic, invalid, irrelevant and perverse.' Johnson's description of the nineteenth-century novel is, in fact, quite as inadequate as was Snow's account of the modernist experiment. For him, its wrongness is that it tells a story—and 'telling stories is telling lies'.[3]

These irritable territorial definitions have taken place against the background of a critical discussion of contemporary fiction which has been, in this country, decidedly thin; and against a critical lore which has been—and this is important—characteristically moral and prescriptive. We have the Great Tradition. We have John Bayley's *The Characters of Love* (1960), an immediately attractive and sympathetic book—particularly, I suspect, to writers—which distinguishes the literature of Nature from the literature of the Human Condition, and advocates a realism, characteristically English, which depends on love, in author and reader, for characters as separate individuals. Related to this is Iris Murdoch's essay of 1961, 'Against Dryness'—a 'polemical sketch' pleading for a return to the realistic depiction of 'free, separate' characters as a way out of a philosophical solipsism and a simple welfare utilitarianism we have too easily embraced. Iris Murdoch gives clear and good historical reasons why it is not now possible simply to mimic the nineteenth-century realists, and certainly her novels do not themselves do so. Nonetheless, her prescription is roughly the same as John Bayley's. We must *learn from* tradition— from Shakespeare, and the nineteenth-century novelists, especially the Russians. Bernard Bergonzi's *The Situation of the Novel* (1970) is extremely sympathetic to Bayley's position; it does, though, share B. S. Johnson's anxious sense that modern English realism is 'no longer novel', but depends on exhausted forms and concepts. The paradox is, according to Bergonzi, that the most vital contemporary literature is also totalitarian and dehumanizing, and as for his examples of that vitality they are French and American, not English: Heller, Pynchon, Burroughs, Mailer, Robbe-Grillet, Genet. There are similar anxieties in David Lodge's *The Novelist at the Crossroads* (1971); Lodge's crossroads mark the paths pointing away from realism, but he nonetheless offers 'a modest affirmation of faith in the future of realistic fiction'—a faith that can be reasonably born out by a look at the kinds of novels many writers today are publishing.

Behind that Great Tradition, there is, of course, the spirit of 'Tra-

[3] B. S. Johnson, *Aren't You Rather Young to be Writing Your Memoirs?* (London, 1973), pp. 12 *et seq.*

dition and the Individual Talent'. 'But we *know* so much more than they did', protests Eliot's hypothetical artist, asked to contemplate his forebears; 'Precisely,' replies the voice of authority, 'And they are that which we know.' It was Eliot who complained that our literature was a substitute for religion, and so was our religion. Respect for the tradition of the realist novel is apparently a very rooted fact, and is inextricably involved in a very complex set of responses to the decline of religion and the substitution of a Religion of Humanity. The fictional texts of the Great Tradition are indeed the texts of the Religion of Humanity; and many novelists now seem to feel that they exist in some uneasy relation to the afterlife of these texts, as the texts themselves once coexisted with the afterlife of Genesis and the Gospels. They are the source of enlightenment, but not true. Or not true, for us.

Thus it seems that much formal innovation in recent English fiction has concerned itself, morally and aesthetically, with its forebears; and in a way for which I know no exact parallel in other literatures. This has its dangers: as Nathalie Sarraute declared, in 'Rebels in a World of Platitudes', the true enemy of good art is not mass society or technology, but 'the only real, the deadly danger, the great works of the past',[4] which must be absorbed and rejected simultaneously. This is, of course, the anxiety of influence, of which Harold Bloom is the prophet.[5] This anxiety, in the English novel now, seems to operate in odd ways—with and against the moral force of the Great Tradition, which still exerts its power, to produce forms sometimes limp, sometimes innovatory, sometimes paradoxical, occasionally achieved, and sometimes simply puzzling. The state is recognizable; but traditional critical methods for the study of influence and of plagiarism are often distracting here. When Dr Leavis isolated the ways in which James's *The Portrait of a Lady* is a reworking of part of Eliot's *Daniel Deronda*, he was pointing to a kind of 'reader's greed' in the writer which is, in fact, perfectly characteristic of George Eliot's own work. I take it that some need both to re-read, and to better, certain stories that caught her imagination was behind her own reworking of an episode from Gottfried Keller in the climax of *The Mill on the Floss*; of the description of George Sand's *Jacques* as a

[4] Nathalie Sarraute, 'Rebels in a World of Platitudes' in *The Writer's Dilemma: Essays from the TLS* (London, 1961), pp. 35–41.

[5] See Harold Bloom, *The Anxiety of Influence: a Theory of Poetry* (New York, 1973).

Saint Theresa born out of his time, in *Middlemarch*; or of the animated tableaux from Goethe's *Wahlverwandtschaften* in *Daniel Deronda*. Not parody, not pastiche, not plagiarism—but a good and greedy reading, by a great writer. The phenomenon, then, is not novel. And yet it inevitably looks different in modern novels—because of the pressure of the past, because of the accumulation of literary criticism, and because of the weight of anxiety as it shows itself in modern form.

II

Perhaps a paradigmatic case is the development of the career of Angus Wilson. In an illuminating interview with Jonathan Raban, Wilson said, 'I nearly always feel when I'm writing a scene that this has been written before.' Raban comments, 'But life itself tends constantly to the second-hand; our responses are so conditioned, our behaviour so stereotyped, that it is immensely hard for us to extricate ourselves from these literary precedents which plot the course of our own feelings and actions.' Wilson's 'literariness', Raban adds, is a function of his characters, who read and use literature to interpret their lives, and is not, in this, like 'the formal allusiveness of most modernist writing'.[6] Indeed, the hero of Angus Wilson's first novel, *Hemlock and After* (1952), is a writer, Bernard Sands. And Angus Wilson requires of his reader that he inhabit Sands's experience, including the writing, but imaginatively, in a 'realist' way. The essence of this experience is a vision of aimless evil which undercuts the meliorism of Sands's traditional humanist position, and comes perilously close to undercutting the Religion of Humanity itself. Sands is, like George Eliot, like Angus Wilson, a person who controls an acid wit and a natural cruelty in the interests of justice. His opponent, fat and smiling Mrs Curry, the procuress, is a two-dimensional Dickensian vision of something irrational, predatory, and powerful. Both characters are nineteenth-century, the good one centrally 'realist' in morals and presentation, the bad one (whom the reviewers found paradoxically 'thin' at the time) suggesting, with hindsight, possibilities of 'experimental' fictional techniques, derived from Dickens's grotesque. (Dickens has been behind other 'experimental' variants of realism, notably those of Paul Bailey.)

[6] Jonathan Raban, 'Angus Wilson: A Profile', *The New Review* I, 1 (April, 1974), pp. 16–24.

Meg Eliot, in *The Middle Age of Mrs Eliot* (1958), remains, I think, Wilson's most successful attempt at the Jamesian ideal of sustained, inner imagining of a character. She, too, is literary, and has her personal collection of texts, characterized as 'the escape she and David had found in the past. *Emma, The Mill on the Floss, The Small House at Allington, The Portrait of a Lady* ... the basic necessities of the voyage.' Reviewers and critics pounce on literary clues in our time. It has been pointed out that all these novels have impulsive, passionate heroines, whose fate is to suffer from forcing their own fantasizing vision on reality; that Meg Eliot is in their tradition and is, indeed, their heir. But there are germs of discomfort here. The novels are explicitly 'an escape to the past'; Meg's identification with the heroines brings no access of wisdom, but a child-like evasion of present misery. David's literary work, like his boyhood pleasure in 'the sad futilities of Emma Bovary's debts', is an evasion of reality. Is this like George Eliot's exposé of Dorothea's desire to dedicate herself to 'Milton, when he was old', or is it a doubt about literature itself?

Literary references are also central, obtrusive and pervasive in *No Laughing Matter* (1967), but in different fashion. The Matthews family's Game deals with unpleasant realities by parody, pastiche, farcical mockery. The Game discovers, exploits, elaborates the sexual, political and aesthetic traits of the characters. It is a primitive, crude and vigorous form of the art of the writer, Margaret, the actor, Rupert, the twee 'writings' of the self-deluded Susan, the high camp of Marcus. The characters use the Game, and the Game, directed by Angus Wilson, uses them. He derealizes them with overt manipulation, in lengthy parodies of Ibsen, Shaw, Chekhov, Bennett, framing them in a plurality of styles. The result is not realism, but is intimately and uncomfortably related to it. This is because, although Wilson's insistence on the 'second-hand' quality of his people and their world renders them papery and insubstantial, they do nevertheless think and feel, and author requires of reader an imaginative response to thought and feeling which belongs with realism.[7] A reverberation is set up between their literary factitiousness and their own sense of this, corresponding to their author's sense of a similar problem in himself and his work, which produces a new, a novel kind of acute disorder and discomfort in the reading experience. This discomfort is intensified in *As If by Magic* (1973), to which I shall return. In that novel, as Raban

[7] There is a very helpful discussion of this aspect of *No Laughing Matter* in Malcolm Bradbury's *Possibilities*, to which I am indebted.

says, the characters proceed by asking themselves 'How would Birkin, or Myshkin, or Alice, or a Hobbit have felt about this . . .': their answers to these questions produce ludicrously parodic behaviour: the texture of the novel is insistent on its own farcical fictiveness, suggesting that all life is a ghastly fiction 'behind' which stands no ratifying or eternal vision of a corresponding reality. When Alexandra declares 'I know I am a fictive device' we are aware that we are out of the world of the realist novel and its norms and in the familiar world of the experimental novel, which proclaims its own artifice and comments on its own procedures. What I want to emphasize at this point is the curiously symbiotic relationship between old realism and new experiment, the way in which Alexandra as 'device' grew out of Meg as typical humane reader.

III

An analogous sense of the ambiguous power and restrictiveness of the tradition goes to create the difficulties readers have with the surface of Iris Murdoch's work. She calls herself a realist, and claims that she is in the English tradition: her progress as a whole has been in the opposite direction from Angus Wilson's.[8] *Under the Net* (1954) contains elements of deliberate parody and surreal joke, and is partly a philosophical game with Wittgenstein and Sartre. It corrects, or re-reads, *La Nausée* by rewriting scenes of it. Iris Murdoch complained that Sartre 'had an impatience, fatal to a novelist proper, with the *stuff* of human life . . .' and lacked 'an apprehension of the absurd, irreducible uniqueness of people, and of their relations with each other'.[9] Critics have ponderously accused Miss Murdoch of failures in density—'the serious novel calls for intensity of characterization' says F. R. Karl, whereas Iris Murdoch's comedies 'frequently decline into triviality'.[10] This criticism fails to recognize that *Under the Net* is a fable *about realism*, a conceptual game about the need for the concepts, language and emotional movements of a new realism. It is not intended itself to be a densely realist work.

Her later novels are the result of a sustained attempt, moral and formal,

[8] I have discussed this in my book *Degrees of Freedom* (London, 1965) in Chapter 2.

[9] Iris Murdoch, *Sartre, Romantic Rationalist* (London, 1953), p. 75.

[10] F. R. Karl, *A Reader's Guide to the Contemporary English Novel* (London, 1963), section on Iris Murdoch.

on the realism she and John Bayley admire. When I read *The Bell* in 1959, I felt that something odd was happening: I was able imaginatively to inhabit a fictional universe, to care about the people and their fate, in what I judged to be a 'good' book, in a way I thought, then, was confined to my reading of nineteenth-century novels and my stock of non-literary 'bad' books or children's books. By *An Unofficial Rose* (1962), my sense of achieved imaginative reality was much more strained. The reason was the obtrusive presence of Henry James, and with him, of John Bayley's reading of *The Golden Bowl*; of Jane Austen, and with her, of Lionel Trilling's reading of *Mansfield Park*. This is difficult, as I suspect the imaginative process involved for Iris Murdoch in writing *An Unofficial Rose* was not essentially different from George Eliot's greedy reworking of Goethe. *An Unofficial Rose* cannot be called parodic, but a trained reader senses its relation to the past in a way that makes its fictional world less accessible, less immediate to the imagination.

Related to this, maybe, is a frequently voiced view that Miss Murdoch is confining her attentions to the 'wrong' kind of characters, an 'irrelevant' group of the upper bourgeoisie. In terms of her own morality, there is no reason why she should not do so. Free and separate persons can be studied in any social setting. I think part at least of the readers' dissatisfaction is aesthetic, to do with the pressure of the Tradition, which was made by such a society, for such a society, and helped to create and perpetuate it. These are the people of James's and Forster's fiction, and this, perhaps, makes them feel artificial and unreal even where they are not. 'Man is a creature who makes pictures of himself and then comes to resemble the picture,' Miss Murdoch has said. The world she studies has already 'come to resemble' the world of the Victorian and modernist novelists, having seen itself in their mirrors. To be realistic about this world is to encounter pervasive and powerful images of it, in itself, in novels, in readers, which make the imaginative process thinner, more second-hand, more difficult. *An Unofficial Rose* is curiously like *The Middle Age of Mrs Eliot*, even down to its setting and controlling imagery of natural and artificial flowers. They are alike in their attempt on density, and in the literary reverberations which intensify and thin that attempt.

Later still, Miss Murdoch achieved, I think, a striking degree of success as a realist by shifting, partly, her model. The plots of several later novels are parodies, overt, acknowledged by the characters, of Shakespearean plots. *The Nice and the Good* (1968), *A Fairly Honourable*

Defeat (1970), *The Black Prince* (1973) play games with *A Midsummer Night's Dream, Much Ado, Hamlet*. These plots could be called experimental devices, obtrusive, making no claims to psychological probability, or development, such as George Eliot or James would have felt essential. They, too, are related to Dickens's comic plotting. Their formality has liberated an imaginative space for reader and character to inhabit; their artifice has created a new–old language for realism. It is this kind of discrimination that makes wholesale advocacy, or rejection, of particular periods and writers, as models, so unhelpful.

In this context one might be able to place the disturbing power and ambiguous effect of David Storey's *Radcliffe* (1963), a novel that derives its terrible energies from a combination of personal obsession, genuinely new realistic observation of things hitherto unobserved, and the absorbing literary greed of huge talent. Storey once spoke of the split in himself that developed when he was playing professional rugger in the North to support himself as a student at the Slade in London. *Radcliffe* is about the split, in the artist, between mind and body, mirrored in the split between labourers and a decadent aristocracy, placed against the tradition of English puritanism and the disturbing central figure of Cromwell. Radcliffe and Tolson, intellectual and workman, in their violent attempts either to become incorporate with each other or to destroy each other, mirror, Radcliffe declares in his visionary insanity, 'the split in the whole of Western society . . .' and 'the division that separates everything in life now, *everything*'. The novel makes a heroic attempt at an aesthetic totality like that of the great modernists, offering its protagonists as types of fundamental truths, historical, social, religious, intellectual, biological together, incorporating precise factual records of tent-contracting work with a neo-Brontë, neo-Gothic visionary Yorkshire landscape, a Christian theory of guilt with a Freudian theory of culture, and all with a series of daemonic literary parodies that are almost, not quite, a new form in themselves.

The early chapters of *Radcliffe* I found, on a first reading, paradoxically new and exciting because they had placed, realist, density of observation and imagination. The style was cool, controlled and very energetic: one had a powerful sense of an impending fictional world both thought out and realized. Storey has said that the opening was inspired by the opening of *Madame Bovary*. It reads as a pure example of the greed of novelist-as-reader. The major voices behind the rest of the novel are Lawrence and Dostoevski. The relation between Tolson and Radcliffe draws on those of Gerald and Birkin, Myshkin and Rogozhin. The style swings wildly between the phantasmagoric, grotesque of an American-Gothic comic drama, and a Lawrentian intellectual nagging and insistent noise. Radcliffe's fate is Myshkin's, withdrawn, insane, in a silly peace, dead. Lawrentian hollyhocks sprout under Wuthering Heights. It is as though Storey had made as ferocious and doomed and violent an attempt to incorporate literature as Tolson and Radcliffe make on each other. One could compare this to Thomas Mann's incorporation, in *Doctor Faustus* of Goethe, Nietzsche, Dostoevski, but the effect is entirely different. Angus Wilson's parodies are joky and papery: Thomas Mann's an act of intellectual appropriation and cultural commentary: Storey's are almost vampiric. That they spring from the same uncomfortable relation to a Tradition as those of Murdoch and Wilson is undeniable, and the reader's sense of muffled power and involuntary thinness is analogous. But it is not the same.

IV

The relation to past novels brings certain firmly 'realist' works and certain declared experimental works curiously close together. John Fowles, in *The French Lieutenant's Woman* (1969), writes a Victorian novel within a novel. Within this story the reader is allowed, invited, both to experience imaginatively the sexual urgency and tension it evokes, and to place such imagining as a function of that kind of story, that kind of style and, Fowles suggests, that period of history. Obtruded authorial comments offer a 'modern' justification of this procedure that has a faintly Murdochian ring. Chapter 12 ends with a Victorian rhetorical question: 'Who is Sarah? Out of what shadows does she come?' Chapter 13 opens with a 'modern' authorial statement:

> I do not know. The story I am telling is all imagination. These characters I create never existed outside my own mind. If I have pretended until now to know my characters' minds and innermost thought it is because I am writing in (just as I have assumed some of the vocabulary and 'voice' of) a convention universally accepted at the time of my story: that the novelist stands next to God . . . But I live in the age of Alain Robbe-Grillet and Roland Barthes; if this is a novel, it cannot be a novel in the modern sense of the word.
>
> There is only one good definition of God: the freedom that

allows other freedoms to exist. . . . The novelist is still a god, since he creates (and not even the most aleatory avant-garde novel has managed to extirpate its author completely); what has changed is that we are no longer the gods of the Victorian image, omniscient and decreeing; but in the new theological image, with freedom as first principle, not authority.

Fowles's understanding of Victorian life and literature is crude and derived from the Bloomsbury rejection of it, which makes his technical nostalgia fascinating as a phenomenon. His theory of 'freedom' leads to the experimental alternative endings to the novel, which painfully destroy the narrative 'reality' of the central events, which have happily withstood authorial shifts in style, interjections and essays on Victorian reality. Fowles claims he did not control his characters, but his projected endings do not suggest a plurality of possible stories. They are a programmatic denial of the reality of any. The future tense, like the future, is a creative lie—necessarily a fiction, as George Steiner has pointed out. But these alternative endings are neither future nor conditional, but fixed, Victorian, narrative past. They therefore cancel each other out, and cancel their participants, rendering Fowles as arbitrary a puppet-maker as he declared his desire not to be. For the writer, whilst the plural endings are possibilities in the head, they intensify the reality of the future world. For the reader, now, they reduce it to paperiness again. (Fowles can manipulate tenses better than this. Chapter 16 opens with some authorial sagacities and apostrophes about Victorian life, and continues in the present tense, with Ernestina's reading of *The Lady of La Garaye*. Two paragraphs later, Fowles is back with his love-story between Sarah and Charles, and in the habitable past tense. *The Lady of La Garaye*, extensively quoted, is thin, high Victorian emotional cliché, possible for Ernestina to be moved by then, blandly farcical now. The present tense, cinematic, distancing, displays her, and it, for judgement. The reader effortlessly and pleasurably switches from watching to imagining with the change of tense. It is a nice game, a typically English experimental game, with layers of literary precedents and nostalgias.)

Such habits of reading can lead to 'framing' of passages not presumably intended for it. Here, in another author, is Lord Ryle, pondering his possible love for a woman who

wasn't even really in his taste. Too sharp, too narrow, not free enough. He hadn't been meeting many women, it was a chance and a pity that she had come along. She wouldn't have suited him, nor would he have been much good to her.

In all that he was probably right. There was another reflection which wouldn't have consoled him. The chances with possible partners whom one met produced a sense of fatality: so ought the chances of possible partners whom one didn't meet. The division bell had rung just as Ryle was about to be introduced to Jenny Rastall. As it happened, and it was pure chance, they didn't speak to each other that night, and were not to meet again until it was too late. . . .

It was possible that they were, as Ryle's old mother would have said, made for each other. No one could predict that for certain, there was no one alive who knew them both well, and there was only one test, which they alone could have proved. From their habits, affections, tastes and natures though, it seems more likely than not that they could have fitted one another: certainly more completely than with anyone they actually found. Which, in his mood that evening Ryle, not a specially sardonic man, would have considered not a specially good joke.

This is a Trollopian authorial interjection, of the chatty kind that James considered a wanton violation of realism, a 'suicidal satisfaction in reminding the reader that the story he was telling was only, after all, a make-believe'.[11] But, in the context of Fowles's games with authorial interjections, this chapter-ending of C. P. Snow's looks like a game with the conventions of plot, character, probability. It discusses what did not happen, what could not have happened, what the character 'would consider' a good joke. Snow is no aesthetician: the qualities he prizes are 'a living tradition; reflection; moral awareness; the investigating intelligence'.[12] His novels, judged by Jamesian criteria of social realism, or verisimilitude, have been found thin and dry. Yet large areas of Snow's *In Their Wisdom* (1974), if they are read as a self-conscious game with a modern neglect of Victorian themes (death, money) and devices (authorial omniscience), take on the same derivative papery energy as Angus Wilson's puppet-show.

V

All I have so far said could be considered reflections on the use, conscious and unconscious, of the *dèja-dit* in current fiction. I would go

[11] Henry James, 'Anthony Trollope' (1883), reprinted in *The House of Fiction*, Leon Edel (ed.), (London, 1957).
[12] See Rubin Rabinowitz, *op. cit.*, p. 98.

further and claim that much aggressively 'experimental' fiction uses much more distracting devices in part to legitimize echoes of old styles and straightforward realisms. J. G. Farrell writes omniscient prose, about the past, in the past tense, using a tough narrative voice to prevent his work appearing to be either pastiche or uneasy current Victoriana. But much of John Berger's G. (1972) has the same virtues—real, concrete imagining of the past, somehow permitted to be by a politically and linguistically self-conscious framework. The same is true of B. S. Johnson's holes, serifs, columnar and shuffled printed surfaces. Through and athwart them we glimpse a plain, good, unfussy, derivative realist prose that can somehow only come about by declaring that *that* is not what it meant to be, not what it meant at all.

Parody and pastiche are particularly literary ways of pointing to the fictiveness of fiction, gloomily or gleefully. And there is now, amongst some novelists, an almost obsessive concern with the nature of truth and lies, with the problems of veracity, which has also taken oddly 'literary' forms. Some of this concern is to do with the history of realist fiction, and later of modernism. George Eliot's scientific 'experiments in life' illustrated laws of probability and development which are now seen much more as hypothesis and much less as 'truth' than in her time. The aesthetic unities of the high modernists can be experienced as reductive. The apparent flux of *Mrs Dalloway*, even the resistance of Indian reality to Western vision and plotting in *Passage to India*, are in fact controlled, orchestrated by the writer's metaphors for chaos. And these idiosyncratic visions are only too easy to reject if they seem to claim the status of truth, especially if the reader is looking for 'the truth'. Virginia Woolf's metaphors require an assent which seems, in certain moods, and particularly for writers, too simple and too exclusive to grant.

There is also our increasing sophistication about the way in which we construct our own world. We study theories of perception and illusion, which show how our biology and its history condition our vision. We study our languages and their limitations, again in terms of biology and history. We deflect our attention from what we perceive to the way in which we perceive it, and this has had it's effect on the structure of the novel. Iris Murdoch, discussing Sartre's view of the sickness of language, claimed that 'our awareness of language has altered in the fairly recent past. We can no longer take language for granted as a medium of communication. We are like people who for a long time looked out of a window without noticing the glass—and then one day began to notice this too.' This self-consciousness made the poet feel that 'the whole referential character of language had become a sort of irritant or stumbling block. It was as if the poet began to see the world with a dreadful particularity. . . . To lose the discursive "thingy" nature of one's vision and yet to feel the necessity of utterance is to experience a breakdown of language.'[13] This raises problems for the realist novelist even more than for the poet, as Miss Murdoch knows: it is part of Jake's conceptual problem in *Under the Net*.

Gabriel Josipovici, in *The World and the Book* (1971), isolates what he calls 'demonic analogy' as a function of modern self-consciousness about language. For Dante, analogies revealed the mirroring of eternal verities in temporal phenomena. For modern writers

> to discover correspondences in the world around us does not lead to the sensation that we are inhabiting a meaningful universe; on the contrary, it leads to the feeling that what we had taken to be 'the world' is only the projection of our private compulsions: *analogy* becomes a sign of *dementia*. . . . We become aware of it with a shock of recognition, suddenly realizing, what we had dimly sensed all along, that what we had taken to be infinitely open and 'out there' was in reality a bounded world bearing the shape only of our own imagination. . . . The effect of demonic analogy is to rob events of their solidity.[14]

Events are also robbed of their solidity, it has frequently been suggested, by the nature of 'modern reality' itself. I am chary about using this phrase, which means all things to all men, from the black heaven untenanted of its God to the television screen flickering with silently screaming children flickering with napalm, or alternatively with the Galloping Gourmet's flambéd soufflé flickering with burning brandy, from social descriptions of 'real' homeless families and 'unreal' jet sets to psychological deductions from the observed effect on kittens of raising them in a vertically striped or horizontally barred 'environment'. 'Reality' in fiction is ambiguously and uncertainly related to 'true facts'. Dostoevski's phantasmagoric and frenetically jerky plots result partly from his fascination with the *improbable* truths of newspaper reports, the murderer who surrounded his corpse with little open bottles of disinfectant to keep off flies. Mary McCarthy in

---

[13] Iris Murdoch, *op. cit.*, pp. 26–7.
[14] Gabriel Josipovici, *The World and the Book* (London, 1971), p. 299.

The Fact in Fiction argues intelligently that the traditional 'facts' of the social novel are now hard to recognize, whilst we are culturally obsessed by facts, Hiroshima, Auschwitz, which are unimaginable because 'their special quality is to stagger belief'. Such facts render our local world 'improbable, unveracious'. She concludes: 'the novel, with its common sense, is of all forms the least adapted to encompass the modern world, whose leading characteristic is irreality.'[15] B. S. Johnson and Giles Gordon, largely without examples, likewise claim that 'modern' reality as opposed to 'nineteenth-century' reality, is 'chaotic, fluid, random', and our fictional forms must reflect this.[16]

B. S. Johnson is obsessed by truth-telling. So is Iris Murdoch, whose precisely moving rhetoric in 'Against Dryness' offers a placing of the word 'reality' in a philosophically and historically meaningful context. Johnson's truth-telling entails the abandoning of 'stories' as lies, and reduces his subject-matter to a carefully structured autobiography. Iris Murdoch's truth-telling involves an abandoning of solipsism, a recognition that 'reality' is other than ourselves, an Eliot-like ideal of the impersonal artist, a return to the 'hard idea of truth' as opposed to the facile idea of sincerity. Roquentin in *La Nausée* sees that there are 'no stories' because what exists is formless: Miss Murdoch says art is 'adventure stories', a necessary technique for discovering truth. Non-realistic autobiography: 'impersonal' story-telling—exactly opposite solutions to the problem of the nature of lies and the difficulty of truth.

In *Albert Angelo* (1964), Johnson uses Albert the architect as a paradigm of Johnson, the poet, supporting himself by supply teaching. He plays games—a hole in page 149 reveals a knife-blow which on page 153 is revealed to be the death of Christopher Marlowe, the future glimpsed in the book being in fact the historical past. This is part of the 'playfulness' of a novel which is reminding us of its own status as artefact, but Johnson in his outburst at the end claims that his intention in making the hole was 'didactic: the novel must be a vehicle for conveying truth, and to this end every device and technique of the printer's art should be at the command of the writer. . . . To dismiss such techniques as gimmicks, or to refuse to take them seriously, is crassly to miss the point.' I find this hard to focus or understand.

[15] Mary McCarthy, 'The Fact in Fiction'.
[16] B. S. Johnson, *op. cit.*; Giles Gordon, New Fiction Society publicity material for the collection *Beyond the Words*, Giles Gordon (ed.), (London, 1975).

'Truth' in this context is general enough to be meaningless. Clearer
is the outburst in which he explodes his illusion:

—fuck all this lying look what im really trying to write about is
writing . . .
—im trying to say something not tell a story telling stories is
telling lies and i want to tell the truth about me about my experience
about my truth about my truth to reality about sitting here writing . . .

Aesthetic solipsism, certainly, and a genuine desperation. Later in
this section Johnson discusses his fictive substitutions: the girl was called
Muriel not Jenny, Balgy was in Scotland not Ireland, the dogs ate
Fidomeat not Felixmeat. . . . Lies, lies, lies, rages Johnson, and cannot,
dare not, be interested in the imaginative process which compels
people, writers, to effect such substitutions. Yet this process is an essential part of human thought. He is a case of a born writer, part paralysed, part humiliated, part impelled, part sustained, by an absurd
and inadequate theory which is nevertheless a clue to the anxieties of
subtler men.

A more complicated response to the problem of veracity and the
fictive is Julian Mitchell's *The Undiscovered Country* (1968). This
consists of two parts, the first a realist, indeed, factual narrative by
the 'true' Julian Mitchell, supported by a cast of real people and a plot
of real events, about his fictional friend Charles, author of the *New
Satyricon*, which is the second part. Within this veracious and conventional first part the two writers discuss the nature of fiction, including their view that they live in a 'post-literary' age, and the
difficulties of the novel, which is 'an impure art-form, inextricably
rooted in the real world'. Charles criticizes the unreal conventionality
of 'Julian's' (factual) earlier novels, on the ground that they are reticent
and untrue. The 'sincere' and certainly *déja-dit* ideas and form of this
realist section themselves take on a new, riddling energy and opacity
when seen as part of the formally unreal, demonically analogic fable,
the *New Satyricon*, itself a parody of 'possibly the first novel' and
containing gratuitous fables, parodies and puns (James Bond, pop
music, rubber fetichist news sheets, possibly, Julian teasingly tells us,
actual news sheets, since impossible to parody). The *New Satyricon*
provides versions, visions, analogues of episodes in Part I, which
change these. It also provides a 'framing' literary critical structure,
written by naive Julian about Charles's 'real' meanings—and this
includes a parody of literary critical procedure. The novel as a whole,

blandly riddling, secretly violent, provides an energetically literary criticism of the relation of the novel, the writer, and his world. It plays games with truth, lies, and the reader, teasing him with the knowledge that he cannot tell where veracity ends and games begin. It is the game all novelists play anyway, raised to a structural principle.

In this context one could add Muriel Spark's later games with plotting and fictiveness, in which the characters act as surrogate plotters, image-makers, newspaper-informers. One could add Fowles's *The Magus* (1966), a ponderously literary game with the writer as demiurge or puppet-master, and the most recent work of Dan Jacobson, whose *The Rape of Tamar* (1970) and *The Wonder-Worker* (1973) are interested in narration, narrative manipulation, and indeed the reasons for 'telling stories' at all. *The Rape of Tamar* is particularly interesting in that its base narrative is an 'inspired' biblical text, a canonical episode. Its narrator-manipulator presents it as a political, aesthetic and religious paradigm. Dan Jacobson's early *A Dance in the Sun* (1956) seems to me one of our few clear, good and strong examples of straight realism. He has said he felt a compulsion to describe South African society, which has not been described. In England, he wondered about the value of fiction, and felt that London had been too often described already. This suggests an oblique response to the pressure of the Tradition and the presence of the texts: what his early work proves is that realist narrative, in English, is not in itself either impossible or *déja-dit*. It is a question of subject-matter, as much as of the age of the form.

VI

Finally, three examples of novels which embody, in very different ways, the problems I have been discussing: an awareness of the difficulty of 'realism' combined with a strong moral attachment to its values, a formal need to comment on their fictiveness combined with a strong sense of the value of a habitable imagined world, a sense that models, literature and 'the tradition' are ambiguous and problematic goods combined with a profound nostalgia for, rather than rejection of, the great works of the past. The novels I have chosen are Iris Murdoch's *The Black Prince* (1973), Angus Wilson's *As If by Magic* (1973) and Doris Lessing's *The Golden Notebook* (1962).

The Black Prince, like *Under the Net*, is best read as a fable about the difficulties of realism, or truth-telling. It contains, like *Under the*

Net, two novelists, one prolific and bad, one silent and good—at least in his own opinion, since he is the narrator, condemned (wrongly?) for the murder of the other. Baffin, the bad, distresses people by collecting the 'facts' of their lives into his fiction, which Bradley characterizes as 'inquisitive chatter and cataloguing of things one's spotted', or 'a congeries of amusing anecdotes loosely garbled into "racy stories" with the help of a half-baked unmeditated symbolism. ... Arnold Baffin wrote too much too fast. Arnold Baffin was just a talented journalist.' If Baffin is journalistic, Bradley is crystalline, holding the Murdochian, Eliotean ideal of impersonality and 'truth', believing in long suffering and apprenticeship, unable to speak at all. The novel is in fact Bradley's very Baffinesque account of his love for Baffin's daughter and its effect, tragic, comic and literary. A central episode turns on Bradley's disquisition on the paradoxical 'truth-telling' in *Hamlet* where Shakespeare, the impersonal genius, wrote a riddling play in which he himself was in fact, for once, the central character, flayed like Marsyas by an Apollo both orderly, loving and cruel. Shakespeare, the true artist, of course combines Baffin and Bradley, reticence with prolific professionalism, endless facts with lucid poetry. *Hamlet* is Shakespeare's purification of the language by a riddling truth-telling. It 'transmutes his private obsessions into a rhetoric so public that it can be mumbled by any child. He enacts the purification of speech, and yet also this is something comic, a sort of trick, like a huge pun, like a long almost pointless joke. ... Being is acting. We are tissues and tissues of different *personae* and yet we are nothing at all. What redeems us is that speech is ultimately divine.'

Bradley's tragi-grotesque account of his suffering is enclosed in fictive editorial matter written by Apollo Loxias, and containing various partial and very self-referring postscripts 'by' several of the characters. Apollo is the puppet-master, explicitly, of this novel, setting the artists, including Shakespeare, dancing in their excruciatingly funny agonies. Bradley writes Murdoch-like prose on the difficulty of describing 'characters', and claims that his 'thin layered stuff of ironic sensibility ... if I were a fictive character, would be that much deeper and denser.' Apollo refutes the idea that he himself might be fictive. 'I can scarcely be an invention of Bradley's, since I have survived him. Falstaff, it is true, survived Shakespeare, but did not edit his plays. I hear it has even been suggested that Bradley Pearson and myself are both simply fictions, the inventions of a minor novelist. Fear will inspire any hypothesis. No, no, I exist.' Apollo, too, assures

Julian Baffin that 'Art is to do with joy and play and the absurd. . . . All human beings are figures of fun. Art celebrates this. Art is adventure stories.'

So the *Black Prince* is a playful adventure story, a comic game, containing fiction within fiction, commentary (and allusion to commentary, Shakespearean, Murdochian) within fiction, ideas about realism endorsed by unreal fictional gods. It does not itself purify the language—Bradley's adventures are Murdochian farce and Murdochian tragi-comedy, his thoughts speak the language of her aesthetic essays which, in our time, are startlingly clear and vernacular. It raises the question of truth and lies, and offers an endless series of receding, unattainable, focused images of truth, but nothing believable, nothing habitable. Like *Under the Net*, it stands beside realism, a papery charade indicating in riddles what it is not doing, but is intensely concerned with.

As If by Magic is also a 'literary' artefact, symbiotically involved both in realism and in the modernist aspirations to the completeness of myth. The central theme of 'magic' incorporates the economic 'miracle' of the new rice, Magic, in underdeveloped economies, the new Oriental, Arthurian, astrological and Tolkienesque cults of the 1960s flower children; and sexual-Lawrentian magic, a rescuing of our culture by 'good sex', transfiguring the Dark Gods into beneficent spreaders of sweetness and light. The novel proceeds by indiscriminate literary parody. Hamo, the rice geneticist with his servant, Erroll, is Frodo with Sam crossing Middle Earth; he is an Arabian Nights prince in search of The Most Beautiful Boy; he is a character from a Feydeau farce, or Victorian pornography, falling about, smashing things, disguising himself. Alexandra uses English literature to interpret life and also to plot the novel, rescuing the charlatan (at least nine-tenths) Swami from his incensed followers by recalling in quick succession Toad disguised as a washerwoman, and Panks exposing Casby in *Little Dorrit*. There are parodies of the Angry Young Men (in Alexandra's father) and threadbare identifications—Alexandra comes to see Hamo's clumsiness as Myshkin's divine idiocy.

The novel contains a collapsed myth, in the sense that all the characters are out to redeem the Waste Land with fertility magic: but Hamo's death at the hands of an incensed mob is neither Dionysian nor Orphic, his body is simply a 'marionette', and the sex-magic of Ned, Roderigo and Alexandra, designed to redeem the aridity of Birkin's failure to love both Gerald and Ursula, produces a child who is explicitly not allowed to represent harvest or fulfilment. At the end of the novel, Alexandra rejects him as a symbol: unlike Helen's child at the end of *Howards End* he will neither reconcile opposites, close circles, inherit the earth nor play with the grain. 'We've had enough of Forster's harvest predictions. Things may have turned sour for all of us, but we must not heap it all on *him*.' Alexandra rejects both literature and stories. After her 'plotting' success with Toad and Panks, she stops short of seeing her fatigue in terms of Frodo's. 'She said to herself, enough of superstitious imagining. A story is a story is a story, even a good one, like the *Lord of the Rings*.' And five lines from the end of the book, having become Shaw's millionairess, she cries 'Damn English Literature!', as though brushing away mental cobwebs. Literature too is a magic spell, an illusion between men and reality.

As If by Magic is nihilistic, but it does not, like Nietzsche and Mann, open windows on blackness with a grim delight in reversals of meaning. It works by reducing everything to the ridiculous, in an intensely, inexorably, exclusively literary way. And it is not the absurd it indicates, it is simply the ridiculous. It is like an onion consisting of allusion, parody, interpretation, misinterpretation, imitative plot and trumped-up analogy, but an onion encasing no green growing point, and putting out no roots. The comparison with Mann is instructive. Mann, writing *Dr Faustus*, discovered, he said, 'my own growing inclination, which I discovered was not mine alone, to look upon all life as a cultural product taking the form of mythic clichés, and to prefer quotation to independent invention'. Mann cannibalized the facts of Nietzsche's life, the forms of Dostoevski's fiction: his book has, as R. J. Hollingdale says 'an airless, a horribly airless quality; it smells of the midnight, and worse of the *midday* lamp'. An analogous airlessness permeates *As If by Magic*, but the differences are instructive. Mann was monstrously curious as a writer—he had to *know about* music, tuberculosis, syphilis, in heaped factual detail. Angus Wilson's rice, although clearly researched, was researched, one feels, as a *literary symbol*. Mann's book has an extraordinary vitality, however airless, even if it was, as he said it had to be, the vitality of *fleurs du mal*. Wilson's book is paradoxically less vital because of his residual liberal humanist warmth and duty towards his characters. He feels morally compelled to appreciate and understand Alexandra's true being, from the inside, and his display of this moral effort curiously vitiates the papery energies of his puppetry without really allowing the reader to care for that 'fictive device' he has so respectfully put together. Further, the presence of this moral nostalgia for Forster's procedures curiously blurs Alexandra's rejection of Forster's metaphors. These moral confusions and formal blurrings are also characteristic of our time.

The Golden Notebook began, Doris Lessing has said, as a combination of a novel about artistic narcissism, about art, about the 'problems of the artist', and a literary-critical book which would be a series of stylistic exercises combined 'in such a way that the shape of the book and the juxtaposition of the styles would provide the criticism'. The two books in one would have a shape 'so enclosed and claustrophobic —so narcissistic that the subject matter must break through the form'. The novel has indeed an airlessness, but it also has a realistic power, almost unique amongst the novels I am discussing, which derives from the fact that in this case form and subject-matter are not a seamless garment, that the subject-matter is not the form, is more and other than it, and does indeed break through.

The novel is about the writing block of the novelist Anna Wulf. During the description of the source, form, symptoms and demolition of this block, Anna, and her author, go into most of the formal problems I have raised in this essay. The nostalgia for Tolstoy, and for Thomas Mann, is raised by Anna's reviewing; the novels she reads, she declares, are typically journalistic, reports on unknown areas of the world, undescribed communities. They reflect psychological and cultural splintering. 'Human beings are so divided, are becoming more and more divided, and more sub-divided in themselves, reflecting the world, that they reach out desperately, not knowing they do it, for information about other groups. ... Yet I am incapable of writing the only kind of novel which interests me: a novel powered with an intellectual or moral passion, strong enough to create order, to create a new way of looking at life.' The novel itself is subdivided, Black, Blue, Red, Yellow notebooks, separating money from politics, from autobiographical facts, from fictional exercises. Journalism is debased realism: Doris Lessing is also penetrating about Iris Murdoch's 'crystalline' alternative, the desire for myth, symbol, dream as a deeper reality. Anna's dialogues with her psychoanalyst show mistrust, and even contempt, for her analyst's facile respect for Art, her assumption that if a dream-vision can be named or placed as myth or folk-tale, Icarus or the Little Mermaid, then that gives it a satisfactory form, allied to the world of the primitive. Anna insists, neurotically and wisely together, that civilization, truth, consist of a capacity to resist such primitive aesthetic wholenesses and delights. Her dreams nevertheless punctuate the novel with a power, colour, and certainty that are part of its patchwork toughness and fascination. They work as symbols do work, in dreams, in life. They do not become a submythology, nor daemonically reduce intelligent Anna to being their puppet.

Anna Wulf is also obsessed by the relations between truth, veracity and fiction. Large parts of the novel are concerned with her relation to her own first novel, a large commercial success, which she now dislikes, feeling it was the product of a corrupt nostalgia for her life during the war, and such nostalgia breeds 'stories' 'like cells under a microscope'. During the novel Anna tries to reconstruct the 'real' events that were transmuted into that fiction. The reader on the other hand is offered increasingly simple and corrupt versions of it—American film scenarios, projected televison musicals, conventional literary reviews, dogmatic Communist reviews, each reducing it to their own form of banal or farcical cliché. Anna asks herself 'Why a story at all. . . . Why not simply the truth?' But truth is hard, stories do indeed breed like cells, the issue is complex. She makes attempts on the factual, the 'true fact' of Dostoevski and B. S. Johnson, in various ingenious ways. She replaces her diary at one point by a series of newspaper snippings, mostly about freedom and violence, of the kind Mary McCarthy said rendered fictive fact 'irreal'. She attempts a detailed, unmediated account of one day of her life, not 'selecting' what she records, not arranging it. This record turns out to be identifiably 'false', like the crystalline dream images. She writes that she had assumed that 'If I wrote "at nine-thirty I went to the lavatory to shit and at two to pee and at four I sweated," this would be more real than if I simply wrote what I thought.' She discovers that thought, concepts, a directing intelligence are as necessary to our sense of truth as Iris Murdoch has said they are.

She broods about the vanishing 'character', in relation to the real people behind the rejected first novel. She writes of them that some were 'good', some 'nice', some not good or nice, and that most people who knew them could recognize and use these simple classifications, although 'these are not words you'd use in a novel, I'd be careful not to use them'. She remarks that personality can still be recognized by gesture in films, yet has become hard to depict in novels, remembers Maryrose's smile, and declares 'All this talk, this anti-humanist bullying, about the evaporation of the personality becomes meaningless for me at that point when I manufacture enough emotional energy inside myself to create in memory some human being I've known.' The novel is full of characters: the novelist-character's personality disintegrates almost to collapse, under the strain of consciousness.

She contemplates the breakdown of language. Her Communist Writers' Group discuss Stalin on Linguistics and Anna broods on their moral incapacity to criticize his bad semantics, brooding also on 'novels about the breakdown of language, like *Finnegans Wake*', and a recurrent experience of her own, in which words lose their meaning and seem 'like a foreign language. The gap between what they are supposed to mean and what in fact they say seems unbridgeable.' Her parodies in this book are partly explorations of debased languages of cliché. She reads a fantasy story 'by a comrade', out of a genre of communist wish-fulfilments, and cannot tell whether it is to be read as 'parody, irony, or seriously'. She and a friend write parodic stories to explore and expose current literary clichés, and find that editors take them seriously. Such debased group languages create, call for, parody which they cannot recognize. A plurality of such languages, and a despairing consciousness that they exist, make it hard for any 'realist' to imagine an audience that can recognize or place a truth, if it is told.

Related to these perceptions are the layered parallel emotions and styles in the fiction-within-the-fiction, Anna's novel about the end of 'Ella's' love-affair, which parallels her own, but distorts it because the love-affair in the novel is inevitably analysed in terms of 'laws' of breakdown, whereas the experience did not assume breakdown as the inevitable end. Ella, also a writer, works, like Anna, with fictions more papery than her own: women's magazines, containing both lonely-hearts letters and clichéd 'stories'. Anna remarks that she could retell her first novel in the person of the sex-obsessed teenager 'in' it by changing a few words here and there and thus the whole style: the Chinese boxes of fiction-within-fiction in *The Golden Notebook* create the most complex example I know of the study of such tensions of whole styles, degrees of 'realism' or vision. They also of course play games akin to Julian Mitchell's with veracity. 'Ella's' son has 'Anna's' lover's name: 'Anna' has a daughter, not a son. And Doris Lessing? A Freudian joke, a writer's joke, a novelist's riddle about truth and fictive-ness. The splendid irony about all this obsessive narcissism and self-consciousness is that the realistic effect of the whole is amazingly reinforced. What Anna cannot do, Ms Lessing does, by an effort of sheer intelligence, political, psychological, aesthetic. It must be added that Doris Lessing's advantage, in this novel, is that she is not necessarily or primarily 'literary'. Anna remarks earlier that all she has left of the novelist is a huge curiosity. It is this curiosity that saves the novelist from aestheticism. Communism is more important in this novel than the Great Tradition, and modern female sex than fictiveness. If it is a book about books about books, it is haunted more by the claustrophobia of bad books than by love or fear of good ones, though these are present. I take it that such untrammelled curiosity is in fact a way out of formal anxiety, and a necessary component of realism.

One of the odd results, for me, of writing this paper, has been an increased respect for Anthony Powell. The thoughts of Nick in the Ritz about the difficulty of writing a novel about English life (in the *Acceptance World*) seem gracefully thrown off, and in fact tell a truth both sober and crucial. Nick thinks about the difficulties of reporting speech in a land where understatement is the normal style of all classes, and how bare facts have 'an unreal, almost satirical ring when committed to paper'. In *Books Do Furnish a Room*, X. Trapnel's outburst about 'naturalism' continues the topic. Its essence is that 'naturalism is just a way of writing a novel like any other, just as contrived, just as selective'. Powell's own contrivances, his own selection, his own manipulation of memory, above all, his vigorous and detailed and controlled curiosity seem to me now gifts of a high order. 'Naturalism's only "like life" if the novelist himself is any good,' says Trapnell. This essay has been concerned with reading, with the morals of literature, with devices and with anxieties. In fact, to be 'good', whatever form you use, takes more primitive gifts of curiosity and greed, about things other than literature. That these gifts are harder to discuss in academic essays is maybe part cause of our contemporary unease.

Note

The following works of criticism and literary theory helped me develop the argument of this essay: Roland Barthes, *S/Z* (London, 1975); Malcolm Bradbury, *Possibilities* (London/New York, 1973); Jonathan Culler, *Structuralist Poetics* (London, 1975); Roger Fowler (ed.), *A Dictionary of Modern Critical Terms* (London, 1973); Barbara Hardy, *Tellers and Listeners: The Narrative Imagination* (London, 1975); Frank Kermode, *The Sense of an Ending* (London/New York, 1967); George Lukacs, *The Historical Novel* (London, 1962); David Lodge, *The Novelist at the Crossroads* (London/Ithaca, N.Y., 1971) and J. P. Stern, *On Realism* (London, 1973). James Vinson (ed.), *Contemporary Novelists* (London, 1972) has valuable informational material on contemporary novelists, and some statements by them; I have also drawn on my own *The Situation of the Novel* (London, 1970), where certain aspects of the argument are more fully detailed.

Other significant discussions of the relation between history and fiction occur in Frank Kermode, 'Novel, History and Type', *Novel*, I (1968), 231–8; Erich Auerbach, *Mimesis: The Representation of Reality in Western Literature* (Princeton, 1953); Robert Scholes and Robert Kellogg, *The Nature of Narrative* (New York, 1966); and Mas'ud Zaverzadeh, *The Mythopoeic Reality: The Postwar American Nonfiction Novel* (Urbana, Ill./London, 1976).

I discuss in some detail the following novelists and some of their writings:

John Berger (b. 1926).
  A Painter of Our Time (1959); *The Foot of Clive* (1962); *Corker's Freedom* (1964); *G.* (1972).

David Caute (b. 1936).
  At Fever Pitch (1959); *Comrade Jacob* (1961); *The Decline of the West* (1966); *The Occupation* (1971) (This, with the play *The Demonstration* (1970) and the essay *The Illusion* (1971), forms *The Confrontation: A Trilogy*.)

B. S. Johnson (1933–1973).
  Travelling People (1963); *Albert Angelo* (1964); *Trawl* (1966); *The Unfortunates* (1969); *House Mother Normal* (1971); *Christie Malry's Own Double Entry* (1972); *Aren't You Rather Young to be Writing Your Memoirs?* (stories) (1973); *See the Old Lady Decently* (1975).

J. G. Farrell (b. 1935).
  A Man from Elsewhere (1963); *The Lung* (1965); *A Girl in the Head* (1967); *Troubles* (1970); *The Siege of Krishnapur* (1973), *The Singapore Grip* (1978).

II

Fictions of History

BERNARD BERGONZI

I

A FEW YEARS ago it was fashionable to call everything a 'fiction'. Fiction was 'fiction', naturally, but so were history, philosophy, and all forms of human discourse. Like most new ideas it had more than one source; but in England and America an immediate influence was Frank Kermode's dazzling essay on the nature of fictional form, *The Sense of an Ending* (1967), which draws on Wallace Stevens, the high-priest of the Supreme Fiction. Another source was the steady infiltration of structuralism. The structuralists talked about 'texts' rather than 'fictions' but the implications were similar. 'Structuralists accept the artifice of all human experience. For them, human experience is grounded in language as an institution. Even our desires are determined by this institution. Men are pronounced to be a function of language, a pronouncement entailing the death, ah at last, of man.'[1] Man, to adapt another phrase of Wallace Stevens, was 'made out of words'. The extreme structuralists refuse to set 'fiction' against 'reality', since 'reality' too is just another text, the text of l'habitude, one more verbal construct.[2] If few people have gone to such extremes in our own more cautious and empirical climate, the supremacy of fiction has still been argued for enthusiastically.

As a speculative instrument the idea has its value, certainly. It was, for instance, illuminating to see just how much the historian had in common with the novelist; both were concerned with originating and sustaining a narrative, with consistency of character, and combining episodic immediacy with over-all coherence. This was, indeed, the rediscovery of an old truth that had been lost sight of, for it was once taken for granted that historiography was a form of literature. In this

---

[1] Merle E. Brown, 'The Idea of Fiction as Fictive or Fictitious', *Stand* 15 (1), p. 40.

[2] Jonathan Culler, *Structuralist Poetics* (London, 1975), p. 140.

analogical sense history can certainly be called a fiction; that is to say, histories are like novels in their formal organization; and like novels, too, in the way in which the historian's feelings and attitudes and values will inevitably colour the narrative, however much he aims at objectivity. Yet it has proved easy and attractive to go beyond this point and suggest that history's claims to be 'about' the real world are invalid; that reality is unknowable, or itself a fiction, and that history is fictitious in precisely the same sense that novels are. I doubt if any historians would believe this, but the idea has appealed to literary intellectuals who like to believe that the world is chaos, and that the best we can do is huddle for protection behind flimsy fictive artifacts;

> Life consists
> Of propositions about life. The human
> Reverie is a solitude in which
> We compose these propositions, torn by dreams . . .

Added to the beguilements of Stevens's fictive music has been the seemingly tough-minded influence of the sociology of knowledge, shown, for instance, in the popularity of such a book as *The Social Construction of Reality* by Peter L. Berger and Thomas Luckmann. This is an absorbing book, but I believe the general influence of the sociology of knowledge to have been baleful and subversive of the possibility of rational discourse (it is not sufficiently realized, though, that the sociology of knowledge is an unstable discipline, since its methods can always be turned against its own practitioners). One has to resist the idea that knowledge is not just a fiction, but an ideologically generated fiction.

If all forms of human discourse are ultimately fictions nothing worthwhile can be said about them, whether in support or modification or refutation: one can only add fictions to fictions. Some decisive objections to the idea of the universality of fictions have been made in a sharp and lucid essay by Victor Sage, who cogently asks, 'If we can only make sense of things through fictions, how do we know of the existence of that which is non-fictional?' Mr Sage continues, 'In addition this extension of the term initiates a set of general conditions for the operation of fictions which makes it either impossible or unnecessary to distinguish between one fiction (say, poetry) and another (say, history).'[3] And of course we do need to distinguish. The novelist and the

---

[3] Victor Sage, 'Fictions', in Roger Fowler (ed.), *A Dictionary of Modern Critical Terms* (London, 1973), p. 73.

poet are freer than the historian, whose fiction-making is at every point checked and governed by the demands of truth-telling, whether he interprets them according to a heroic, Whig or tragic paradigm. However much we regard history as a 'fiction' or a 'text', the contents of history constantly make themselves felt in the texture of our daily lives. As David Lodge has put it with Johnsonian directness: 'History may be, in a philosophical sense, a fiction, but it does not feel like that when we miss a train or somebody starts a war.'[4]

If the assumption that history is just another kind of fiction is unhelpful, indeed untenable, the relations between history and fiction, more narrowly and precisely defined, are still worth considering. They have always been close, as we see in neighbouring languages, from the double sense of 'histoire' or 'storia'. It is open to a novelist to treat the received texts of history as the raw material for literary fiction; or history itself can be rewritten, as in *1066 and All That*, which is indeed a fiction and depends for its comic effect on the reader knowing something about the actual history concerned. Modern American novelists, working in the vein of emphatic fictiveness, or what Robert Scholes has called 'fabulation', have treated history as infinitely malleable, as a text of low and uninteresting organization, whose destiny is to be given point in comic or apocalyptic ways by the novelist; one thinks of Pynchon, Barth, Vonnegut, Hawkes, and Heller. English novelists are less inclined to do this. It may be that the Americans have less history, and what there is has already been turned into myths which lend themselves to literary treatment, whether exalted or deflating. Europeans, perhaps, are more inclined to treat history with respect, avoiding either a passive or a manipulative attitude to it; history is a process which men make, and which in turn makes them; this is in some respects a Marxist view of the matter, but by no means wholly so. Such a dialectical view of history was a feature of the major European novels of the past, even if with the decline of the realistic fictional mode that was its natural vehicle it no longer seems easily available to the contemporary English novelist. But it is still in a powerful if anachronistic way dominant in Solzhenitsyn, working in the great tradition of Russian fiction and certainly not unaffected by his Marxist education, however much he now rejects it.[5]

---

[4] David Lodge, *The Novelist at the Crossroads* (London, 1971), p. 33.
[5] See Martin Esslin, 'Solzhenitsyn and Lukacs', *Encounter*, March 1971.

II

The historical novel has often been favoured by Marxists, who claim a particularly intimate relationship to the processes of history, and was the object of a magisterial treatise by Georg Lukacs. In this context it is instructive to consider the case of David Caute, who is both a novelist and a historian, an intellectual of the left, and a former Marxist (one should add that, like Orwell a generation ago, Mr Caute devotes much energy to criticizing his comrades on the left). Early in his career Mr Caute wrote a historical novel, *Comrade Jacob* (1961), which was set in seventeenth-century England soon after the execution of Charles I. It describes the rise and fall of the egalitarian Digger community set up by Gerrard Winstanley and ultimately suppressed by Cromwell. Caute paints a good picture of the community and the principal characters in its story, but his novel is shackled by a rigid Marxist *schema*; it is a *roman à these* rather than a genuine novel of ideas, though there is no doubt about its author's intelligence and literary skills. In his next novel, *The Decline of the West* (1966), Caute tried to penetrate the heart of the historical process in our own day. It is a long, naturalistic work set in contemporary Africa, in an imaginary country which is the setting for revolutionary violence and brutal repression. Here, too, one finds a prominent thesis, about the collapse of imperialism and the final stages of capitalism. It is the kind of book known to blasé reviewers as a 'block-buster' and its naturalism is in literal ways raw and bleeding. There is a potent mixture of elements in *The Decline of the West*; high-flying intellectualism, indicated by the solemn appropriation of Spengler's title; sex, violence, atrocities; and large unassimilated chunks of the recent history of the Congo and Algeria (Caute has written a short study of Frantz Fanon). It is a striking, ambitious book, quite unlike the work of most English novelists of Caute's generation, though it cannot be called a successful novel. And for all its superficial sophistication it is naive in its confident use of naturalistic conventions at precisely the time when more reflective novelists were beginning to question them.

How Caute now regards *The Decline of the West* is uncertain, but it is worth noting that, in his next and very different novel, *The Occupation*, there are references to a work called *The Rise of the East*, which seems to have much in common with Caute's previous novel, and is the subject of frequent disparaging comment by the principal characters. *The Occupation* represented a decisive break with Caute's past; it formed part of a trilogy, the other constituents being a play, *The Demonstration* and a book-length essay, *The Illusion*, subtitled, 'An Essay on Politics, Theatre and the Novel'; all three appeared in 1971. The play and the novel describe the misadventures of an English academic called Steven Bright, who is also supposed to be the author of the essay. Steven Bright has different identities in *The Occupation* and *The Demonstration*; in the former he is a novelist and historian in his mid-thirties, temporarily teaching in a university in New York; in the latter he is in his forties and is professor of drama in an English university. In both works, however, he is a serious-minded intellectual of the left, subjected to humiliation and comic outrage by revolutionary students, who destroy his manuscripts (though prudently he has already circulated copies to friends). How far, and how thoroughly, the two versions of Steven Bright represent *personae* for David Caute is not a question to speculate about here. But in *The Illusion* 'Steven Bright' certainly speaks with David Caute's own voice; one finds the same combination of darting, urbane intelligence, seriousness, breadth of reading and mild pervasive anxiety in Caute's book of essays, *Collisions* (1974). Considered as criticism and cultural speculation, *The Illusion* is first-rate, but its quasi-fictional presentation prevented its ideas from getting the right sort of attention. Early on in that book the author asserts, 'Realism is burnt-out, obsolete, a tired shadow of a once-living force. It has to go.' It was the kind of protest quite often heard from English novelists in the late sixties and early seventies, as they grew tired of an established tradition, but in fact realism has many aspects and is far from easy to dispose of.[6]

In Caute's development this assertion represented a new access of reflexiveness and a seeming rejection of the conventions he had tried to employ in *The Decline of the West*. It was also a defiance of the literary ideals of the Old Left and the central Marxist tradition; notably represented by Lukacs's attempt to draw into the cause of progress and historical inevitability not just the historical fiction of Sir Walter Scott, but the whole of nineteenth-century bourgeois realism, against the twentieth century modernism which he found so distasteful. In *The Illusion* Bright-Caute argues for an alignment of revolutionary art and radical politics; for a literature and theatre that will be dialectical in the play between art and reality—*contra* the structuralists, who are

[6] See, for instance, the studied defence of realism in the title-essay of David Lodge's *The Novelist at the Crossroads*, and in J. P. Stern's *On Realism* (London, 1973).

scathingly treated in *The Illusion*, Caute believes in distinguishing between the two—and for an exposure of the essentially illusory nature of fictional and dramatic realism, and the necessity of alienation as Brecht understood it. Brecht is, in fact, the hero *of The Illusion*, where Caute regards him with all the fervour of a recent convert. Caute's rejection of the Old Left is satirically illustrated in *The Occupation* by Hamilton Snout, an ageing socialist hack writer and editor; Snout praises Bright's *The Rise of the East* as a triumph of socialist realism in contrast to the shallow experiments of modernism. There are all sorts of indirections in *The Occupation*, but Caute may here be both presenting a caricature of Lukacs and disowning *The Decline of the West* as just the sort of book Lukacs might have praised if it had ever come his way.

The Occupation enacts the ideas and attitudes that are speculatively set out in *The Illusion*. It is an antirealist novel which systematically undermines the illusion of a sustained dramatic fiction. Caute dwells on the problems of composition, intervenes in the narrative and directly addresses the reader. The novel owes much to Caute's own new allegiance to Brecht and *Verfremdung*—equally evident in theatrical terms in *The Demonstration*—but it also shows how easily a revolt against convention can itself become a convention. *The Occupation* is, in fact, an example of what David Lodge has described as the 'problematical' novel, where the act of writing is part of the novelist's subject, and which explores the paradoxical relations between art and life. There have been many instances in English fiction during the past twenty years. One can refer to Doris Lessing's *The Golden Notebook* (1962), to Lodge's own novel, *The British Museum is Falling Down* (1965), Julian Mitchell's *The Undiscovered Country* (1968), discussed at some length by Lodge in *The Novelist at the Crossroads*, the whole fictional oeuvre of the late B. S. Johnson from *Travelling People* (1962) onwards, John Fowles's *The French Lieutenant's Woman* (1969), and the later novels of Muriel Spark. It is noticeable, too, that Dan Jacobson who established his reputation as a mainstream realist, a mode which he used very impressively in *The Beginners* (1966), later turned to forms of problematical fiction in *The Rape of Tamar* (1970) and *The Wonder Worker* (1973). Beckett, Borges and Nabokov have been important influences, but in any case the tradition of problematical fiction is of considerable antiquity, older, in fact, than that of the sustained realistic illusion; it reaches back to *Tristram Shandy* and beyond that to *Don Quixote*, which Caute praises enthusiastically in *The Illusion*.

Discussing his own work Caute has said that, 'perhaps the tension between man's private and public existences is the central "problematic" of my thinking and writing',[7] which is a grand way of putting it. In *The Occupation* the tension is exhibited but not resolved. In his private existence Steven Bright is a depressed Herzogian kind of modern intellectual; he relates himself to the world by fantasies; he is impulsive and accident-prone; his sexual life is fraught with humiliation and anxiety; he is betrayed both by his mistress in America and his wife, whom he still loves, back in England. In the public dimension Bright tries to respond to the pressures of history in the America of the late sixties: Vietnam, racial conflict, the politicizing of the universities, urban guerillas. But whatever gestures he makes towards public commitment Bright's real preoccupations and obsessions remain resolutely private. Despite its fractured and alienated surface, *The Occupation* remains at heart a straightforward novel on a familiar theme; one could easily imagine it being rewritten in a traditionally realistic form, which is not true of more profound instances of the problematical mode. In places it is funny, as Caute energetically exploits the possibilities of comic effect in the clashes between private and public, fantasy and fact. But it is, in a strange way, not as funny as it ought to be; Steven Bright's struggles and defeats too often pro-voke embarrassment rather than mirth. When I say that *The Occupation* has a familiar theme I am referring to the way it fits into a genre of fiction of which there have been many recent examples: the novel about the misadventures of an Englishman, and particularly an English academic, in America.[8] Even the problematical treatment of this theme has become familiar, as in Thomas Hinde's heavy-handed *High* (1968) or Lodge's witty and stylish *Changing Places* (1975). *The Occupation* is not, any more than *The Decline of the West*, a wholly successful novel, even though the reasons for failure are very different Yet Caute is not to be dismissed as a writer, however defective he is as a novelist. The problem may be, if one recalls T. S. Eliot's judgement that Henry James had a mind too fine to be violated by ideas, that Caute has too many ideas, and too much intellectual energy, to be a novelist. I have already compared him in passing with Orwell, and the comparison seems appropriate; Orwell, too, was an immensely talented writer who wrote novels even though they were not his natural medium.

[7] James Vinson (ed.), *Contemporary Novelists* (London, 1972), p. 244.
[8] See Bernard Bergonzi, *The Situation of the Novel* (London, 1970), p. 21.

The Occupation invites comparison with a novel by a committed Marxist intellectual, John Berger's *G.*, which won considerable praise and attention when it appeared in 1972. *G.* is more radically problematical and would certainly resist rewriting in conventional terms. It tries hard to undermine illusion and explode the form of the novel, whilst at the same time opening the narrative to significant tracts of history. Berger, too, is concerned with the inter-action of private and public; among other things the book is a modern treatment of the Don Juan myth; the 'G' of the title standing for Giovanni. Thomas Pynchon, the author of *V.*, might have suggested the terse title to Berger and influenced him in other ways as well. Like Pynchon, Berger is interested in dramatic but unfamiliar episodes in turn-of-the-century European history, though as a Marxist he sees more significance in them: the bloody repression of a workers' demonstration in Milan in 1898 is a decisive defeat for revolutionary aspirations; the first crossing of the Alps by aeroplane is both a triumph of the will for the Peruvian aviator who accomplished it and a technological breakthrough; Trieste on the eve of the Italian declaration of war on Austria in 1915 is a cockpit of conflicting nationalisms.

Against such backgrounds Berger tells the story of his latter-day Don Giovanni, though to talk of telling a story is misleading; we are never allowed to forget that this is a book by John Berger, and that if he wants to break off the narrative and tell us about his dreams, or a visit to a Parisian laundry or the near-impossibility of writing, then no-one can stop him. As his other writings show, Berger is a superb essayist and in *G.* he allows himself full liberty to blur the distinction between writing essays and writing fiction. All this is in marked contrast to the Hegelian insistence of Lukacs and Goldmann on the substantiality of literary genres. If one commentator is to be believed, Berger intended, in his own way, to maintain the dialetical attitude to history of nineteenth-century fiction: 'In this chronicle, Berger has set himself the vast task that Tolstoy undertook: that of depicting how each one of us is history in that we are both monumentally shaped by events and, in small measure, by the mere act of inhabiting our skins, influence their course.'[9]

This may serve as an account of Berger's aims but hardly of the impression that one gets from reading *G.*, which seems to me vivid in its local detail but self-indulgent and indefensibly baffling in its total effect. Some of the shrewdest criticism of *G.* was written by David

9 Shirley Toulson, in James Vinson (ed.), *Contemporary Novelists*, p. 118.

Caute, who might have been expected to approve in principle, since it represented precisely the kind of alienated break with realistic convention that he had argued for in *The Illusion*; in practice, though, he had many reservations about it. He noted, first, the continuing division between the public and private aspects of Berger's sexually adventurous hero: 'although presented as a radically alienated product of bourgeois hypocrisy, he also emerges as a type of existential hero completely devoid of bad faith'. He adds that it is not apparent whether Berger sees G. as the product of a particular society or an expression of 'timeless' rebellion and defiance. Caute also remarks on the way in which Berger's style and idiom, which seemed so excitingly new to English reviewers in 1972, was itself just another convention, familiar enough in the contemporary French avant-garde: 'one notices that Mr Berger attempts to translate Cubism into literary terms by employing and rather over-taxing many of the devices used in recent years by Sarraute, Sollers, Butor and the other novelists who have said farewell to naturalistic certainty and divinely certified mimesis'. Caute's conclusion is worth quoting at length, both as a just assessment of G. and as an implied limiting judgement on some of his own beliefs about the alienated novel:

> the modern writer must either yield some territory to the *dramatic* heritage of fiction or risk alienating his readers in the wrong way. To emphasize that the failings of G. are the result of a rich endowment of talents and of a bold, experimental intelligence which distrusts the safe, mediocre and provincial, is not to explain these failings away. One comes away from G. as from many modern paintings: provoked and stimulated, yet baffled and faintly resentful.[10]

Both Berger and Caute, it seems, share a common dilemma. Profoundly influenced by Marxism, they wish to relate the private and the public, and to show how History directs human lives and is directed by them. But the literary form which in the past has been most amenable to registering the operations of history—partly, perhaps, because of its overlapping closeness to historiography itself— is the novel of traditional realism, the novel of Scott and Balzac, of Tolstoy and Solzhenitsyn. And this form, it is commonly argued, both by Marxists whose taste is later than Lukacs's, and by non-Marxists, is outmoded and unavailable for truly serious expression. B. S. Johnson,

[10] David Caute, *Collisions* (London, 1974), p. 146.

for instance, throughout his too short life as a writer, conducted a fierce polemic against the realistic novel. Not, indeed, that Johnson was inclined towards supreme fictions, fantasies and fabulation, since he believed that 'writing fiction is telling lies'. Aggressively self-absorbed, even solipsistic, his principal aim was to make his own experience clear and memorable to himself, and he was quite indifferent to the response of possible readers. In fact, Johnson's objection to the traditional novel was not to mimetic realism, of which he himself was a conscientious practitioner when writing description (though he believed the cinema could do it better), but to its implied claims for narrative order and coherence. He was particularly dismissive of the idea of 'story-telling', of keeping the reader interested in what happens next: 'The drunk who tells you the story of his troubles in a pub relies on the same curiosity.'[11] Johnson was here being not only rather snobbish but aesthetically perverse. The basis of narrative is, I believe, not a contingent cultural artifact but a primeval power of the human mind; however sophisticated his conscious art, the novelist has more in common with the drunk telling stories in a pub than he may like to think.[12]

Despite Johnson's strong, even dogmatic convictions about his art, or possibly because of them, he was never able to make really adequate and convincing use of his striking talents as a writer, whether in the Sternian jokiness of his first two novels, *Travelling People* and *Albert Angelo* (1964), or in the obsessive recreation of his own past, distanced by formal devices, in *Trawl* (1966) or *The Unfortunates* (1969). Yet his last, posthumous novel, *See the Old Lady Decently* (1975), looked like a promising development and made Johnson's death seem all the more tragic. In this work Johnson moved outward from his own experience, though still staying close to what he regarded as verifiably 'true', in order to tell the life story of his own mother up to the moment of his conception. Parts of the account he is forced to invent, but much of it he tells from what he knows. The personal narrative, however, alternates with impersonal ones. There is a series of apparent guidebook extracts about famous places in British history, though with the actual names left out, which Johnson used to represent the growth of Britain in the past and in its decay in the present century.

[11] B. S. Johnson, *Aren't You Rather Young to be Writing Your Memoirs?* (London, 1973), p. 15.
[12] See Barbara Hardy, *Tellers and Listeners: the Narrative Imagination* (London, 1975).

Other passages gave a similar survey of the British Empire in its hey-
day. Johnson regarded the collapse of the British Empire as beginning
during the First World War at Ypres, and there are many references
to that war and abuse of Field Marshal Lord Haig. Finally, the early life
of Johnson's mother up to the year of his birth in 1933 is paralleled with
a series of journalistic vignettes illustrating the social and political
history of those years. One suspects that Johnson may have been directly
influenced by neo-Brechtian developments in the theatre, such as
Oh! What a Lovely War! See the Old Lady Decently is no closer to being
a traditional well-made novel than Johnson's other books—less so, indeed, than some of them—and its formal devices are often arbitrary.
Nevertheless, it works better than many of his other novels—partly,
I suspect, because Johnson had more to write about in it. There is
nothing Tolstoyan in Johnson's attempt to relate the personal and
the historical: but it is significant that he should have been impelled to
make it.

III

One of the recurring problems of contemporary English novelists is
a fundamental lack of material. This much is apparent in many run-
of-the-mill realistic novels about middle-class adultery, teenage revolt
or whatever; and the advent of the problematical novel has had a
bad effect insofar as it has permitted authors to write at length about
nothing other than the fact that they are writing. This is solipsism
with a vengeance, and has provoked an exasperated parody from a
reviewer: 'In front of me, six books. They are on my desk, which is
facing me. Next to them is my typewriter, an Olivetti Lettera 22.
Beyond that, the window of my study. Beyond the window, the
garden, with one apple tree poking wintry fingers into a cracked
Wedgwood sky . . .'[13] There are more possibilities than this, even for
the writer of problematical fiction, and Johnson's late interest in history
has suggested what they might be. The times, for a contemporary
Englishman, are neither secure nor cheerful, but for a novelist with
a sufficient historical sense and the right combination of concern and
detachment they could be remarkably interesting and rewarding.
And some of the most talented English novelists have indeed found
them so, like Angus Wilson in *No Laughing Matter* (1967), which
ranges panoramically over English life from 1912 to 1967. More
recently, Malcolm Bradbury in *The History Man* (1975) and Margaret

[13] Paul Bailey, 'Beyond All This Fiddle', *Observer*, 9 March, 1975.

Drabble in *The Ice Age* (1977) have tried to pin down not just the public events but the shifting sensibility and flavour of the 1970s, in very particular phases: 1972 in *The History Man*, 1975–6 in *The Ice Age*. Both novels, for all their inexorably observant notations of things and behaviour, are pervaded by an idea of historical crisis. Such fictional engagements with the times are courageous, since the novels risk becoming dated in the short term with no certainty of moving in the longer term into the timeless order of literature; they reflect the paradox inherent in the concept of 'contemporary history'. Bradbury's eponymous central figure, the sociologist Howard Kirk, acts out the Marxist claim to a special intimacy with History, but he is as much a victim of the process as its master. Towards the end of *The Ice Age*, not long before he disappears into an East European prison camp, Drabble's hero, Anthony Keating, a television journalist turned property developer, reflects, 'I am nothing but a weed on the tide of history.'

There are other ways of bringing a sense of history to fiction. There are, for instance, those distinguished, extended works derived more or less directly from personal experience in the Second World War, like Olivia Manning's *Balkan Trilogy* (1960–65), set in Rumania and Greece, and the late Paul Scott's *Raj Quartet* (1966–75), set in India. Beyond this, though, lies the possibility of writing historical fiction proper, not in an antiquarian spirit, but with a sense of the interpenetration of past and present, and of the extent to which our own collective past still affects us.

One living English novelist who is profoundly possessed of such a sense is John Fowles; *The French Lieutenant's Woman* is a brilliant novel, of deserved fame. As it is discussed elsewhere in this volume I shall refer to it only briefly here. It reveals, of course, a remarkable capacity to enter the way of life and state of mind of Victorian England, or an aspect of it, achieved by a combination of extensive research and intuitive understanding. Fowles shows, too, immense skill at recreating, in a particular distanced way, the narrative movement, the solid characterization, the descriptive care, of the nineteenth-century realistic novel, that supposedly obsolete and unavailable form. All of which is commented or enlarged on in the author's commentary from the vantage point of 1969 (some would simply say it is 'undercut' but this seems to me an overused piece of critical shorthand). It is a novel in which the realistic and problematical elements are so cunningly interwoven that it is impossible to keep them in a steady perspective, as in a drawing by M. C. Escher. As Malcolm Bradbury has said, it can be taken, first, as 'a very Whig novel, a novel about emancipation through history, with Victorian hypocrisy and ignorance yielding up to modern truth and authenticity, to good faith and freedom. . .'. But another reading can see it equally as 'a novel of ironic counter-pointings in which the present may make no such triumph over the past, in which emancipation is also terrible exposure, a loss as well as a gain'. And there is another possibility, 'which is that the modernist fiction is what is being questioned, being attenuated and modified by the substance and realism of Victorian fiction'.[14] I will merely add to this two further considerations. In the first place, the author's commentary on the action, though no doubt seeming highly innovatory to readers used to the Flaubertian and Jamesian canons of dramatic form and an invisible author, is different only in degree, not in kind, from the practice of Cervantes or Fielding. Even the author's occasional appearances in person have antecedents in the obtrusive Thackerayan stage-manager. In the second place, Fowles's vision of Victorian England, though scrupulously presented, is very much what we are already inclined to see; the element of obdurate unfamiliarity is kept at a minimum. This much is apparent if we consider the sources of the many epigraphs for the chapters. Marx and Darwin are there, and Matthew Arnold and Clough and the Tennyson of 'Maud' and 'In Memoriam', but not such equally representative Victorians as Macaulay or Samuel Smiles or Thomas Arnold. Even the large-eyed, taciturn, impulsive personality of the heroine, Sarah Woodruff, may reflect, as a sceptical friend once remarked to me, a particular fashion in feminine style of the sixties, a Julie Christie type. There is, in fact, a possibility that as well as its deft interweaving between the texts of 1867 and 1969, *The French Lieutenant's Woman* may acquire yet a further dimension of historicity as 1969 ceases to indicate the present and becomes itself part of the past.

There can be no doubt, though, that Fowles's novel forces one to think again about the possibilities both of fictional realism and of the function of history in fiction. Much of the recent revolt against realism has had a limited target in mind, the kind of realistic novel written out of unreflective cultural habit, and a conviction that the forms of nineteenth-century fiction have unchanging validity. J. P. Stern has convincingly argued that realism refers to much more than a particular way of writing, or a form of mimesis. He sees it as a fundamental

[14] Malcolm Bradbury, *Possibilities: Essays on the State of the Novel* (London, 1973), p. 258.

mode in all narrative, even though in such stylized forms as epic and romance it will have a subordinate place. Realism, for Stern is concerned with recognition and understanding and assessment, those moments where, in a remote and unfamiliar literary context, and across the centuries, we achieve a sense of human community. Realism, Stern writes, is anti-ideological and is concerned with a human world of shared meanings and values:

> the world of care: of scrounging and getting and being concerned over the possession of things; but also the world of giving and freeing and loving; the world of movement and change which knows no arrest. Of the fact that reality changes realism is more fully, more intelligently aware than any other literary mode: what it implicitly denies is that in this world there is more than one reality, and that this denial is in need of proof.[15]

In theory one could deny that there is such a world, for ideological reasons, or because one believes that reality is chaos without trace of rationality or possibility of true communion. It is still, though, the world in which we all, novelists, critics and readers, have to live our daily lives. Given a sufficiently broad understanding of realism there is no need to dismiss it.

IV

To return to the recent literary situation, one acknowledges that many novelists have reacted against the convention of unreflecting realism, and turned in a number of possible directions: towards fantasy and fabulation; towards documentary, such as the 'non-fiction novel' of Truman Capote or the 'new journalism' of Tom Wolfe; or towards the alienated, the self-aware and the problematical. And, as I have argued, the problematical mode, which seemed defiant and liberating, has itself become just another convention, by an inevitable process of cultural stabilization. Codes and conventions can be used and modified and extended but never completely escaped. The argument that the novel of traditional realism was the product of a past phase of history—the epoch of bourgeois individualism and naive empiricism as some would put it—and has now become obsolete could seem very convincing. But it was based on a partial and not a total relativism. The assumption that, whereas Scott or Balzac or Tolstoy are no longer acceptable models, Beckett or Borges or Nabokov are, is fundamentally

15 J. P. Stern, *On Realism* (London, 1973), p. 54.

vulnerable. A really radical scepticism might conclude that all models are equally arbitrary and therefore equally available, in an extension of the process described by Peter L. Berger, in another context, as 'relativizing the relativizers'.[16] By a 'negation of a negation' one might, after all, arrive at a new realism that would not be an inevitable or habitual cultural mode, but one possibility to be freely chosen by the novelist—out of a full knowledge of all the possible choices he might make. It would be a reflective realism, aware of the conventionality of fiction, whilst open to the world of experience; as a matter of deliberate choice and consideration for the reader it would preserve the traditional formal decorum of the novel whilst using the insights of problematical fiction. There is a possible analogy in the work of those contemporary painters who have moved through surrealism or abstractionism to discover a new and self-aware form of representational art, which retains their earlier discoveries.

There is one contemporary British novelist who seems to me to have given, in his recent work, remarkable evidence of the possibilities of a conscious realism, and of the use of history in fiction, two concepts which clearly converge and overlap. I am referring to J. G. Farrell, who was born in 1935. His early novels, published between 1963 and 1967, are not of great interest, though it is worth remarking that the first of them, A Man From Elsewhere, hints at qualities to be developed in Farrell's later books. It is unusally impersonal for a first novel, being set entirely among French people in Provence; the plot is about the attempt of a young Communist journalist to expose and unmask a famous novelist, once a Communist, who is dying. The novel deals with large questions of politics and history, containing many ideological discussions, and recollections of the French Resistance and the Warsaw Rising. As a novel it is flat and unconvincing, being too much of a cerebral construct, although it shows Farrell's readiness to appropriate other cultural codes into his fiction; a dominant—and unassimilated—influence on the writing is the contemporary French cinema.

But Farrell did not become an important novelist until the publication of Troubles in 1970 and The Siege of Krishnapur in 1973. Both works are, in a sense, historical novels, and both focus on crucial moments in the rise and fall of British Imperialism. Troubles is 'about' the Irish struggle for independence in 1919–21, and The Siege of Krishnapur is 'about' an episode in the Indian Mutiny in 1857. Such bald summaries are, of

[16] Peter L. Berger, A Rumour of Angels: Modern Society and the Rediscovery of the Supernatural (Harmondsworth, 1971), pp. 43–65.

course, misleading. Farrell is concerned with history, not in the abstract, but in its effect on individual human lives, and with the extent to which it serves as a metaphor for the present. He has written an interesting note about his intentions:

> One of the things I have tried to do in *Troubles* is to show people 'undergoing' history, to use an expression of Sartre's. The Irish troubles of 1919–1921 were chosen partly because they appeared to be safely lodged in the past; most of the book was written before the current Irish difficulties broke out, giving it an unintended topicality. What I wanted to do was to use this period of the past as a metaphor for today, because I believe that however much the superficial details and customs of life may change over the years, basically life itself does not change very much. Indeed, all literature that survives must depend on this assumption. Another reason why I preferred to use the past is that, as a rule, people have already made up their minds what they think about the present. About the past they are more susceptible to clarity of vision.[17]

For Farrell, as for J. P. Stern, reality is indivisible. It is an emphasis worth recovering at a time when the sociology of knowledge insists that it is not. Farrell's real achievement in these novels is to be equally aware of the demands of history and a shared reality, and of the conventional nature of fictional making. My point can be best illustrated by invoking a great novel of the early twentieth century that was also concerned with both history and fictionality, E. M. Forster's *A Passage to India*, a masterpiece of realism and symbolism. Its famous opening sentence has been often discussed as pointing ahead to the locus of the novel's action and to the heart of its symbolic structure; 'Except for the Marabar Caves—and they are twenty miles off—the city of Chandrapore presents nothing extraordinary'. Compare the openings of Farrell's novels; 'In those days the Majestic was still standing in Kilnalough at the very end of a slim peninsula covered with dead pines leaning here and there at odd angles.' (*Troubles*). 'Anyone who has never before visited Krishnapur, and who approaches from the east, is likely to think he has reached the end of his journey a few miles sooner than he expected.' (*The Siege of Krishnapur*). Farrell's sentences are very like Forster's, may even recall him. There is the same detached and knowledgeable descriptive register, the same calmly assured tone (given a further dimension in the first three words of *Troubles* by the use of the Biblical 'In those days'). At the same time,

---

[17] In James Vinson (ed.), *Contemporary Novelists*, pp. 399–400.

they focus attention on the places that are the physical locations of the novels' action, and, equally, their metaphorical centres. From the beginning Farrell shows himself adroit at the manipulation of multiple fictional codes.[18]

In the code of realistic narrative, *Troubles* tells the story of Major Brendan Archer. Demobilized after war service he travels in 1919 to Kilnalough in rural Ireland, to join his fiancée, daughter of Edward Spencer, owner of the Majestic Hotel. The engagement was half-hearted, he knows Angela mostly through correspondence, and when he gets to the Majestic she shows very little interest in him. Soon after his arrival she retires to her room, seemingly ill, though Archer can neither see her nor find out anything definite about her condition. Conscious that he feels no great love for Angela he accepts this situation, and settles down to an inactive life at the Majestic. Then, when he is away on a visit to Dublin, he receives a telegram telling him that Angela has died; he returns to find that she had all along been dying of leukaemia. He still stays on at the Majestic, mainly because he is falling in love with another girl, Sarah Devlin, who is beautiful, eccentric and forceful. She flirts with Archer, but refuses to take him seriously. Archer's attempts to unravel life at the Majestic, to resolve the mystery of Angela, and his long fruitless attempts to advance his relationship with Sarah provide plenty of novelistic interest, in a hermeneutic code of mystery-solving.

Brendan is a familiar novelistic type; perceptive and intelligent, but lazy and weak-willed, or perhaps so traumatized by wartime experience that he needs a long period of inactivity to recuperate. At all events he spends most of his days idly pottering about in the Majestic, which is one reason why Sarah despises him. He does, however, embody other values than those of Kilnalough and Ireland. As an Englishman, an officer and a gentleman, he maintains a certain detachment

---

[18] I am here employing one of the more useful and usable innovations of structuralist criticism, the idea that a novel can be regarded as a network of intersecting codes, as in Roland Barthes's *S/Z*, rather than a set of superimposed levels of meaning. The latter model, which has long been common in Anglo-American critiques of fiction, raises troublesome questions of priority of importance. Again, the structuralist model makes it easier to relate the aesthetic and formal on the one hand, and the historical and social on the other, since all can be seen as separate constituent codes of the total work. Or, in rather different terms, the historical and social can be regarded methodologically as constituent fictions in a larger fiction, which in no way commits one to reductively regarding them as 'only' fictions.

about the way of life in which he becomes more and more immersed. He is also a liberal, basically sympathetic to the cause of
Irish independence, which puts him at odds with the Anglo-Irish,
Protestant group centred on the Majestic and the Spencer family.
Yet for all their Unionist allegiance, they strike Archer on his arrival
as characteristically Irish: ' "How incredibly Irish it all is," thought
the Major wonderingly. "The family seems to be completely mad." '
He is, incidentally, referred to as 'the Major' throughout the narrative,
which is one way of distancing him, of establishing him as a role and
function in contrast to the rich and over-blown personalities of the
Spencer family. Through Archer's eyes Farrell portrays the mad
fecklessness of Irish life; a literary *idée reçue*, no doubt, but steadily sub-
stantiated in everything that Archer discovers. Even Edward Spencer's
fanatical Toryism and assertion of his Unionist allegiance strikes the
well-bred Major as wild and unbalanced. But Edward, rather mad at
the beginning of the story, becomes more and more so as it develops.

Farrell is, in fact, making deliberate use of a familiar set of literary
codes and conventions about the charming eccentricity of Irish life,
and particularly those that deal in a comic or elegiac way with the
decline of the Anglo-Irish gentry; many writers have used and developed them: Somerville and Ross, Elizabeth Bowen, Henry Green, and
Iris Murdoch. There is no doubt that Farrell, who comes from an
Anglo-Irish family, knows intimately what he is writing about, but
the experience is mediated via literary codes. And in his treatment of the
great rambling, decaying structure of the Majestic Hotel Farrell draws
on the conventions of the Gothic novel. Once, years before, the
Majestic had been the centre of a glittering and fashionable social life.
When Archer arrives in 1919 it has fallen on evil days, though it still
keeps a nucleus of elderly guests. The building is vast but neglected;
rain comes through the roof, rooms are abandoned as they become
uninhabitable, plants from the hothouse proliferate and extend their
tentacles everywhere, innumerable cats breed and multiply. No one
quite knows how many rooms there are, staircases and corridors lead
nowhere in a strange arbitrary way. As Archer explores it, the
Majestic presents the fascinating menace of Mervyn Peake's Gormen-
ghast. The treatment is unashamedly literary, but Farrell puts great
imaginative power into establishing this atmosphere. And on occasion
one is aware of other sources than the Gothic novel. In this passage, for
instance, Farrell seems to be recalling one of the familiar images of the
surrealist cinema:

A great quantity of rain-water collected on the sagging flat roof of the Prince Consort wing and presently it relaxed under the pressure, allowing a cascade to empty itself with a musical roar into a grand piano which had been left open and on its side, with one leg amputated.

In every sense the Majestic is central to the book and diminishes the human characters. It is not just a static symbol, but is malignly active in decay, and the progress of the novel can be traced by the inexorable processes that point towards its final collapse: the multiplication of cats, roots thrusting up through the parquet flooring, great sections of the roof falling off in a storm; cracks appearing and ominous creaks sounding in the structure. But the symbolic meaning of the Majestic functions, as it were, centrifugally as well as centripetally, pointing outwards to expanding areas of historic significance. It works, first, as a sign of the decline of the Anglo-Irish Ascendency who had built the Majestic and patronized it in its days of glory; next, the collapse of British rule in Ireland being enacted throughout the novel; and finally and most generally the impending dissolution of the British Empire, still in the future in 1919. *Troubles* is both rich in symbolic implication and precise in its historical references: the Black and Tans move into the district, atrocities and assassinations are reported, and at length negotiations begin in London between the British Government and the rebels. And a global context is established by the intermittent quotation of newspaper reports showing what was happening in the rest of the world: Bolshevism in Russia; D'Annunzio entering Fiume; race riots in Chicago; massacre at Amritzar. It is an effective if unsubtle way of emphasizing the novel's historicity.

Troubles is not easily summarized, though one can certainly describe it, in the first place, as a realistic novel. But it is the work of a cunning and conscious realist, who knows just how much convention is involved in the writing of realistic fiction. *Troubles* is also symbolic, comic, elegiac and historical. Farrell writes with faultless precision and delicacy, and a remarkable command over a wide range of registers, from evocative metaphorical description to humorous dialogue. This novel is, without doubt, one of the triumphs of recent English fiction.

The Siege of Krishnapur is equally brilliant, though of less rich implication. Being set so much further back in time it relies entirely on research and historical imagination, without the particular element of authenticity that Farrell brought to *Troubles* from his personal knowledge of Irish life. Structurally, though, the two novels are similar;

in *The Siege of Krishnapur* the siege of the residency by the mutineers is a long continuing process, with a succession of expectations and resolutions, which corresponds to the unfolding of the narrative. Historically the novel presents a tiny and remote but perfectly representative fragment of Victorian civilization facing violent destruction. The plot is a beautiful mechanism; hints and rumours that all is not well in British India build up, through an opening section of fashionable life at Calcutta, until war and rebellion break out at Krishnapur and the siege commences. Then each day is a record of privations and contrivances, of steady encroachments by the besiegers and of occasional sallies and successful stands by the defenders. It is unquestionably exciting and full of suspense. A sceptical reader might reply that this was '*Boys' Own Paper* stuff'. And so in a way it is; insofar as Farrell is here using Victorian adventure fiction about the Empire as a major code in his narrative, though at the same time conveying meanings and implications that would have been quite inaccessible to the original writers or readers of such stories.

At the heart of the action stands an official of the East India Company, still governing India at that time, Mr Hopkins, whose title is the Collector of Krishnapur. A large, handsome, fastidious man, he is capable and far-seeing. Anticipating trouble, he fortifies the residency in good time, so enabling the European community to take refuge in it when the mutineers descend on Krishnapur. And during the siege he is the natural leader of the garrison, morally and because of his natural resourcefulness. He represents the confident, scientific, expansive side of the Victorian consciousness, and is very sympathetically presented by Farrell, even though some of his attitudes and enthusiasms seem a little ridiculous to the modern reader. The crucial experience of Hopkins's life was the Great Exhibition of 1851 when all the treasures and achievements of Victorian civilization had been displayed. He prides himself on being a whole man with a capacity to appreciate both art and science:

> The study was the Collector's favourite room; it was panelled in teak and contained many beloved objects. The most important of these was undoubtedly *The Spirit of Science Conquers Ignorance and Prejudice*, a bas-relief in marble by the window; it was here that the angle of the light gave most life to the brutish expression of Ignorance at the moment of being disembowelled by Truth's sabre, and yet emphasized at the same time how hopelessly Prejudice, on the point of throwing a net over Truth, had become enmeshed in its own

toils ... Yet Art did not hold sway alone in the Collector's study for on one corner of the desk in front of him there stood a tribute to scientific invention; he had come across it during those ecstatic summer days, now as remote as a dream, which he had spent in the Crystal Palace. It was the model of a carriage which supplied its own railway, laying it down as it advanced and taking it up again after the wheels had passed over. So ingenious had this invention seemed to the Collector, such was the enthusiasm it had excited at the Exhibition, that he could not fathom why six years should have passed away without one seeing these machines crawling about everywhere.

Farrell shows a remarkable capacity to identify with the less familiar and accessible preoccupations of the Victorians. He is very much at home too with their intellectual controversies. One sees this in the agonized religious reflections of the Padre, who is convinced that the siege is a very particular mark of God's disfavour, and in the bitter arguments about medical treatment between the two doctors, Dunstable and McNabb, one old-fashioned and one advanced, which on the outbreak of cholera in the besieged community become quite literally a matter of life and death. Set against the energetic positivism of the Collector is George Fleury, a sensitive and aesthetic poet, a passionate Romantic, who represents another side of Victorian sensibility, and one more familiar to us. Like other late-Romantics Fleury also longs to prove himself as a man of action; and, true to the conventions of the adventure story, he has the opportunity to do so when he takes up arms during the siege.

Thus does Farrell embody many aspects of Victorian civilization. His sense of period, shown not only in his awareness of circumstantial detail but in his capacity to give life and conviction to unfamiliar modes of thought, is extraordinary and in no way inferior to John Fowles's. But *The Siege of Krishnapur* is more than a convincing historical novel, and a gripping tale of adventure, though it is both of these. Its themes are very much part of our own day: the disruption and overthrow of European imperialism throughout the world, of which the Indian Mutiny was an early anticipation; and the precariousness of civilization itself, once, in the Whig reading of history, thought to be moving inexorably from strength to strength. At the end of the novel Farrell shows the Collector, long after the siege, having to consider other and less complacent ways of understanding his civilization; 'Perhaps, by the very end of his life, in 1880, he had come to believe that a people, a nation, does not create itself according to its own best ideas, but is shaped by other forces, of which it has little knowledge'.

In these two novels Farrell seems to me to have broken out of the impasse that many British novelists have lately found themselves in. Far from abandoning realism as useless, he has rethought its possibilities. In *Troubles* and *The Siege of Krishnapur* he has shown both a respect for the past and a vivid sense of how it has made us what we are; this, truly, is the historical imagination at its finest, combined with impeccable fictional invention. His achievement, though inimitable, might still be exemplary.

POSTSCRIPT

Just before this essay went to press I had the good fortune to read in proof J. G. Farrell's latest book, *The Singapore Grip* (1978). Although I can only respond impressionistically after a single reading, it seems to me a very fine novel, which continues the methods and aims of *Troubles* and *The Siege of Krishnapur* and which can be discussed in the terms that I applied to those works. Like its two predecessors, *The Singapore Grip* begins with a calm, detached, Forsterian opening: 'The city of Singapore was not built up gradually, the way most cities are, by a natural deposit of commerce on the banks of some river or at a traditional confluence of trade routes. It was simply invented one morning early in the nineteenth century by a man looking at a map.' *The Singapore Grip* continues—and perhaps concludes—Farrell's delineation of various phases of British imperialism: it is set in Singapore, among the British business and official community, during 1941-2. We see first the foolish, complacent continuation of peacetime ways and habits of thought, despite the growing threat of war with Japan. Then comes the Japanese invasion of Malaya in December 1941; the ensuing defeat of the British forces; the retreat down the pensinsula and, two months later, the surrender of Singapore, which Sir Winston Churchill was to describe as 'the worst disaster and largest capitulation in British history'. This, more than any other single event, marked the collapse of the British Empire. Farrell writes throughout in a large and sombre historical perspective, but with characteristic energy, inventiveness and humour, delighting in the rich, exotic spectacle of the great imperial city on the eve of its downfall. As in *Troubles*, he moves easily from one mode of writing to another, switching from satirical social comedy at the expense of the English community, to detailed accounts of the history and economics of the rubber trade, and in the later sections to vivid descriptions of battle. An immense amount of research has gone into the book, though all its elements combine into an imaginative unity. It is longer, bolder and less tightly structured than *Troubles* and *The Siege of Krishnapur*, though, as before, the unfolding of the narrative is paralleled by a developing process in the events, involving much excitement and suspense: in this case the threats and then the fact of Japanese invasion and the subsequent military campaign. Farrell links *The Singapore Grip* to *Troubles* by bringing in a central figure from the earlier novel, Brendan Archer. Now in middle age and a confirmed bachelor, he is still generally known as 'the Major' although he has long left the army. In the new novel he lives a fairly inactive life on the fringes of the business world. Despite his mild, recessive temperament he is increasingly the hero of *The Singapore Grip*, taking an active part in civil defence and fire-fighting during the heavy Japanese air-raids that precede the attack on the city. As in *Troubles*, Archer sometimes appears as the only sane and integrated man in a collection of people who are in various ways eccentric, malign, foolish and impractical. Whereas in *Troubles* his principal foil had been the mad hotel-owner, Edward Spencer, in *The Singapore Grip* it is the even madder rubber tycoon, Walter Blackett, who cannot take the war seriously even when the Japanese army is at the outskirts of Singapore. Farrell's characters frequently tend to caricature, albeit subtle caricature, and he is clearly interested in extravagant or unbalanced personalities. In this respect there is a Dickensian strain in his art. There is much else to be discussed in this dense and original novel; but a closer examination will take time and successive readings. It is evident, though, that *The Singapore Grip* relates naturally by theme and method to *Troubles* and *The Siege of Krishnapur*, and that together these three novels form a major contribution both to modern English fiction and the literature of imperialism.

Note

On women writers, the best general study so far is Ellen Moers, *Literary Women* (New York, 1976); also see Patricia M. Spacks, *The Female Imagination* (New York, 1975); S. J. Kaplan, *Feminine Consciousness in the Modern British Novel* (Urbana, 1974); Elaine Showalter, *A Literature of Their Own* (Princeton, NJ, 1977), and P. M. Spacks (ed.), *Contemporary Women Novelists* (Englewood Cliffs, NJ, 1977).

Doris Lessing (b. 1919): *The Grass is Singing* (1950); *Martha Quest* (1952); *A Proper Marriage* (1954); *Retreat to Innocence* (1956); *A Ripple from the Storm* (1958); *The Golden Notebook* (1962); *Landlocked* (1965); *The Four-Gated City* (1969); *Briefing for a Descent into Hell* (1971); *The Summer before the Dark* (1973); *The Memoirs of a Survivor* (1974). Some of her criticism is in Paul Schlueter (ed.), *A Small Personal Voice* (New York, 1974); also see her 'Preface' to *The Golden Notebook* (New edn., 1972) and 'On the Golden Notebook', *Partisan Review* 40 (Winter 1973).
Criticism: The most useful book is Paul Schlueter, *The Novels of Doris Lessing* (Carbondale, Ill., 1973); also A. Pratt and L. S. Dembo, *Doris Lessing: Critical Essays* (Madison, Wis., 1974). See also Margaret Drabble, 'Doris Lessing: Cassandra in a World Under Siege', *Ramparts* X (1972), C. J. Driver, 'Profile', *New Review* I, 8 (November 1974), and Mark Spilka, 'Lessing and Lawrence: The Battle of the Sexes,' *Contemporary Literature* 16 (1975).

Margaret Drabble (b. 1939): *A Summer Bird-Cage* (1963); *The Garrick Year* (1964); *The Millstone* (1965); *Jerusalem the Golden* (1967); *The Waterfall* (1969); *The Needle's Eye* (1972); *The Realm of Gold* (1975); *The Ice Age* (1977).
Criticism: Real criticism on Ms Drabble is sparse, but see N. S. Hardin, 'Interview with Margaret Drabble', *Contemporary Literature* 14 (1973); Virginia K. Beards, 'Margaret Drabble: Novels of a Cautious Feminist', *Critique* 15, 1 (1973) (repr. in Spacks, *Contemporary Women Novelists*) and M. V. Libby, 'Fate and Feminism in the Novels of Margaret Drabble', *Contemporary Literature* 16 (1975).

Angela Carter (b. 1940): *Shadow Dance* (1966); The *Magic Toyshop* (1967); *Several Perceptions* (1968); *Heroes and Villains* (1969); *Love* (1971); *The Infernal Desire Machines of Dr Hoffman* (1972); *The Passion of New Eve* (1977).
Criticism: Lorna Sage, 'The Savage Sideshow: A Profile of Angela Carter', *New Review* 39/40 (June/July 1977).

Beryl Bainbridge (b. 1934): *Harriet Said . . .* (1972); *The Dressmaker* (1973); *The Bottle Factory Outing* (1974); *Sweet William* (1975); *A Quiet Life* (1976); *Injury Time* (1977); *Young Adolf* (1978).
Criticism: 'Beryl Bainbridge talks to Yolanta May', *New Review*, 33 December) 1976); Pat Garrett, 'The Sad, Mad, Funny World of Beryl Bainbridge', *Women's Journal*, April 1978.

(For notes on Iris Murdoch and Muriel Spark, see elsewhere in this volume.)

III

Female Fictions: The Women Novelists

LORNA SAGE

I

WOMEN WRITERS are at the sensitive centre of English fiction. Many of the qualities that have distinguished English novels from American and European ones derive from the much greater part women in England played in determining the characteristic form. By the mid-nineteenth century it was pretty well accepted that one of the bonuses of female unfreedom was that women had become the custodians of 'culture'—were experts in all the fragile threads and treacherous currents that made up society's tone, men having neither time nor taste for such vital details. Mrs Ellis's address to the daughters of England in 1843, for example, made the point eloquently:

> If then for a man it is absolutely necessary that he should sacrifice the poetry of his nature for the realities of material and animal existence, for women there is no excuse—for women, whose whole life from the cradle to the grave is one of feeling rather than of action; whose highest duty is so often to suffer and be still; whose deepest enjoyments are all relative; who has nothing, and is nothing, of herself; whose experience, if unparticipated, is a total blank; yet whose world of interest is as wide as the realm of humanity, boundless as the ocean of life, and enduring as eternity![1]

This figure, living in and through others, 'whose deepest enjoyments are all relative', is one of the major characters of English fiction, of course. She acts too as a persuasive model for the ideal novelist, so that, from Richardson to James to Angus Wilson, men have been tempted into literary transvestism, impersonating not only women-as-subjects, but women-as-perceivers, because of the special suffering leisure that is supposed to make them so acute.

The recent fortunes of this tradition reveal its extraordinary resilience.

[1] Sarah Ellis, *The Daughters of England: Their Position in Society, Character and Responsibilities* (1843), p. 124.

Yet at the same time, they hint at its demise—or, if not that, a profound change in its status and significance. The novel, as a vehicle for plots of continuity (Mrs Ellis's 'relative enjoyments'), and as itself a genre favouring the prolific, continuous writer—both aspects of the feminine connection—has become a lot harder to believe in. So have the canons of moral taste conceived in that nagging dialogue between self and others, freedom and servitude. Post-war women novelists find themselves mapping out the limitations of the tradition they are working in. Having sensitive antennae—as convention dictates—they register the ways in which the knowable world that has sustained so much English fiction is disintegrating, and making sensitive antennae perhaps redundant. Some of them (Doris Lessing for example) have recorded the dissolution of that model major character (and novelist): the woman who creates herself in the lives of others. All of them have the sense of being faced with rather abstract and primitive choices (about the *nature* of freedom, or the *definition* of self) which gnaw away at the foundations of a tradition that depends on the limitation of choice. The rich constrictions James and Virginia Woolf suffered and enjoyed have now, to a great extent, to be self-imposed. Things have changed—things to do with both the nature of women and the novel form—but the habit of continuity goes so deep in English writing that it disguises and papers over such changes. Often the result is fiction that is consciously, but nonetheless damagingly, provincial.

II

The greatest exemplar of continuity is Iris Murdoch: *Under the Net* (1954) was a first novel much influenced by Beckett, and therefore half in love with silence, but the eighteen novels since then have given that love, if not the lie, then at least a distant and respectful flavour. She is prolific, wordy and confident. Any one book may, like the first, suggest a deep scepticism about the value of writing; but her *oeuvre* denies doubt. She has become a figure of comfort and reassurance on the fictional scene: whilst most of her contemporaries seem to grow more uncertain, or more metaphysical and thin, she retains a justified belief in her own robust productiveness. Reading any particular novel, one is always conscious that there are other plots waiting in the wings—equally elaborate and surprising—which could have happened and probably have or will. There is a festive rhythm in her writing: *The Nice and the Good* (1968), acknowledging it, punned on the Puckish coincidences of *A Midsummer Night's Dream*, and so did *The Sacred and Profane Love Machine* (1974), as though the writing had become, like the seasons, a regular miracle. Her self-echoes, unlike those of her influential, exiled elders (Beckett or Nabokov), are not really jokes, or desperate gestures provoked by penury of soul; they are rather the careless off-spin of her fertility.

She more and more resembles one of those nineteenth-century writers whose novels appeared in serial form, and began being read before they were finished. Though, of course, with this difference, that for her it has been a matter of conscious commitment, not general convention. She has spelled out her position on the novel's role: it should not be a philosophical fiction, instead it should conjure up an exemplary chaos, a densely populated world that generates random couplings and partings, and lets in some of the unreasonable speci-ficity that protects us against our easy abstractions.[2] It's an argument that touches on the kind of literary metaphysics that would question the activity of writing itself, but only to measure Miss Murdoch's own distance from such inhibiting conclusions. Just as her novels have combined contempt for language with an unrivalled fluency and gusto in its use, so too her sketch of the critical scene turns theoretical scepticism into a reason for confidence.

In effect, she argues that the inadequacy of language is only depres-sing and obsessive for those schools of thought which identify the written word (word for word) with the nature and extent of ex-perience. She would presumably see such doctrines as aesthetic variants of behaviourism. If you spread words like a thin, synthetic plastic coating over things, and refuse to believe that anything escapes, then (on her view) it is hardly surprising that you arrive at a Midas-like poverty. If, on the other hand, you admit that reality eludes words, then their shortcoming are an occasion for celebration, and novels can be made out of their unending approximations and wasteful clashes. This explains how she can manage to be at once anti-utilitarian and anti-idealist, disliking equally what she calls the 'journalistic' and 'crystalline' fashions in modern fiction: they both take the act for the essence, neither can see beyond the edges of its own idiom. Indeed, for her they are the opposite sides of the same coin, since a world reported in the style of documentary is the consequence and corollary of an inner world of autonomous, crystalline fantasy.

[2] Iris Murdoch, 'Against Dryness', *Encounter* XVI (January 1961), pp. 16–20.

Her novels are conceived, each time, in opposition to the whole set of choices apparently on offer for the contemporary writer: she seems set against the very idea that there is such a freedom of choice—presumably because it represents 'Welfare State' thinking applied to literature. Her ties to the nineteenth-century tradition, so evident in the nostalgia with which she alludes to the 'rich receding background'[3] of reality in Victorian novels, act as a (welcome) reminder of unfreedom. The sense of such a pressure from elsewhere, from the past, seems a guarantee of belonging—not being shapelessly and pointlessly 'free'. Though she perhaps nowhere says so exactly, she is obviously in deliberate reaction against the modernist attitudes to literature she characterized so well in her book on Sartre:

> The novelist, too, seemed now to turn to literature as to a metaphysical task whereon the sense of the universe was at stake. Compare the attitude of Proust to his work with that of Tolstoy or even Conrad. The writings of the two latter show forth, are nourished by, their answers to life's questions; Proust's work *is* his answer to life's questions. The human task has become a literary task, and literature a total enterprise, wherein what is attempted might be called reconciliation by appropriation.[4]

Demystifying this 'metaphysical task' has become a major function of her novels, and while she has adopted with relish the various new devices of style and structure that the novel's brooding upon itself has thrown up, she has done so without in the least accepting the wider, demoralizing implications. *The Black Prince* (1973), for instance, set its hero's egocentric narrative in a context of wildly (and mutually) contradictory accounts from the other characters, and yet in the end failed (quite deliberately) to close the magic circle and query the author's own status. It could, after all, have been told in the omniscient third person—there would have been much lost in the way of local effect, but nothing of consequence in 'placing' the story as a whole. Miss Murdoch conspicuously lacks the literal-minded consistency of, say, Nathalie Sarraute or Christine Brooke-Rose, who are genuinely uncertain about where they stand, and hand on that uncertainty to

---

3 'Against Dryness', *loc. cit.*, p. 20.

4 *Sartre, Romantic Rationalist* (1953), Fontana Library 1967, p. 43. For a fuller exposition of Iris Murdoch's continuing battle with the metaphysics of fiction see Lorna Sage, 'In Pursuit of Imperfection', *Critical Quarterly* 19, 2 (Summer 1977), pp. 61–68, a review article on her novel *Henry and Cato* (1976).

the reader in the form of stylistic puzzles. Her notion of integrity is looser, messier and (in the negative sense of the word implied above) more anti-*literary*.

That this connects her with the 'other-centred' model of fiction is clear; she herself uses such terms—*Middlemarch* is 'that brilliant study of being-for-others',[5] or again, 'We need to return from the self-centred concept of sincerity to the other-centred concept of truth'.[6] One of her early heroines, Dora in *The Bell* (1958), was made to realize, 'When the world had seemed to be subjective it had seemed to be without interest or value.' And though later heroes and heroines have been more plausibly muddled (Dora was bullied into very uncharacteristic clarity by an impatient author), most of them glimpse daylight through the gaps in their armour. *A Word Child* (1975) affords a striking example: its narrator-hero, Hilary Burde, has made himself safe against experience by adopting an attitude of passive malice, avoiding choices and chances, timetabling his life by dinner engagements and mapping it by stations on the Inner Circle. He aspires to total culturelessness, and does it mainly by translating everything into dead words (so that meals become menus, and 'shepherd's pie and beans' no more and no less appetizing than '*caneton à l'orange*'), but as usual the plot's elaborate engine, Miss Murdoch's device for humiliating people who want to contain experience, exposes how fake his acceptance is. He too comes to confess, 'I had raged at the accidental but had not let it in any way save me from my insistence upon being the author of everything.'

A similar recognition underlies her own dialogue with her readers. Each new novel will claim all one's present involvement, and yet it will *not* claim to garner up the past or mortgage the future in the way would-be great books do. The novels present themselves as objects for consumption rather than contemplation, despite being a great deal richer and more various than disposable 'popular' novels ever are. In almost every book there is a submerged argument that says that these persons, these particularities, bereft of the dignity of typicality or the resonance of 'character', should suffice. Even a cast list (Hilda, Rupert, Morgan, Julius King, Axel, Simon, Tallis Browne)[7] reveals how slight her people are—completely plausible, but far too individual to re-member. The organizing images and myths, too, are localized and

[5] *Sartre*, p. 60.
[6] 'Against Dryness', *loc. cit.*, pp. 19–20.
[7] The cast list of *A Fairly Honourable Defeat* (1970).

acclimatized in each book, not allowed to form any grand over-arching scheme, even though they may be enduringly important to the author as part of her own mental furniture. A minor example: in *The Flight from the Enchanter* (1955) the final scene was a tableau— 'Rosa sat down on the edge of the sarcophagus and plunged her hand into the cool water. . . . Mischa was standing beside her with a glass of wine. She took it in a dripping hand and he sat down opposite to her on the edge of the sarcophagus.' The image was borrowed from Titian's 'Sacred and Profane Love', a painting that provokes exactly the erotic casuistry the plot needed; and of course, almost twenty years later, Titian provided the structure for the wife/mistress oppo-sition in *The Sacred and Profane Love Machine*. The echo, however, is not a sly hint at some secret code, rather the reverse—an indication of Miss Murdoch's capacity for keeping her favourite images under control.

Over the last ten years the density and particularity of her writing have become its most characteristic features. If the plots seemed once to expend their energies in feats of permutation (*A Severed Head*) now they burgeon into sub- and parallel structures rather like the multi-plying narratives of late Dickens in *Our Mutual Friend*. The turning point may have been *The Red and the Green*, her only historical novel, set in Ireland in 1916, which though it competes utterly unsuccessfully with Yeatsian mythology does seem to have signalled a surge of vital curiosity about the sheer differentness of people's lives, and their secure location in time and place. The number of opaque, separate worlds she can imagine for her characters seems far from exhausted, as does her versatility in finding ways for them to impinge on each other, in bed and out. Indeed the very sexual 'accidents' that used to seem so shocking now look at least as morally robust as all those fictional Victorian marriages. She is a go-between, a pandar, an entrepreneur: an appropriate twentieth-century mutation of the nineteenth-century lady 'whose deepest enjoyments are all relative'.

And yet, for all the confidence, it would be difficult to think of another contemporary writer so irritated by the idea that there is some other kind of book, which she is not writing and deeply dis-approves of, but which nonetheless lurks in the background as a phantom project. In nearly every one of her novels there is a character haunted Casaubon-like by this Platonic idea: Mor in *The Sandcastle* 'was writing a book on the nature of political concepts. He was not making very rapid progress with this work. . . .'; Marcus (*The Time of the Angels*) 'had taken two terms' leave from his school in order to write a book . . . a philosophical treatise'; in *An Accidental Man* someone nearly gets killed for producing a manuscript ('Why did you hit him, really?' 'I didn't like his novel. It was muck, you know, muck.') and the whole murderous plot of *The Black Prince* is perhaps really about authorial rivalry. The Great Books seldom get written, but if by chance they do (like Barney's memoir in *The Red and the Green* or Rupert's life-work in *A Fairly Honourable Defeat*) they end up torn apart in disgust and scattered like confetti. That task, you are meant to feel, is archaic, irrelevant, fake—the magicians and manipulators are withered people, the would-be philosopher-rulers are arid and sterile. Only those masters of ceremonies who develop a personal interest in other people's pleasures and pains—'moral greed' is Miss Murdoch's name for it—are allowed to have any real insight. Fictions must console not by their shapeliness or writtenness or perfection but by their energy and curiosity, and their continuance. A telling instance is Monty in *The Sacred and Profane Love Machine* who writes successful detective novels, but likes to think of himself as a 'serious' writer: he's finally persuaded to abandon his pretentious and abortive scheme, and to carry on with the shameless formula. It may be vulgar, sensational and routine, but then so is life.

Miss Murdoch's novelistic world defines itself against the metaphysical task, and this is why—though it sounds paradoxical—the vitality, variousness and sheer frequency of her productions indicate not only her strength, but her limitation too. Her conviction that human and literary ends are at odds means that her writing does not have to be exact or demanding, and usually is not. Failure (of a special kind, more interesting, you are meant to feel, than success) becomes almost the aim. Her characters, despite the recantations, never seem to achieve the openness their author wants from them—*that* she has to symbolize by bits of randomness, things or creatures from another dimension: the flying saucers in *The Nice and the Good*, a drifting balloon in *The Black Prince*, the illegitimate, unwanted child Luca in *The Sacred and Profane Love Machine*, 'a visitor strayed over the border from another world' who is briefly accepted by the adults, and even learns to talk, but ends shut up in an institution. His fate is the fate of the elusive, real, contingent world. We glimpse it at moments when living gets too complicated, surprising and intense for us, but we cannot sustain the insight, it slips away into some fourth dimension and is lost. You need sensitive antennae indeed to detect such presences. In any case, Miss Murdoch's main achievement is not that she offers brief peeps at unadulterated Contingency, but that she has contrived to displace and postpone the bleak prospect of self-doubting, self-conscious fiction. The 'moral greed' she awakens and feeds depends for its very existence on *not* querying the author's nature or status—each new novel is unsatisfying, both to its author and its readers, and addictive because it's unsatisfying.

III

Iris Murdoch's writing remains, however, the most plausible instance of continuity with the 'relative' values of the nineteenth century. Elsewhere, the attempt to lay claim to a special area of sensitivity and insight untainted by professionalism—the division between (male) utility and (female) culture—is much more obviously a defensive move. Margaret Drabble's novels best illustrate this: almost too well, it might seem, since she takes a certain rueful pride in letting her readers know that *she* knows there are many areas of experience beyond her vision. That, though, is the kind of disarming gesture that should not disarm, because (as in conversation) it so often carries the implication that those excluded possibilities were anyhow overrated. If Iris Murdoch seems a modern mutation of the grand Victorian mass-producers of fiction, Miss Drabble is in many ways a contemporary Mrs Gaskell—there is the same technique of domestic inventory (both for furnishings and emotions), the same overt embarrassment over the role of author, even the same insistent quotation from the Bible and Bunyan.

People are characterized far less by their looks or their talk than by their domestic interiors: 'Simon, sinking into the corner of a deeply-upholstered off-white settee, and resting his feet on a luxuriantly waving, almost grotesquely verdant, silky rug, reflected how much affluence was, quite simply, a question of texture.' This detail from *The Needle's Eye* (1972) consigns Nick and Diana to limbo—their sitting room has been assembled from scratch and without conviction, its pleasureless pneumatic luxury (like their marriage) has no past, and no future; the only genuine feeling it expresses is the anxiety to avoid offence, to neutralize all sharp edges and pressure points. It contrasts eloquently with Rose's scruffy domain, which rouses in Simon memories of the background he and his smart friends have so sucessfully (and disastrously) escaped. His fate is sealed the moment he recognizes 'The tea-cosy, the bundle of knitting, the ticking clock, the arm chairs, the round tin tray, they were all objects that he had not seen for years, and here they all were, well-worn, well used, lived with.' It is hardly an exaggeration to say that these inventories provide the most dramatic life of the book: they measure the characters' grip on life, what they've made of it in the most intimate sense ('Her alliance with the objects around her had irradiated her, transformed her'). Rose's tea-cosy and tin tray are touchstones, talismans that guarantee continuity with the past, signal her capacity to be 'weathered' and matured. It's on the analogy of her furniture that Simon learns to appreciate Rose's skinny frame and crows' feet.

However, when the same time-honoured descriptive formulae are applied to people's invisible inner states their familiarity becomes deadening and drab. A favourite schema is the set of three—a verbal three-piece suite?—'cement, concrete, plaster', or 'comic, dreadful, grotesque', and it is one that is worked very hard in reading behaviour: 'Sally's husband actually gave him a look of sympathy, a look of commiseration, the look of one who knew the problem, admired his inability, and slightly deplored his own success.' Rose's reported consciousness falls into the same rhythm—'no exemption, no cancelling of bonds, no forgetting'; 'the darknesses, the struggles, the anguished reassessments that lay ahead'. There is a monotony about this writing which is perhaps less obvious when things are being listed than when fears and hopes are strung out in the same way, but which must account in part for the lack of urgency and depth in the book's effect. The standpoint of the observer dominates, even when people are observing themselves; there is nothing inward or problematic that escapes translation into commentary. It is striking, too, that the mental inventories seldom reveal ambiguities or potential contradictions, instead they are emphatic and amplificatory—'there was depth, there was power, there was a force that would not, could not accept any indulgence or letting off'. It seems doubtful whether, despite what it says, such language can really convey the inner obligation it is trying to describe. There is very little in these people that is truly private, they exist within the same steady, rather shallow focus whether Rose is analysing herself, or Simon is doing it (which may be a different way of making the point that Miss Drabble can't 'do' men). The message, in *The Needle's Eye* as in the earlier books, is about finding a way to carry some of the accumulated strength and sad experience of the past into the founding of the future, but the

writing suggests that the spiritual goal, the holy city whose image
dominates the novels, is not a city at all, perhaps not even a village,
but a cluttered sitting-room.

Lone individuals and wide spaces are anomalous. There are signs of,
course, that the author herself feels hemmed in by her point of view;
in *The Needle's Eye* the most surprising aside of this kind is an inset
paragraph completely at adds with the drab, anxious tone of the
characters:

> . . . Lovely Miss Lindley, striding across the asphalt playground to
> that building that looked like a prison but thanks to her and people
> like her was not one: let her so forever stride, ask no questions about
> her future or her past. . . . Do not seek to disbelieve it, do not dis-
> turb her with disbelief, because she is, there she walks. . . . Do not
> believe that she does not, could not exist. O lovely Miss Lindley.
> O almost confident apostrophe.

This set-piece is noticeably literary and out-of-place; the author
sounds alarmingly sprightly, and embarrassed at her own draing, as
she gestures at the things the book does not do—at the high style, at
frank comic artifice, at characters who are not obliged to comment
interminably on themselves, at characters, in a word, fully *fictional*.

In *The Realms of Gold* (1975) the people are more mobile and some
of the settings far from homely ('mosaic pavements, rippling fountains,
heavenly Musak') but family inventory still frames the plot: the heroine
Frances Wingate is a fairly celebrated archaeologist, freed by talent and
money from most of the domestic pressures; her children are nearly
grown up, her marriage has been painlessly disposed of, and what
scars she does bear become her, making her (more convincingly than
dreary Rose) 'a person with a history survived'. Inevitably she is
drawn to explore the ties she has rejected (her stalemated love affair,
her many-branching, spiteful, melancholy family); however she does
it with gusto, and injects new life into the role of cultural observer by
wanting (and even sometimes grabbing) what she sees. Her self-
commentary is full of greed and curiosity, and the contrasts between
her way of life and those of her re-discovered relatives are altogether
more comic and shocking than the rather tired rooted-versus-rootless
oppositions of *The Needle's Eye*. One of the book's triumphs is the
description of the life of Janet Bird, dragging out a furious, baffled
existence on a new estate, with a bewildered new baby, surrounded by
stainless steel wedding presents and dreaming of atrocities.

But if the familiar territory is mapped with more vividness and humour, the familiar omissions have also become more overt. The book seems to have been planned so that Frances's reimmersion in human complications should contrast with her cousin David's deepening loneliness and detachment (she the archaeologist, he the geologist savouring the earth's indifference to human habitation). Frances is a survivor, David represents the opposite impulse towards the perfect, the inorganic and the dead. However David is most noticeable for his absence: he cannot convincingly exist in a style devoted to accumulation, and in a defiantly cheerful preamble to Part Three of the novel, Miss Drabble says as much:

> The truth is that David was intended to play a much larger role in this narrative, but the more I looked at him, the more incomprehensible he became. . . . Imagine him, David Ollerenshaw, standing there . . . indefinably English, indefinably odd, with the oddness of one who spends much time alone, thinking about inhuman things. Watch him, as he begins to stumble, a small figure against a small volcano, down the mounds of pyroclastic rubble, back to his new car. Tomorrow he sets sail for Africa.
>
> And we can leave him there, on the eve of departure, and return home to Frances Wingate; she is a more familiar figure, a more manageable figure in every way.

David wanders again and again beyond the boundaries of his author's sympathy and vision, joining the ghost-characters of fiction—like Mrs Gaskell's John Barton, who was meant to be the centre of her 'Tale of Manchester Life', but whose abstract political hatred put him beyond the pale, so that half way through the book she says (sadly, but with relief) 'Let us leave him'.[8] Miss Drabble is less disturbed by her inability to imagine 'inhuman things', and credits them with less reality (John Barton departs from view to commit a murder, David one can't imagine doing anything definite). In *The Realms of Gold* her explicitness about her limitations is almost celebratory; whatever threat David represents, in his incurious, empty way of perceiving, and his separateness, is shoved aside by the familiar, listable objects she has always been at home with.

IV

If one were to synthesize the ghost-novel—the negative book Miss Murdoch's misguided characters keep trying to write, the one where

[8] *Mary Barton* (1848), Chapter XVII.

Miss Drabble's vagrant geologist would be in his element—it might well be written by Muriel Spark. It would be a novel structured with metaphysical finality and economy, arrogantly contemptuous of accident, and shamelessly given over to fine writing. Not all of Mrs Spark's novels, of course, are so exactly contrived, but her best and most characteristic work (starting with her first novel *The Comforters* in 1957, and culminating in *The Driver's Seat* (1970), *Not to Disturb* (1971) and *The Abbess of Crewe* (1974)) is thoroughly at odds with the unsmart, cluttered styles so far discussed. The very outline of her writing career spells discontinuity: she became a novelist in her late thirties, after her conversion to Catholicism, when her taste for paradox and her dislike of 'Protestant' introspection were already decided; and when the success of *The Prime of Miss Jean Brodie* (1961) made her an international best-seller she became an expatriate, first in America, then in Rome, living with much of the panache her role as author predicted. Her novels have often dealt with people who exist in their projections of themselves (notably her first 'Italian' book, *The Public Image* (1968)) and have in their turn been often dramatized and filmed, confirming the impression of glamour and unreality.

'Image' and 'scenario', in their public relations and political usage, are the terms that seem best to describe the substance of her novels: 'image' for character, 'scenario' for plot. Cameras, tape-recorders, all the most up-to-date means of reproduction and record (and forgery) are in evidence in her stories—not as alien presences either, but as reminders that the contemporary reality she portrays is rotten with fiction. However, it would be misleading to represent her as alto-gether rootless: she certainly has 'influences' (Beerbohm, for example, and Waugh) and some of her most memorable and alarming figures, like Miss Brodie and the Abbess remain 'ladies' and British to the (empty) core. What sets her apart from her contemporaries is not that she is untouched by tradition, but that she reads the tone and direction of English culture very differently. From her point of view its most fascinating aspect is people's capacity for bland inconsistency and heroic snobbery, which she connects (in the Abbess, for instance) with the most apparently un-English frauds and self-delusions, like Watergate. Again, her women resemble Miss Murdoch's in being pandars and manipulators, but are very different in their coolness, brittleness and lack of curiosity; women's fertility and other-centred-ness is likely in her books to take the comic, contemptuous form of Heloise (*Not to Disturb*)—'She looks at her stomach as if to discern by a kind of X-ray eye who the father truly might be. "There was a visitor or two," she says. "I must say, there did happen to be a visitor or two about the time I caught on." ' What women are especially good at perceiving is not the particular, but the general condition; they are open to impersonal insights ('the Id tends to predominate over the Ego'). The old jibe that females are all outside, all image, takes on a different meaning in the context of Mrs Spark's unremitting scepticism about anyone's capacity to have coherent intentions. Lise in *The Driver's Seat*, ruthlessly tracking down the stranger who is to kill her, satirizes the notion that people possess characters. Her reckless emptiness is that of someone caught up in a role.

Mrs Spark's vision is so blatantly selective that there would be little point in claiming it was truer than that informed by moral greed, feeding off the detail of people's lives. She too makes a point of her limitations:

> 'Who were those people banging at the back door and ringing at the front?'
> '. . . One of them's a masseuse that I haven't seen before.'
> 'And the other?' says Lister.
> 'The other didn't say. I didn't ask.'
> 'You did right,' Lister says. 'They don't come into the story.' (*Not to Disturb*)

However, she has a high reputation amongst critics—for two main reasons. One is that her cruelly predestined narratives (with the present tense that allows the future to seep, as it were, into the present, and the present into the past) fit very well into the most currently desperate (and therefore most convincing) theories about the novel. Fictions that stress the corruptions of fiction, as in the liar paradox, are international currency, so that the idiosyncratic scepticism of Mrs Spark connects her not only with the inheritors of the *nouveau roman* in France, but with American writers like Joyce Carol Oates, whose novels and stories document on an epic scale the erosion of the moral 'I' by patterns of violence.[9] The other reason is that (as befits someone who doesn't distinguish between image and essence) she writes with an elegance and economy that invite analysis. She has the great advantage (from the critical point of view) of not posing the problems of unevenness, redundancy or awkwardness.

[9] Miss Oates's latest novel *Childwold* (1977) does this with devastating literalness: her heroine thinks of herself in the *second* person.

V

Doris Lessing poses all these problems. Although she is the most original and impressive of the women novelists, her work is also fragmented, repetitious and sprawling. *The Golden Notebook* (1962) came to terms with the fluidity—or rather, discontinuity—of her various authorial selves, but its fractured form was a Pyrrhic victory. Her two most recent books *The Summer before the Dark* (1973) and *The Memoirs of a Survivor* (1974) once again demonstrate the opposing poles between which she moves: more or less observed social reality on the one hand, and visionary dispatches from somewhere on the frontiers of mental space on the other. In one version she seems thoroughly immersed in the traditional role. It is hard to recall a more exact and subtle praise of women as guardians of the living texture of place and time than this passage from *The Four-Gated City* (1969), describing bomb-damaged London in the late 1940s, when Mrs Lessing arrived from Southern Rhodesia:

> ... Iris, Joe's mother, had lived in this street since she was born. Put her brain, together with the other million brains, women's brains, that recorded in such tiny loving anxious detail the histories of windowsills, skins of paint, replaced curtains and salvaged baulks of timber, there would be a recording instrument, a sort of six-dimensional map which included the histories, lives and loves of people, London—a section map in depth.

Even here the conscientious materialism which survived her break with official Communism takes her a long way from 'taste' as understood by Miss Drabble. But her pursuit of literal truth takes her a lot further—into the alien territories of gothic and science fiction; she has written about madness in such a way as to allow herself and her readers to suspect that *she* is mad; and (perhaps most unforgiveably, in terms of inherited decorum) she has failed to be humorous and ironic at the crucial moments when a wry gesture of understanding would purchase acceptance for her disturbing revelations.

Irony is so important because it is the main way of retaining authorial immunity; when it is discredited the familiar observer-manipulator becomes just another fallible character, as novelist Anna does in the opening scene of *The Golden Notebook*. Anna finds herself suddenly resisting the urge towards 'making it humorous', 'the safe tone' (' "Yes, it's all very odd ..." ') of quizzical mockery and self-deprecation, 'half-laughing, plaintive, rueful'. Meeting with her friend Molly after a year, she's alerted to the cosy, conspiratorial flavour of their talk ('if I'm not careful, Molly and I will descend into a kind of twin old-maidhood, where we sit around saying to each other, Do you remember how that man, what-was his name, said that insensitive thing, it must have been in 1947? . . .'). Which is of course itself very accurate, and very funny—at such moments, Anna swops irony for double irony. Nonetheless, the attack on the humorous tone is real—it suddenly seems dangerous because it denies the possibility of real failure, real loneliness. As she looks back at herself and her friends of the left in Africa, Anna spots 'the wrong tone' again and again—'self-punishing, a locking of feeling, an inability or a refusal to fit conflicting things together to make a whole . . . the refusal means one can neither change nor destroy'; or again, 'I know how to watch the jokes people make. A slightly malicious tone, a cynical edge to a voice, can have developed inside ten years into a cancer that has destroyed a whole personality'. It's not necessary to labour the point: the cure is worse than the disease, the irony that enables her to judge the world, and to contain her own self-love and despair—that seems necessary for survival—turns out to be killing her. From the point of view of the traditional values of criticism, and fiction, this is bound to seem paradoxical: irony's purpose is supposed to be 'to fit conflicting things together'. Mrs Lessing, though, sees it as a means of containing, and insulating, potential irritants—in the body politic at large, as well as the individual, as in the treatment of 1960s satire in *The Four-Gated City*:

> . . . in spite of (because of?) society's never having been more shrilly self-conscious than it is now, it is an organism . . . whose essential characteristic is the inability to diagnose its own condition. . . . There is a new phenomenon, or one conceived to be new: the creature, sullenly alerted, all fear, is concerned for only one thing, how to isolate it, how to remain unaffected. The process is accomplished, in this society, through words . . . communism, traitor. . . . Or anger, or commitment, or satire.

One of the main temptations that faces her heroines is to rest in the double irony of watching humour and awareness defeat themselves (' "Yes, it's all very odd . . ." '). They take instead to cultivating their despair, courting insecurity, looking for portents of the new too amorphous and too far beyond the pale to be processed and spat out—'if society is so organized, or rather, has so grown, that it will not admit what one knows to be true, will not admit it that is, except as it comes out perverted, through madness, then it is through madness and its variants it must be sought after.' (*The Four-Gated City*)

Five sections of *The Golden Notebook* of course are titled 'Free Women', a phrase that starts as double irony in the cosy complicities of the opening scene, and comes nastily true as Anna gets more graceless, lonely and desperate—'I want to be able to separate in myself what is old and cyclic, the recurring history, the myth, from what is new, what I feel or think that might be new'. What's being jettisoned—as the language shows, with its vehemence, stiffness, and anxious literalness—is the convention that women, and especially novelists, rule their worlds by cunning indirections. Mrs Lessing's exposure and fragmentation of the person of the author has proved very important to the Womans' Liberationists: not a qualified acceptance of a change in mores (nor breaking taboos on the unmentionable, like menstruation) but the revelation of an aggressively diffuse, unformed, uprooted state of being, in which anything is possible. This makes her a difficult and deeply embarrassing writer; she is moving always away from synthesis, from 'maturity', and towards an embryonic future that seems primitive, formless, magical—in which individuals are more isolated than ever, shapeless strangers communicating by overlapping nightmares and dreams, plucking their knowledge out of the ether.

The Four-Gated City chronicles the breakdown of decorum most completely, ending with Martha's search for documentation on the discoveries she's made by experimenting with her own psyche. Once she exorcizes her fears of seeming dotty and indecent, she finds plenty of it, in fantasy writing, in hermetic philosophy, in the quotations from Sufis that are taken out of the text, and made into epigraphs:

> Organs come into being as a result of a need for specific organs. . . .
> In this age of the transcending of time and space, the complex of
> organs is concerned with the transcending of time and space. What
> ordinary people regard as sporadic and occasional bursts of telepathic
> and prophetic power are seen by the Sufi as nothing less than the
> first stirrings of these same organs . . .
>
> (IDRIES SHAH, *The Sufis*)

Assembling an alternative tradition, however, does not help very much when its pillars are themselves so suspect, so redolent of pseudo-science and pseudo-religion. Mrs Lessing is right that one is trained to shrink from this stuff, unless it is safely packaged in a sub-genre (science fiction) or tacitly admitted to be mere metaphor. And for good reason: at best, these ideas provide a crude, amateurish framework for describing mental events compared with the long-elaborated, much-practised complex of attitudes she has discarded. The curse of the new turns out to be that its range of expression is so limited as to make it seem rapidly familiar, even banal (original as in original sin).

Briefing for a Descent into Hell (1971) suffers from these difficulties; its spiritual odyssey is a weary frenzy, often awakening echoes that belong to the ready-made properties of literary fantasy, rather than to tentative, newly discovered areas of response. What its breathless flow strives for (interrupted by the probing exasperated tones of the two psychiatrists effecting their cure) is a view of the human world without benefit of the middle-distance perspective of sanity, at once god-like and myopic: 'To celestial eyes, seen like a broth of microbes under a microscope . . . it begins to sense itself as one . . . where the scummy film transcends itself, here and here only, and never where these mad microbes say I, I, I, I, I, for saying I, I, I, I, is their madness. . . .'

The Memoirs of a Survivor (1974) is more explicit about the drabness and despair the 'free' psyche encounters along with the ecstatic release of becoming 'a note in the harmony'. It describes the decline and fall of a city, the whole superstructure of civic and personal identity dissolving into tribal masses, squalid and devouring, 'everyone tasting and licking and regurgitating everyone else'. Paralleling this repulsive and frightening process, the narrator finds the edges of her own perceptions blurring and opening out uncanny new dimensions. Her experience is no longer just hers: the blank, dead wall of her room becomes transparent and dissolves, so that she can step through into other lives in inner space. It is like (or rather it *is*, no simile is intended) the development of an extra sense, and an extra wordless mode of communication, growing out of civilization's decay.

Mrs Lessing's teasing, fragmentary description of what happens when the sitting-room walls, and the solid habits of feeling they enclose and preserve, fall away, is an appropriate tailpiece because it suggests both excitement and a new poverty—'That world, presenting itself in a thousand little flashes, a jumble of little scenes, facets of another picture, all impermanent, was folding up as we stepped into it, was parcelling itself up, was vanishing, dwindling and going.' So much has been lost, 'cancelled out' as she says: the picture, shorn of landmarks and touchstones, becomes a matter of juggling with two dimensions. In place of characters, there are primitive, fluid creatures—networks of physical sensations and metaphysical intuitions, undoubtedly alive, but without personality or conscience. Not that these new mutants are altogether unrecognizable: Mrs Lessing looks (and is) a lonely, marginal figure these days in the context of her generation of English novelists, but she is a benevolent, tutelary presence on the American scene. (For instance, in her autobiography *Flying* (1975) Kate Millett records calling on Mrs Lessing in London, not so much as an illuminating encounter, but as an act of almost automatic, daughterly reverence.) Though her particular, home-made mystical naturalism exercises no obvious influence, her experiments in uprootedness and her refusal to ironize herself into respectability have had an extraordinary exemplary force. Joyce Carol Oates (again) typifies the kind of writing:

> A mysterious, unfathomable revolution seems to be taking place in our civilization ... characterized by loss of ego, by experiences of transcendence among more and more people, especially younger people ...[10]

This is not (as the earnest tactlessness of the style announces) revolution as consummation—the elaborate flowering of self—rather, it is conscious vandalism.

Freedom, breaking down the careful balance between self and others on which the solidity and continuity of the traditional novel depended, is at once exhilarating and unexpectedly depressing. Endless choices can mean no choice at all (when everything is a portent, nothing is). This is perhaps the source of the underground connection between Mrs Lessing's kind of novel and Mrs Spark's; though one pursues the severely truthful while the other enjoys good lies, they both operate in a world where the distinction between 'Ego' and 'Id' has utterly collapsed, and where the novelist's task is inevitably a metaphysical task. One consequence of this is that 'novel' has to cover works as wildly different as *Briefing for a Descent into Hell* and *The Abbess of Crewe*—the genre itself is coming apart at the seams, and shows few signs of reassembling. There is little one can predict about the attitude the author will take up towards her readers, except that it will be, perceptibly, something taken up, with an edge of arbitrariness and defiance, rather as the heroine of *The Summer Before the*

10 *New Heaven, New Earth* (1976), p. 246.

Dark experiments with putting on and taking off again the role of attractive woman.

> She walked away out of sight . . . took off her jacket . . . showing her fitting dark dress. She tied her hair dramatically with a scarf. Then she strolled back in front of the workmen, hips conscious of themselves. A storm of whistles, calls, invitations. Out of sight the other way, she made her small transformation and walked back again: the men glanced at her, did not see her.

A sorry parody of the woman 'who has nothing, and is nothing, of herself; whose experience, if unparticipated, is a total blank. . . .'

VI

The most successful and sinister of the newer 'generation' of women novelists are hardened to dressing up: their choices of forms and settings seem to have come from the theatrical costumiers. Angela Carter's Kings Road Gothic, for instance, or Beryl Bainbridge's self-enclosed, feebly crazy settings, where people are destroyed by panic and timidity, and where one's trapped into watching them as if they were creatures in a zoo. Miss Bainbridge belongs in fact to the same generation as Margaret Drabble, but is worlds away in sensibility and style. Her career began abruptly in the 1970s with the now characteristic formula, brief, bleak and suggestive (a couple of earlier, more rambling novels having been stricken from the record), and her imagination feeds avidly on the daily disasters chronicled in the newspapers (a suburban siege, for instance, in *Injury Time* in 1977) as well as on early memories of the austere, shell-shocked 1940s (*The Dressmaker, A Quiet Life*). What's distinctive about her fictional world is the coincidence of lovingly rendered domestic drabness and seaminess with violent events which her lucid, exact style persuades you to accept as just as 'normal' as (say) the hamster dying, or the dirty dishes in the sink. Her characters, and most noticeably her heroines, are alienated from their own emotions by the routines of family life, so that they react to 'Gothic' intrusions with shocking, hilarious resignation, and even efficiency. The neatness, economy and hard humour of the writing (her closest affinities are predictably with a split-off sub-genre, the detective thriller) are a tacit satire on the traditional woman's novel, the mode of concern and other-centredness. In some ways her plots, which often reverse causation to make passive fear the source, rather than the effect, of violence, resemble Muriel

Spark's, except that the point being made is a social rather than a theological one. It no longer seems necessary to cultivate baroque beliefs in order to arrive at that eerily splintered portrayal of character.

Angela Carter, too, explores the pathological, corrupt effects of passivity, and relishes still-lifes and other tableaux suggestive of arrested existence—though with a great deal more self-consciousness ('life imitating rotten art again,' as one of her characters thinks in parenthesis). She has a throwaway expertise in the delights of suffering —'we fought a silent battle of self-abnegation and I won it, for I had the stronger character' (*Fireworks*, 1974)—and her novels and stories take shockingly for granted that people *are* their roles. Her creative career to date has been a witty, elaborate, many-sided and passionate attack on 'reality' (i.e., the traditional consensus) and hence of course on 'realism'. The earlier books contented themselves with miming the decay of experience into dream and fantasy, but since *Heroes and Villains* (1969) her writing has become much more boldly speculative, and the dividing line between her human characters and the dolls, puppets and erotic icons they like to play with has become increasingly blurred. Symbols of exploitation and ecstasy—a Hollywood siren, a Transylvanian count, a tribe of sexist centaurs, a Reichian scientist— conspire to oust the ordinary universe, and yet ('A critique of these symbols is a critique of our lives') they are portayed with a paradoxical, mocking seriousness, almost with an anthropologist's careful curiosity. The effect is at once regressive (back to fairy tales and myths) and adventurous, since she explores her property box of images so coolly and subversively. Her style, formed more by French literature than English, and crystallized by a spell in Japan, is exactly adapted to rendering surfaces and fashions of behaviour with a conclusiveness that subtly denies essence—or rather, relocates it. She is of course a 'Gothic' writer, but her Gothicism consists less in the nature of her properties and figures than in her obsessive and analytic attitude to them—the splintering of consciousness that she assumes as a routine condition of life and of writing. As author, she plays a part, volun- tarily, experimentally, temporarily; she switches from pastiche of romantic movies to pastiche of science fiction with conscious agility; and her 'characters', thanks to this Frankensteinish skill, exchange roles and even (in *The Passion of New Eve*, 1977) sexes, with monstrous plausibility. Such bizarre fictions may simply represent a Gothic footnote or interlude, as they seemed to in the nineteenth century. However, their rootlessness, the strangeness, vulgarity and arbitrariness of the ideas they use to interpret the times, are harder, now, to classify as eccentricities. They haunt the novel of continuity, these negative presences and 'eldrich guerillas' (Angela Carter's jokey phrase). They are already crowding it out of existence.

Note

Samuel Beckett.
   Life and works: Deirdre Bair, Samuel Beckett: A Biography (New York, 1978) is
the one 'life': also see John Calder (ed.), Beckett at Sixty: A Festschrift (London,
1967) and James Knowlson, Samuel Beckett: An Exhibition (London, 1971). The
main bibliography is Samuel Beckett: His Works and His Critics (Berkeley/Lon-
don, 1970), supplemented with John Pilling, Samuel Beckett (London, 1976).
   Criticism: Beckett's work is covered in almost every critical series on modern
writers, but two stimulating studies are A. Alvarez, Beckett (London, 1973),
with some useful dissents, and Hugh Kenner, A Reader's Guide to Samuel
Beckett (London, 1976), which supplements his earlier Samuel Beckett: A Critical
Study (London, 1965). Richard Coe's Beckett (London, 1964) valuably relates the
earlier fiction to philosophical influences; Vivian Mercier, Beckett/Beckett
(Oxford, 1977) studies the importance of the Irish background. Martin Esslin
(ed.), Samuel Beckett: A Collection of Critical Essays (Englewood Cliffs, NJ,
1965) selects from major studies. More specific anthologies are J. D. O'Hara
(ed.), Twentieth-Century Interpretations of Molloy, Malone Dies, The Unnamable
(Englewood Cliffs, NJ, 1970) and Katherine Worth (ed.), Beckett the Shape
Changer (London/Boston, 1975). John Calder, London, publish A Journal of
Beckett Studies.

Malcolm Lowry.
   Life and works: the standard life and best analysis of the career is Douglas Day,
Malcolm Lowry: A Biography (New York, 1973; London, 1974), supplemented
by Tony Kilgallin, Lowry (Erin, Ont., 1973) and M. C. Bradbrook, Malcolm
Lowry: His Art and Early Life (Cambridge, 1974). Also see H. Breit and M.
Lowry (eds.), Selected Letters of Malcolm Lowry (Philadelphia, 1965; London,
1967), and Margerie Lowry (ed.), Malcolm Lowry: Psalms and Songs (New York,
1975). For publications by and about M.L., see Earle Birney and Margerie
Lowry's bibliography in Canadian Literature 8 (Spring 1961), 9 (Summer 1961),
11 (Winter 1962), 19 (Winter 1964) and W. H. New, A Malcolm Lowry Check-
list (Boston, 1978). J. Combs, Malcolm Lowry, 1909–1957: An Inventory of His
Papers . . . (Vancouver, 1973) itemizes the major collection of his mss., at the
University of British Columbia.
   Criticism: main studies are G. Woodcock (ed.), Malcolm Lowry: The Man and
His Work (Vancouver, 1971); W. H. New, Malcolm Lowry (Toronto, 1972);
R. H. Costa, Malcolm Lowry (New York, 1972); Anne Smith (ed.), Malcolm
Lowry (London, 1978). Also see D. Edmonds's pioneering 'Under the Volcano:
A Reading of the "Immediate Level" ', Tulane Studies in English XVI (1968),
63–105; A. Pottinger, 'The Consul's Murder', Canadian Literature, 67 (Winter
1976), 53–63; R. Binns, 'The Lowry Fringe', Canadian Literature, 72 (Spring
1977), 91–2; J. Arac, 'The Form of Carnival in Under the Volcano', PMLA 92
(May 1977), 481–9. A Malcolm Lowry Newsletter appears twice yearly from
Dept. of English, Wilfrid Laurier University, Canada.

IV

Beckett, Lowry and the Anti-Novel

RONALD BINNS

I

THE CONVENTIONAL account of the development of the postwar English novel as a movement from prewar experimentalism to postwar realism has tended to displace or to overlook a good number of writers of experimental stamp—like William Golding or Lawrence Durrell—who are recognized in critical discussion to be of importance, but held to lie outside the mainstream.[1] Certainly, for a satisfactory record, we need to think not in terms of one tradition or line of development, but of at least two. Thus, we would need to centre in the alternative line the work of two of the most important writers to produce fiction in the postwar decade: Samuel Beckett and Malcolm Lowry. They are writers usually displaced from the English sequence, yet they both stand in oblique yet significant relation to contemporary English writing; they are not, on the face of it, very similar writers, yet they have certain ground in common. The social novel has had no appeal for either writer; and in the context of the development of fiction in the English 1950s it is significant that Beckett (b. 1906) and Lowry (b. 1909) belong to an older generation than almost all the other writers who came to prominence in the 1950s and 1960s. Further, in a period when provincialism and localism were strong forces in English writing, they made their lives and found many of their artistic sources and influences elsewhere: indeed they chose a conscious displacement. Both sustained an internationalist view of the arts, established complex canons of reference and influence, and became indeed exemplary modern expatriates, writers 'unhoused,' to the extent that they are regularly claimed as belonging to traditions of writing other than the British.

[1] One critic with an alternative emphasis is Robert Scholes, whose *The Fabulators* (New York, 1967) does recognize the importance of a fictive and fable-making tradition.

Yet, in other respects, they have the appearance of being contrasting kinds of writer. They went in different directions: Lowry to Mexico and Canada and to a romantic solitude, Beckett to *avant garde* Paris. Lowry died in obscurity in 1957; just around this time, Beckett was beginning to establish a massive international reputation through the success of his play *Waiting for Godot*. Their subsequent reputations have followed very different courses. Lowry's posthumous fame has taken a long time to develop; however, with the gradual publication of the novels and stories left unpublished at the time of his death, his career has come more sharply into focus, his importance has grown much clearer, and there is much recent publication on his work. *Under the Volcano* (1947) is now widely accepted as a masterpiece; however, the more experimental fiction of Lowry's last ten years has found rather less critical approval. Indeed the dissonant narrative form, and the weight of private, biographical reference that dominates it, have largely been interpreted as an expression of imaginative poverty, artistic incompleteness, and alcoholic collapse. By contrast, Beckett's career is now stabilized as a model of calm and order. Over the last twenty years, he has gone on to publish a variety of novels, stories, plays for radio, television and stage, and a filmscript; each has been instantly recognized as offering a new adjustment of perspective on that minimal, absurdist world of futile endurance which has become identified as 'Beckettian'. There has been an enormous body of commentary, and his reputation is worldwide; he holds the Nobel Prize. However, despite all this, he remains a deeply reticent figure, rarely giving interviews, never appearing in public, and emerging only infrequently to direct the production of one of his plays. Where Lowry has, in many ways, won most attention through his life story, powerfully represented in Douglas Day's biography, Beckett has offered us remarkably little material towards a life. When the narrator of the last of *Texts for Nothing* (1955) remarks 'get out of here and go elsewhere, go where time passes and atoms assemble an instant, where the voice belongs perhaps, where it sometimes says it must have belonged, to be able to speak of such figments', the last laugh, for the present, is Beckett's.[2] Whether or not the 'figments' are of the

[2] Since writing this, Deirdre Bair's *Samuel Beckett: A Biography* (New York, 1978) has appeared. Reviewers have suggested, however, that the substantial biographical information it contains is, paradoxically, at odds with her stress on the confessional character of Beckett's prose; the relation of the art and the life continues to remain problematic. See Richard Ellmann, 'The Life of Sim Botchit,' *New York Review of Books* XXV, 10 (15 June, 1978), pp. 3–4, 6–8.

imagination or, as sometimes seems the case, genuine biographical recollections remains, until a biography appears, impossible to decide.

Lowry and Beckett are indeed different kinds of modern writer: one romantically assertive, the other infinitely recessive. With Lowry we are involved in the drama of the life, with Beckett we are put on the defensive; and it is the impersonal elements in his fiction—narrative form, metaphysical wit—which attract immediate attention, rather than the often human, emotional content which is nonetheless strangely secreted in Beckett's limpid prose. Norman Mailer, sceptically observing the beginnings of the cultural phenomenon of Beckett, noted the ways in which critical deference muted reactions to his work.[3] And that deference has become ever more pronounced over the last twenty years, when Beckett has been critically acclaimed as one of the greatest living writers—though his fiction is probably read scarcely at all outside university campuses, and premiere seasons of his latest plays fail to pack London theatres. Scholars have tended to emphasize the control, the coherence, the systematic evolution of his career, and it has become a post-modernist or absurdist ceremonial. However, if we contrast it with Lowry's, we get some insight into the difficulties and uncertainties of direction which have underlain the production of experimental fiction in the years since 1945—difficulties and uncertainties which call into question the confident claim, made in many quarters now, that the modern novel *must*, by stylistic and historical necessity, be the anti-novel.[4]

For one firm assertion of such a belief, we might look to Gabriel Josipovici's influential, structuralist-biased study of modern fiction, *The World and the Book*. Josipovici proposes that the traditional naturalist fiction pretends to be actually reproducing reality, but in fact it uses worn-out conventions of reality in order to establish a spurious objectivity. In the era of a zero degree of writing, he celebrates the novel of lexical foregrounding, where text is prior to or other than the world; the modern novel is, he says, the anti-novel. And the modern anti-novel is a text which plays with naturalistic techniques to create a world which seems lifelike, but which suddenly crumbles 'when the work reveals itself as a "pure object".' The reader, suddenly aware

[3] Norman Mailer, *Advertisements for Myself* (London, 1968), p. 253. There is a profitably qualified response to Beckett's fiction in Frank Kermode, *Modern Essays* (London, 1971), pp. 205–19.

[4] See, for example, John Barth, 'The Literature of Exhaustion', repr. in M. Bradbury (ed.), *The Novel Today* (London and Manchester, 1977), pp. 70–83.

that what he is reading is not reality, life, but truly a fiction, a man-made object, is pitched 'into reality'.[5] Though, oddly, he does not make Beckett a central instance, and gives more weight to, say, Saul Bellow, Josipovici makes a significant case for the kind of writing that Beckett has come to represent for many readers, the literature of self-conscious text. For a minor example, we might take this from *Malone Dies:*

> An aeroplane passes, flying low, with a noise like thunder. It is a noise quite unlike thunder, one says thunder but one does not think it, it is just a loud, fleeting noise, nothing more, unlike any other.

The conventional simile is introduced only to be negated, questioned, shown as sloppy and imprecise; the text comes to the surface, but we are given more 'reality'. Our problem is to place the feature; Josi-povici's approach to the idea of the anti-novel echoes an increasingly popular trend in modern criticism against realism as a literary mode. So, in his study of the French *nouveau roman*, Stephen Heath attacks realist fiction for its linguistic innocence in supposing that reality is objectively available, and transcribable through the referential medium of prose; he then praises those self-conscious fictions—from *À la recherche du temps perdu* and *Finnegans Wake* to current *nouveaux romans*—which he sees as exploiting language as process, thrusting the reader into an uncertain world of verbal games, offering 'a dramatiz-ation of the possiblities of language'.[6] Traditional areas of fictional concern—society, history, the individual—thus are seen to involve a misuse of language, literary value being located instead in the plurality of meanings which a text displays, creating uncertainty and doubt in the reader. In *Structuralist Poetics*, Jonathan Culler raises similar ob-jections to realism, and to fiction as a communication of ideas, beliefs and experiences, preferring 'problematic' anti-realist narratives dealing in ambiguity and verbal play.[7]

This school of thought is influential and critically vigorous; how-

[5] Gabriel Josipovici, *The World and the Book* (London, 1971: paper, 1973), p. 308, 304.

[6] Stephen Heath, *The Nouveau Roman: A Study in the Practice of Writing* (London, 1972), p. 22.

[7] Jonathan Culler, *Structuralist Poetics* (London, 1975). For other key accounts of the structuralist approach, see Culler, 'Structuralism and Literature', in Hilda Schiff (ed.), *Contemporary Approaches to English Studies* (London, 1977), pp. 59–76; Barbara H. Smith, *Poetic Closure* (Chicago, 1968) and Robert Scholes, *Structuralism in Literature: An Introduction* (New Haven, 1974).

ever, there are various objections we might make to its central tenets. The immense fertility and variety of realist writing is far too easily written off as conformist; the view of such fiction as being unself-consciously imprisoned in culturally conditioned linguistic codes runs the risk of over-determination; other, larger areas in which a novelist experiences both freedom and constriction tend to be ignored by structuralist critics in their account of a text. As Culler elsewhere crucially admits, 'literary works never lie wholly within the codes that define them',[8] and the careers of Beckett and Lowry make only limited sense if we interpret their fiction solely according to formal criteria. By this sort of account, Beckett, especially, emerges as a central figure of that strain of contemporary writing which has abandoned traditional humanist notions of culture, and which has come to be defined as 'postmodernist'. Leslie Fiedler, for example, includes Beckett in his inventory of writers who usher in the new age 'of myth and passion, sentimentality and fantasy',[9] though the style of Beckett's anguished wit and his mandarin allusiveness in fact seems contradictory to the emphasis Fiedler is intent on making. Rather more helpful is Gerald Graff's distinction between 'untroubled' celebratory postmodernism (the kind with which Fiedler is concerned) and an ironic, disillusioned, backward-looking postmodernism, with Beckett occupying a major position as an early exponent of the second type.[10] Clearly there is in Lowry and Beckett a radical aesthetic self-consciousness and a commitment to experimental narrative, but the problem is to give it definition.

Beckett's 'experimental' bias has of course long been clear. His distaste for realism and the 'vulgarity of a plausible concatenation' is stridently articulated in his first book, the critical monograph on *Proust* (1931). It is reiterated, more whimsically, in the 'Three Dialogues with George Duthuit' (1949). Lowry's changing aesthetic

[8] Jonathan Culler, *Saussure* (London, 1976), p. 105.
[9] Leslie Fiedler, 'Cross the Border: Close That Gap: Postmodernism', in Marcus Cunliffe (ed.), *Sphere History of Literature in the English Language, Vol. 9: American Literature Since 1900* (London, 1975), p. 346.
[10] Gerald Graff, 'The Myth of the Postmodernist Breakthrough', in M. Bradbury (ed.), *The Novel Today*, cited above, pp. 217–49. For other accounts of Beckett's place in post-modernist writing, see David D. Galloway, 'Postmodernism', in *Contemporary Literature* XIV, 3 (Summer 1973), pp. 398–405; Ihab Hassan, *The Dismemberment of Orpheus: Towards a Post-Modern Literature* (New York, 1971); Hassan, 'Postmodernism', in *New Literary History* III, 1 (Autumn 1971), pp. 5–30.

receives a rather more fragmentary expression, though it is evident in his fiction, which is persistently a speculation about writing. We also may find it as an evolution in his letters, ranging from the early condemnation of writing 'in which the preoccupation with form vitiates the substance' (letter to James Stern, 7 May, 1940) to the reversal of that viewpoint, revealed in the casual analysis of Faulkner's *Intruder in the Dust* as 'only the first part of a novel to be called *Intruder in the Dust*' (letter to Albert Erskine, 5 March, 1949) and other like references.[11] But both writers were persistently impatient with realism, and they shared the experimental bias in much of 1930s aesthetics. For many writers in the interwar period, Joyce was the man who had demonstrated the 'death' of the novel. So, reviewing *Ulysses*, T. S. Eliot had exclaimed that 'the novel is a form which will no longer serve.'[12] And the gigantic scale of Joyce's enterprise, in moving on from realism to turn narrative form, and ultimately even language, inside out, remained exemplary to any modern writer whose ambitions were of the very highest. It is therefore revealing that, when they sought to explain what their experimental work was endeavouring to accomplish, both Beckett and Lowry referred their efforts to the example set by Joyce.

Thus, interviewed in the first flush of fame, after *Waiting for Godot* had been a smash-hit in Paris, London and New York, Beckett remarked:

> The more Joyce knew the more he could. He's tending toward omniscience and omnipotence as an artist. I'm working with impotence, ignorance. I don't think impotence has been exploited in the past. There seems to be a kind of aesthetic axiom that expression is an achievement—must be an achievement. My little exploration is that whole zone of being that has always been set aside by artists as something unusable—as something by definition incompatible with art.[13]

In fact, in contrast to the progression of Joyce's *oeuvre*, where each new work appeared more exhaustive and revolutionary than its predecessors, Beckett came to offer a modern regression. His career, as it developed, actually seemed to reverse the traditional picture of

[11] Quotations from Harvey Breit and Margerie Bonner Lowry (eds.), *Selected Letters of Malcolm Lowry* (London, 1967).

[12] From Frank Kermode (ed.), *Selected Prose of T. S. Eliot* (London, 1975), p. 177.

[13] Interview with Israel Shenker, *New York Times*, 6 May, 1956.

artistic development. Each new work of Beckett's shrank in length; minimal plot, social setting and characterization became yet more minimal. The logical point of termination began to look like silence, the pure blank page. This was the meaning of Beckett for many in the 1960s. But, from the viewpoint of 1970s the perspective is quite different. The myth of regression has collapsed. In retrospect we can see how the apparent dead-ends of Beckett's career are simply staging posts for new ventures. We now get an image of the writer as a free man making artistic decisions, rather than as a metaphysician trapped in the coils of an immutable aesthetic logic. And, as the perspectives change, the question that now arises is whether or not Beckett has managed to match the accepted triumphs of his trilogy, *Molloy, Malone Dies* and *The Unnamable* (written 1947–50).

In Lowry's case such a problem of evaluation does not arise, since *Under the Volcano* is unquestionably his major work. The later work does, however, raise a question of interpretation. For Lowry the 1950s was a decade that began with the glamour of his 1947 success with *Under the Volcano* fast fading (for the last six months of 1950 the novel's sales in Britain earned the writer £2 3s 8d in royalties), and brought increasing difficulties with his publishers. In November 1951, Lowry produced a fifty-page *Work-in-Progress* statement, hoping to persuade his publishers that his unfinished novels and stories would eventually form an interrelated major epic sequence to be called *The Voyage That Never Ends*. Defending his portrayal of the writer-hero in the uncompleted autobiographical novel *Dark as the Grave Wherein My Friend is Laid* (written 1947–9), Lowry argued 'Joyce has surely left *some* regions to explore, even blazed the trail to some he didn't explore himself'.[14] Lowry's efforts to persuade publishers of the value of his fiction, which used Joycean techniques to convey auto-biographical material, met with initial success. Robert Giroux of Harcourt Brace expressed interest, writing that Lowry's scheme 'promises what might be the most important literary project of the decade'.[15] Within two years, however, the project had fizzled out in a heap of unfinished manuscripts. What went wrong? The failure is usually attributed to Lowry's alcoholism. In conjunction with the zigzags of Beckett's later career it could, I think, equally well evidence the strains involved in the writing of 'anti-novels'—even, perhaps, embody a crucial underlying anxiety about the merits of the mode.

[14] *Work-in-Progress*, UBC Collection, 37 (9).
[15] *Selected Letters of Malcolm Lowry*, p. 445.

II

Waiting for Godot is the work which we automatically associate with Beckett's name. It remains his most popular and successful play, and, together with the prose trilogy, it forms the central achievement of his career. It seems significant that it took a play to draw public attention to Beckett as a writer. When he switched from English to writing in French, after the war, his exile as a writer was complete,[16] yet he remained in obscurity. When he switched from fiction to drama he became an instant international success. The reason why becomes clear, I think, if we compare *Waiting for Godot* with a slightly earlier work, *Mercier and Camier* (written 1945). The novel has much in common with the play: two male antagonists enduring a relationship based on an arbitrary accumulation of comic or pathetic non-events. We learn from the first sentence of the novel that Mercier and Camier are on a journey, but its route and destination appear obscure. The anonymous narrator summarizes a part of their conversation as follows:

5. Did what they were looking for exist?
6. What were they looking for?
7. There was no hurry.

This offers a microcosm of the entire novel, and the similarity to *Waiting for Godot* is strong. Instead of having to wait for an arrival, Mercier and Camier are themselves bent on arriving. Implicitly the journey is life, a pilgrim's progress through absurdity to nowhere except, possibly, the extinction of 'that harmless lunacy', consciousness. *Mercier and Camier* gives us a fuller, more eventful version of the absurd than *Godot*, but an equally inconclusive one. Sections of the novel anticipate the flat, ritualistic question and non-answer technique of the play, but most of it is devoted to a parody of the narrative conventions of realism. In comparison with the economy of the play, however, the novel seems to dissipate its comic energy. *Waiting for Godot* gains a tremendous dramatic tension by setting up the mysterious, tantalizing figure of Godot to overshadow Vladimir and Gogo's anxieties. The two tramps, instantly fleshed-out as individuals the moment they appear on the stage, impose meaning on the emptiness

---

[16] For two useful studies of Beckett's bilingualism see chapter six of John Fletcher, *Samuel Beckett's Art* (London, 1967) and Harry Cockerhorn, 'Bilingual Playwrite' in *Beckett the Shape Changer*, pp. 141–59.

with a desperate comic invention next to which the wit of *Mercier and Camier* appears flaccid and redundant:

> What are you musing on, Camier?
> On the horror of existence, confusedly, said Mercier.
> What about a drink? said Camier.

There is nothing in the play as easy and indulgent as that; in contrast to it the novel appears as little more than an amusing bag of tricks, exercising Beckett's talents at a much lower level of engagement.

The unevenness of Beckett's career is further evident from *First Love* (written 1945) and *From an Abandoned Work* (written 1955), two rather flat, strained shorter pieces, separated in composition by the ten years in which he produced his most enduring work. As such minor works are added to the canon we get a clearer view of the false starts and cul-de-sacs in Beckett's development. His frank admission in the Shenker interview that 'The kind of work I do is one in which I'm not master of my material' takes on a new edge as details of Beckett's abandoned manuscripts emerge, modifying the apparent logic of his progress/regress towards shorter and shorter fiction.[17]

This logic, however, only became prominent after the completion of the trilogy, in which Beckett seemed progressively to exhaust even the materials of the anti-novel. *Molloy* (1955), *Malone Dies* (1956) and *The Unnamable* (1958)—all originally written in French between 1947 and 1950—continue to form the core of Beckett's postwar achievement in fiction. Unlike his earlier novels, *Murphy* and *Watt*, they are narrated in the first person; unlike *Mercier and Camier*, the centre of attention is the narrator himself. The three novels have a cumulative impact as we gradually learn that Molloy, Moran, Malone, Mahood, Worm and the Unnamable are each reincarnations of the same garrulous voice. At times the voice claims to be taken over by other voices, but on other occasions it asserts that this is simply a fiction. The effect of this is radically to undermine any confident judgements on the reader's part about the reality of the world conveyed by the prose. The vestigial plot of the first part of *Molloy*—Molloy's desire to 'speak of the things that are left, say my goodbyes, finish dying'—quickly dissolves into a series of uncertain or self-cancelling memories ('It was winter, it must have been winter. . . .

---

[17] For an account of the Beckett manuscripts see Richard L. Admussen, 'Samuel Beckett's Unpublished Writing', *Journal of Beckett Studies* 1 (Winter 1976), pp. 66–74.

Perhaps it was only autumn'). This technique of immediately negating what has only just been said remains one of Beckett's most consistent and disturbing narrative techniques. In both halves of *Molloy*, absurdity and ambiguity accumulate within a highly self-conscious circular narrative structure which leads nowhere except to doubt, hesitation, and, finally, the revelation that the second section is a fabrication. *Molloy* is crammed with materials and techniques designed to shatter the complacency of readers used to more traditional fiction: lyrical expressions of melancholy and despair uncomfortably juxtaposed with jeering outbursts of disgust at human existence; exquisite phrasing which develops into slang and obscenity; pathetic fallacies one moment, anti-romanticism the next; and theological jokes in the Irish comic tradition, which range from simple *double entendre* to sophisticated encyclopedic wit.

Malone Dies takes us further than *Molloy* in that it has a very exact point of termination: death, which strikes Malone down in the very act of narrating his last garbled memories and creative fantasies. The narrative structure is superficially different, split into short sections, mostly a page or two in length, one as short as a single verbless sentence; but the comic techniques and the bleak condition being dramatized echo *Molloy*. At first it seems as if we are being presented with daily diary entries ('Enough for this evening'), but later sections break off in mid-sentence, and start up again jerkily, as though expressive of disintegrating mental processes. The narrator's autobiographical reminiscences prove as unreliable as ever; mid-way through section three he casually interjects, 'All that must be half imagination.' Like Molloy and Moran, Malone is his own literary critic, but with a greater frequency. 'What tedium,' he sighs on each occasion that his imagination begins to run away with him and is seduced into creating a sequence of naturalistic episodes. Malone's weakness in this regard makes him rather more three-dimensional and human than the previous Beckett grotesques, and the author's wit often seems to function at its best when satirizing more traditional areas of novel-writing, as in the marvellous comic image of a house filled with 'multitudes of fine babies ... which the parents keep moving about from one place to another, to prevent their forming the habit of motionlessness.'

With *The Unnamable* all such comforting familiarities are gone. All traces of human landscapes and human situations vanish, and we find ourselves in a hellish void, which contains a voice—a voice which may truthfully be describing the conditions of its anguish and the other voices which appear to possess it, or which may just be living up to its promise of telling stories:

> pick your fancy, all these stories about travellers, these stories about paralytics, all are mine. I must be extremely old, or it's memory playing tricks, if only I knew if I've lived, if I live, if I'll live, that would simplify everything, impossible to find out, that's where you're buggered . . .

More disturbing than the contents, imaginary or otherwise, of the Unnamable's particular hell, is the unstable narrative point-of-view. The novel metamorphoses into something which resembles a kind of automatic writing, in which the narrator is the medium for a babble of conflicting voices. *The Unnamable* bulges with a mad medley of styles, tones and voices. Behind the gibbering, schizophrenic pressure of the narrative, one senses Beckett drawing on his previous experience as a nurse in a mental hospital and putting it to use in the most experimental and disturbing of the trilogy's three texts.

L'Innomable was completed in 1950, and Beckett thereafter abandoned full-length fiction for several years, transferring his attention to his playwriting and to the translation of the trilogy into English. His attack on the naturalistic novel seemed both exhaustive and exhausted, and in 1958 Beckett remarked that he believed it was impossible for him to write another novel. The *Texts for Nothing*, thirteen short pieces written in 1950, are represented as a tranquil afterword to the trilogy, rounding off (with an echo of Sterne) 'its cock-and-bullshit in a coda worthy of the rest.' As a set of variations on well-worn themes, the *Texts* are not among the more compelling of Beckett's works. An exquisite style is put in the service of a set of self-cancelling statements, but the absence of a specified existential condition leaves the work a clutter of familiar ironic gambits, lacking the coherence of the novels.

Structure, however minimal, makes a welcome reappearance in *How It Is*, the full-length fiction which Beckett suddenly produced in 1959. Divided into three parts, the work gives us the narrator's gabbled account of how it is 'before Pim with Pim after Pim'. After the spectral hell of *The Unnamable* the new work plunges us into an earthbound purgatory, through which the narrator crawls, dragging a sack of tinned sardines and a tin-opener. The last item comes in useful when, in a hideous burlesque of human communication which distortedly echoes Kafka's 'In the Penal Colony', he tries to scratch a message in Pim's flesh. Later, the narrator returns to his original breathless solitude, dismissing the skeleton events of the novel as an invention—'never any procession no nor any journey no never any Pim nor any Bom no never anyone no only me'.

The sequence of isolated paragraphs, all of which lack syntax, gives a striking appearance of formal innovation to the novel. On a closer examination, such experimentation offers no significant barrier to an appreciation of the text. The narrative is no incoherent, chaotic babble, but yet another dramatization of a suffering consciousness which manages to formulate its agonies in cool, beautifully cadenced prose. Natural breath pauses take the place of the expected punctuation; we instinctively know where the bridges and breaks in meaning occur:

> my life last state last version ill-said ill-heard ill-recaptured ill-murmured in the mud brief movements of the lower face losses everywhere

A strict order underlies the initial appearance of incoherence.

In the English translation we miss a crucial joke at the end, when the narrative closes by repeating its title, since 'comment c'est' in French sounds identical to 'commencez', a command which returns us to the first page, snapping the narrative shut within its own circularity. The narrator invites us to permutate the order of the text in any way we please, but in practice the offer is rhetorical. We inevitably read the text as a linear structure, and follow it as it decomposes, reconstitutes the elements of its plot, and then decomposes them again. This note of perpetual metamorphosis gives us the feel of the narrator's squirming, anguished thoughts, but simultaneously the painfully self-conscious stops and starts ('something wrong there'; 'I recapitulate') evoke the intimacy of an author caught in the act of composing his manuscript.

In *Ping* (1967) and *Lessness* (1970) Beckett demonstrates that the process of stripping language down can be taken several stages further. The extreme formalism of these pieces, which juggle a handful of words and phrases in mathematically-exact patterns of symmetry, do yield more meaning under close textual analysis than is at first apparent,[18] but whether or not they repay the effort when the natur-

[18] For example, see David Lodge, 'Some Ping Understood', *Encounter* 30, 2 (1968), pp. 85-9.

alistic base has been so radically pruned away remains debatable. However, the apparently diminishing curve of Beckett's career took a sharp change of direction away from the pursuit of minimalism with the appearance of *The Lost Ones* (1972), which marks a return to a more conventional fictional form, complete with sentences, syntax and a stable, even humanized, third-person narrative. The novella portrays a miniature society of two hundred men and women on the brink of extinction. Inside a mysterious cylinder these dehumanized figures engage in an endless, futile circulation, each searching for its lost one, each haunted by the belief that an exit somewhere exists. The narrator speaks wistfully and pityingly of these doomed and pathetic people; the tone is muted, resigned, compassionate, only rarely broken by comic interjections. *The Lost Ones* is Beckett's most allegorical work, but as a vision of the absurdity of human existence it seems stale and secondhand, lacking the compelling power of Kafka's short fiction.

The title of Beckett's latest work, *For To End Yet Again, and Other Fizzles* (1976) is oddly defensive. Its shrugging mock modesty touches that recurring note of contempt, both for literature and for readers, which occasionally erupts through the surface of the writer's prose. As Richard Poirier has remarked, once a writer has discovered his theme, he can either show 'his unabashed confidence in its authenticity, or, by parodies and self-parodies, indicate his discomfort with the appropriateness of any of the styles available to him.'[19] For Beckett such a discomfort, expressed as a perpetual parade of self-mockery and exploded illusions of verisimilitude, has almost always been the norm. But 'Old Earth', the coda to this new collection of short pieces, provides an astonishingly calm, confident revelation of the author in his old age (it is precisely dated 'Paris, August 1974'):

> I turn on the light, then off, ashamed, stand at gaze before the window, the windows, going from one to another, leaning on the furniture. For an instant I see the sky, the different skies, then they turn to faces, agonies, loves, the different loves, happiness too, yes, there was that too, unhappily. Moments of life, of mine too, among others, no denying, all said and done.

This shows that Beckett is still capable of surprises, even if the passage, divorced from the context of Beckett's career, is not in itself exceptional. *For To End Yet Again* shows him keeping his options open:

[19] Richard Poirier, *The Performing Self* (New York, 1971), p. 51.

the title story presents, in the style of *The Lost Ones*, the end of a journey in a featureless desert and the last glimmerings of consciousness, whereas 'Horn Came Always' takes us back to the world of *Molloy*. 'I thought I had made my last journey', the bedridden narrator confesses, 'but the feeling gains on me that I must undertake another.' Beckett seems to be suggesting that the themes of his earlier fiction are still open to exploitation should he so choose. Indeed, 'Afar a Bird' and 'I Gave Up Before Birth' offer brief, linked extensions of a theme which runs through both *The Unnamable* and *How It Is*—that of the hapless narrator musing on the identity of his creator, but threatening to reverse the old slave/master relationship, and offering a dark vision of the author sliding into senility.

The theme of death and last things, at the heart of much of the younger writer's work, inevitably takes on a new edge for a writer in his seventies; and if *For To End Yet Again* shows Beckett casting a retrospective eye over his *oeuvre* and touching it up here and there, it also discloses a growing exploitation of his own legend as subject matter for new texts. The fiction since *How It Is* has largely avoided extreme self-consciousness and formal innovation; and *For To End Yet Again* suggests a graceful rehearsal of new work as much as a valedictory to the old. But Beckett's career still seems to lack a major fiction to equal what he achieved in the late 1940s; whether or not the variety to be found in the new collection expresses self-confidence or aesthetic uncertainty remains for the future to reveal.

III

Five months before he died, Malcolm Lowry heard *Waiting for Godot* on the radio, and promptly hailed it as 'one of the most inspired pieces of bloody-mindedness since the Crucifixion'.[20] He also capped his praise with a sidelong glance at his own work, laconically promising '—coming, the Resurrection'. That Resurrection, the attempt to move beyond the hellish vision of the alcoholic as a damned soul embodied in *Under the Volcano* and write about redemption and peace in 'the voyage that never ends' occupied the last decade of the writer's life. But Lowry never did manage to write his much-dreamed-of sequel that would outshine the masterpiece, though he did achieve a dazzling, if ambiguous, vision of an earthly paradise in the long story 'The Forest Path to the Spring'. Increasingly from the mid-1940s

[20] Unpublished letter to David Markson, 22 February, 1957.

Lowry shifted the focus of his fiction away from the naturalistically-grounded materials of *Under the Volcano*, towards a much more private obsession with the theme of a writer's creative paralysis.

Under the Volcano, originally written as a short story in 1936, is a postwar novel only by the accident of its publication date. In many respects this great romantic drama of the last day in the life of an alcoholic British ex-Consul in Mexico harks back to Lowry's earlier flirtation with fashionable political themes in his 1930s stories. Set on the Day of the Dead, 1938, the novel provides an elegy for the decade as the hero stumbles tragically to a casual death at the hands of a local fascist gang. The novel went through many drafts before Lowry was finally, at the end of 1944, satisfied with it. He took the rather flat, conventional narrative which he had completed in 1940 and radically transformed it, abolishing the third-person narrator and substituting a series of interior monologues, each of the four prin-ciple characters being allotted one or more chapters. By offering us four versions of the tragic events of the Day of the Dead, Lowry renders the reasons for the Consul's self-destructive postures deeply ambiguous. The hero's hints that he is a black magician, a Faust on the brink of damnation, deepen the metaphysical dimensions of the drama of his last hours; but the wealth of detail about contemporary politics brings the tragedy down to earth and gives it a realistic edge. Lowry's deployment of myth is not systematic (though the writer's famous letter to Jonathan Cape suggests otherwise); the analogies with Christ, Hamlet, Ulysses and many other figures invest the Consul with a tragic grandeur which rubs off with each new act of pitiable buffoonery that he performs. Lowry's encyclopedism, his lavish use of billboards, signs, myth, folklore, Mexican history, quotations and parodies of poetry, and allusions to innumerable novels and novelists, makes the novel a bewildering, overwhelming experience on a first reading. The techniques are reminiscent of *Ulysses*, but lack Joyce's mania for pattern and scrupulous regard for verisimilitude. Lowry's persistent irony invests the tragedy with mock-epic features; we are left poised between the image of the Consul as a great tragic hero, the last exemplar of humane, civilized, liberal man, and a less glamorous view of him as a shabby, paranoid self-deluding drunk, sunk amid the ruins of his failed marriage.

By the second half of the 1940s Lowry had become a very isolated figure, cut off from other writers and any knowledge of changing trends in contemporary fiction. In so far as he ever felt himself to be working in a tradition, it was a poet's rather than a novelist's—the timeless tradition of the *poète maudit*, where the writer's legend tends to inform our responses to the actual work. The tragic deaths of his friends Paul Fitte, Nordahl Grieg and Juan Fernando Marquez reinforced Lowry's initial empathy with the role of the suffering, sensitive romantic genius. This identification was made yet more complete for the writer by a single unfavourable review by Jacques Barzun, which rejected *Under the Volcano* as a weak imitation of *Ulysses*, *The Sun Also Rises* and 'other styles in fashion—Henry James, Thomas Wolfe, the thought streamers, the surrealists'.[21] Lowry allowed this review to torment him for years, and he quotes it scornfully in *Dark as the Grave Wherein My Friend is Laid* and *La Mordida*—his abortive sequels to *Under the Volcano*. Salt was further rubbed into the wound when Barzun later published, quite by coincidence and certainly not with Lowry in mind, an article mocking 'neglected genius' which found its work unpublishable, the kind of writer who 'must be Shakespeare or nothing'—in short, precisely the kind of writer that Lowry regarded himself as being.[22] Lowry quotes from this article and makes a jeering reference to 'that fake, Barzun' in his last short-story, 'Ghostkeeper'.

Though cut off from metropolitan cultural groups by his squatter's existence, Lowry did learn something about the expansion of the literary-criticism industry through his enthusiastic reading of academic magazines such as *The Kenyon Review*, *Partisan Review* and *Sewanee Review*. The early 1950s were, in Randall Jarrell's opinion, 'the age of criticism', with academic articles 'astonishingly or appallingly influential'.[23] New Criticism was at its height, emphasizing the irrelevance of the writer, his biography or his intentions to the finished text. For a writer like Lowry, such knowledge proved lethal to his self-confidence and crucially undermined his efforts to write autobiographical fiction. *Dark as the Grave Wherein My Friend is Laid*, his attempt to rewrite *Under the Volcano* as parody, based around the events of his return trip to Mexico in 1945, foundered. Lowry wrote three drafts of the novel and then abandoned it. The shortened, edited

---

[21] Jacques Barzun, 'New Moralists for your Muddles', *Harper's Magazine* (May 1947), p. 487.

[22] Jacques Barzun, 'Artist Against Society: Some Articles of War', *Partisan Review* XIX, 1 (January–February 1952), p. 71

[23] Randall Jarrell, 'The Age of Criticism', *Partisan Review* XIX, 2 (March–April 1952), p. 186.

text published posthumously in 1968 reveals Lowry as the earnest promoter of his own legend.[24] The enigmatic title, actually a line from Cowley's elegy 'On the Death of Mr William Hervey', seems to allude to the suicide of Lowry's friend Paul Fitte as much as to the Mexican friend he abortively searched for on the return trip. Much of the text is a painfully naked account of Lowry's frustrations and fears as a writer, measured against the objectivity and distance achieved in *Under the Volcano*. Lacking such a symbiotic relationship with the masterpiece, Lowry's other 1940s fiction disintegrated. *La Mordida* and *The Ordeal of Sigbjørn Wilderness* remain little more than sketches and notes, elaborating on Lowry's life and writing difficulties.

The crisis was an aesthetic one, and Lowry solved it by abandoning fiction altogether, in order to concentrate on a screenplay of Scott Fitzgerald's *Tender is the Night*. This screenplay, four-hundred and fifty-five pages long in typescript, was never filmed and is still unpublished. It is an impressive, if colourful, imaginative reconstruction, and writing it gave Lowry's morale a much-needed boost. After the collapse of his other projects, he had, after six years, at last managed to produce a dazzling and, above all, *completed* text. Between late 1949 and the end of 1952, Lowry also suddenly seemed to find new confidence in the value of writing autobiographical fiction. In an article in *Life* magazine about the American painter Albert Pinkham Ryder, he found fresh support for his faith in the *poète maudit* ideal.[25] In addition he came across the writings of Ortega y Gasset, and showed a great fascination with the Spanish philosopher's argument that life itself is a work of fiction. Lowry subsequently quoted this idea, in his letters and in his fiction, as a triumphant vindication of the value of fiction about writers and their problems—or rather, Malcolm Lowry and *his* anxieties.

Lowry's best work after *Under the Volcano* is collected in *Hear Us O Lord from Heaven Thy Dwelling Place* (1961), a posthumously published set of seven linked autobiographical stories which he wrote during his sudden burst of confidence in the early 1950s. Four of the stories

[24] This text also raises the question, which faces us in dealing with almost all of the posthumously-published fiction, of whether or not editors should interfere with the manuscripts in this manner. For a critique, see Matthew Corrigan, 'Malcolm Lowry, New York Publishing, and the 'New Illiteracy'' ', *Encounter* 35 (July 1970), pp. 82–93.

[25] See Winthrop Sergeant, 'Nocturnal Genius', *Life* 30, 9 (26 February, 1951), pp. 85–91, 93–6, 101–2. Lowry stole the title of Sergeant's article for one of his own unfinished short stories.

derive from the writer's journey to Europe in 1947–48, and convey his feelings about his role as a writer after the enthusiastic reception of *Under the Volcano* had died down.[26] 'Through the Panama', 'Strange Comfort Afforded by the Profession', 'Elephant and Colosseum' and 'Present Estate of Pompeii', each hark back to a phase when Lowry's creativity was paralysed by the feeling that he had written himself out. They dramatize a state of despair and collapse, yet the experience is distanced, seen in retrospect, and often rendered comic. Against the background of the voyage and visit to Italy—a land which Lowry's heroes immediately associate with the last days of Keats and Shelley— romantic poses are struck, parodied, and then renewed. The theme that literature distorts reality and cheats the reader, darkly evoked in *Dark as the Grave*, receives a series of comic twists. Diction alone, Lowry laconically suggests, is sufficient to turn the writer away from the real towards the mellifluous:

> Silent on a peak in Bragman's bluff.
> Silent on a peak in Monkey Point.
> —Keats could scarcely have written.

In 'Elephant and Colosseum' the whole comic enterprise hinges on the blow dealt to the hero's expectations of a romantic re-encounter in Rome, derived from having just read *Tender is the Night*. Rosemary turns up, but, absurdly, she is an elephant; fiction, we learn, is no guide to reality.

'Strange Comfort Afforded by the Profession' adopts an innovative form, linking newspaper clippings, notebook entries, and interior monologue, in order to subject the *poète maudit* myth to the sceptical scrutiny of Sigbjørn Wilderness. Wilderness, a writer (and Lowry's favourite persona), concludes that romantics like Keats and Poe deliberately put on dramatic poses in their correspondence, as though with one calculating eye on a public readership. The role of *poète maudit*, Wilderness ruefully realizes, is impossible and absurd in a twentieth-century world which cries out 'enjoy Pepsi!—Drink Royal Crown Cola—Dr Swell's Root Beer—'. And yet, having established the ironic distance which lies between himself and the dead romantics, Wilderness suddenly discovers an identity with them and converts his laughter into 'something more respectable': a mock-Keatsian tubercular cough. Behind Wilderness stands Lowry, toying

[26] Enthusiastic, that is, in North America. For an account of the lukewarm English reaction to the novel see Anthony Burgess, 'Europe's Day of the Dead', *Spectator* (20 January, 1967), p. 74.

with his own legend, intensifying the complex interplay of romanticism and irony. The story concludes with a despairing letter from the worst phase of Wilderness's life, but the account of its composition reveals the writer's own effort to transform his life into myth. Much of the irony here depends on our awareness that the letter quoted is obviously one Lowry himself wrote in 1939 and then, typically, kept a copy of for possible later use.[27] Wilderness crosses out the letter, then instantly regrets the action, 'For now, damn it, he wouldn't be able to use it'. But, paradoxically, Lowry himself *does* use it. By a last ironic sleight-of-hand Lowry involves himself in the same process of self-conscious myth-making as Severn, Keats and Poe.

The two outstanding stories in *Hear Us O Lord* are 'The Forest Path to the Spring' and 'Through the Panama'. The former gives us a superbly written account of Lowry's life as myth. Time and place are not identified in this version of contemporary pastoral, and the oblique representation of Lowry's life at Dollarton is further coloured by the use of an anonymous first-person narrator, a musician, who apologizes for his clumsy style. Such protestations remain merely rhetorical; the long, flowing sentences convey the change of the seasons and the rhythms of the natural landscape with a brilliance unmatched since Lawrence's *The Rainbow*. Much of the story's appeal lies in Lowry's accretion of precisely observed simple details—trees, flowers, birds, animals, clouds, mist, sunlight—free of the symbolizing impulse that often chokes his other work. All the same, the story is not simplistic, and though it is often interpreted as the *Paradiso* to the *Inferno* of *Under the Volcano*, the narrative structure resists such easy schematization. The antinomies of hell and paradise are rooted *within* the story, rather than outside it. Nor does Lowry abandon his preoccupation with the vocation of writing in 'The Forest Path to the Spring'. Instead it is disguised as the narrator's discussion of his musical projects which, 'destined to develop in terms of ever more complex invention', echo the equally ambitious scenarios of the *Work-in-Progress* document.

'Through the Panama', explicitly 'a story in the form of notes'[28] with sections 'left deliberately rough',[29] is the most experimental of

[27] The copy does not seem to have survived, but compare Wilderness's letter with the one Lowry wrote to Aiken in the late summer of 1939, *Selected Letters of Malcolm Lowry*, pp. 18–25 (where it is mis-dated).

[28] *Selected Letters of Malcolm Lowry*, p. 267.

[29] 'Note on "Through the Panama"', UBC Collection, 36 (7).

the stories in the volume. The title echoes Lewis Carroll's *Through the Looking-Glass*, and the story also refers to a scene in *Alice-in-Wonderland* when Trumbaugh dreams of seeing a 'seemingly bodiless creature a bit like the Cheshire Cat'. The joke here is that Lowry, born in Cheshire, is writing about Sigbjørn Wilderness, author of novels in the Lowry *oeuvre*, and himself writing in his journal about another Lowryesque character, Martin Trumbaugh. In the face of such dizzying perspectives Lewis Carroll's two books seem to provide ironic, pertinent analogues for some of the central themes in *Hear Us O Lord*. In normal life, we remember, Alice frequently pretends to be two people. After drinking from a bottle she undergoes a series of metamorphoses, holds monologues with herself, and worries about her identity: 'Who in the world am I? Ah, *that's* the great puzzle!'[30]

At the surface level 'Through the Panama' gives a thinly-disguised account of the Lowrys' journey to Europe, 7 November to 17 December, 1947; but the account of the voyage is quickly swamped by lengthy descriptions of his alienation as man and writer, his impressions, torments, fears, hopes and anxieties. 'Through the Panama' develops by a process of accretion rather than a carefully patterned unfolding of image and motif. It resists attempts to organize the fragmentary experience which it conveys; Wilderness goes through multiple transformations of identity, from Trumbaugh, to Firmin, the engineer, the Hungarian, the man who fell overboard, the immigration inspector with his 'unfinished novel', Paterson, originator of the concept of a Panama canal, a man with 'too many novel ideas', and so on. Geography and chronology blur as memories, dreams, literary projects, criticism and a jumble of travel impressions overwhelm the narrative. By using a parallel narrative derived from a history of the canal Lowry dramatically evokes the imaginative truth of a writer's imagination against the mundane rational models of order provided by historians—or 1950s' literary criticism.

'Ghostkeeper' (written 1952–3), probably the last short story Lowry worked on, parodies 'The Bravest Boat', the rather sugary introductory story in *Hear Us O Lord*. This time the marital harmony is disturbed, and the landscape full of sinister omens. The story begins conventionally enough, setting the scene, establishing a precise date for the action; and then, suddenly, all verisimilitude collapses, and the story decomposes into variant plot sketches, analytical interjections,

[30] Lewis Carroll, *Alice's Adventures in Wonderland and Through the Looking-Glass* (Harmondsworth, 1974), p. 36.

the representation of dialogue as merely tentative ('Some such conversation as this ensues'), and a disturbing narrative instability (the
wandering Englishman is blind, then nearly blind, then not blind at
all). Because of this, 'Ghostkeeper' is usually represented as simply an
unfinished text, yet the radical formal features do seem to possess
an internal logic and consistency in relation to the writer-hero's
inability to describe truthfully the ever-receding complexities and
coincidences in the day's events. 'Ghostkeeper' begins with a question:
'What time is it?', but the metaphysics informing the story deny that
identity, temporal or otherwise, can be so easily located in a shifting,
protean world of constant change and mystery. The hero vacillates in
the face of bewildering complexities, and abandons truth-telling in
favour of 'Lex Talionis', a comforting, conventional tale which shuts
out the disturbing reverberations which reality has been shown to
contain. By implication 'Ghostkeeper' is the story the protagonist
should have written, but didn't. Radical form legitimately expresses the
metaphysics of perpetual metamorphosis.

October Ferry to Gabriola (mostly written 1952–54) registers both a
new phase in Lowry's career, and its collapse. After *Dark as the Grave,
Hear Us O Lord* and 'Ghostkeeper', Lowry was presumably aware
that his exploration of the relationship between fiction and reality
was, if not exhausted, becoming dangerously repetitive as a topic.
October Ferry to Gabriola marks an attempt to revert to a more classi-
cally objective form of novel—another *Under the Volcano*, as it were.
For the first time since 1944 Lowry made a serious effort to invent a
non-autobiographical surface plot, without a writer hero. The representation of Ethan Llewellyn as a family man, a car-owner, and a
lawyer quickly breaks down, however, and he remains a solitary
figure, divorced from society or history, with, for a lawyer, an unusual
terror of authority. As squatter, alcoholic and metaphysician, he
acquires all the features of the familiar Lowry hero. Lowry tried to
rationalize these limitations as best he could, claiming that *October Ferry*
was 'not intended to fall into any particular category or obey any of
the normal rules of a novel'.[31] This special form of pleading he even
extended to the text of the novel, giving his protagonist the thought
that 'Nothing was more unreal than a novel, even a realistic novel.'
The naturalistic base of *October Ferry*, an account of a long day's
journey to Gabriola Island, proved to be too weak for the weight of
autobiographical reverie which Lowry chose to incorporate (even

[31] Unpublished letter to Albert Erskine, December 1953.

Gabriola itself, ambiguous symbol of the future, seems to have been selected because of its ironic echo of Lowry's first wife's name, Gabrial). Though he managed to produce accomplished short fiction, Lowry seemed to lose control each time he attempted to write a self-conscious sequel to his masterpiece. In the last months of his life he was still scribbling fragmentary autobiographical notes for insertion into what was, by then, a badly constructed top-heavy narrative. *October Ferry to Gabriola*, intended as a magnificent coda to 'The Voyage That Never Ends', remains, like the epic project itself, a ruin.

IV

Commenting on the tradition of self-parody in modern literature Richard Poirier has asserted that 'Our greatest invention so far remains ourselves, what we call human beings, and enough inventing of the phenomenon still goes on to make the destiny of persons altogether more compelling in literature than the destiny of systems or literary modes.'[32] Fiction, that is, still needs to be about individuals, and human situations of consequence. The best anti-novels, from *Tristram Shandy* through to *At Swim-Two-Birds*, *Pale Fire* and *The French Lieutenant's Woman*, possess such qualities, as do Beckett's and Lowry's finest experimental productions: *Malone Dies*, 'Through the Panama'. When the elements of individuality fade, and the author's abstract formal intelligence begins to take over, the results often end up seeming laboured and less deeply engaging.

Of course, if we deny a central referential value to language, then the notion that individuals and their circumstances can be sensibly expressed in fiction becomes devoid of value. This seems to be Josipovici's viewpoint. He sweepingly adopts a position derived from Wittgenstein to argue that anti-novels prevent us 'from falling into the trap of thinking that meaning inheres in words, objects or events'.[33] Anti-novels, he argues, thrust us back into reality. But reality, as referred to in *The World and the Book*, is an odd place— oddly like the ambiguous worlds of Beckett's fiction, if judged by Josipovici's mystifying *cri-de-coeur*, 'The more we struggle to under-

[32] Poirier, *op. cit.*, p. 44.
[33] *op. cit.*, p. 303. The best empiricist reply to this school of philosophy that I know is Bertrand Russell, *An Inquiry into Meaning and Truth* (Harmondsworth, 1973).

stand the world around us, the harder we look at it and at the past, the greater grows our sense of our own isolation.'[34]

What is missing from *The World and the Book,* and what blunts the edge of its commendation of the virtues of self-conscious fiction, is any acknowledgement of the way in which experimentation itself becomes assimilated, transformed into convention. Writing about Beckett in 1958, Christine Brooke-Rose, herself a significant anti-novelist, had no hesitation in identifying him as the author of anti-novels, remarking that 'the tradition makes a sparse alignment compared with the vast body of "straight" novelists. . . .'[35] That is not true of subsequent developments in contemporary fiction. In the context of the recent glut of anti-novelists (Barth, Coover, Brautigan, Vonnegut, Pynchon, B. S. Johnson *et al.*), it is a writer like J. G. Farrell, quite self-consciously reproducing the features of the naturalistic novel, even down to the heresy of omniscience and guiding authorial commentary, who appears startling and inventive. Looked at from the 1970s Beckett and Lowry seem like links between the great phase of modernism which ended in the 1920s, and the changed climate in fiction of the late 1950s and 1960s. The level of engagement which they demand from the reader is high, and ideally we should read all of their work in order to grasp the consistency of the *oeuvre.* In their best work we see the comic virtues of the anti-novel; in their lesser works and in the zigzags of their careers we also see some of its limitations.

[34] *op. cit.,* p. 312.
[35] Christine Brooke-Rose, 'Samuel Beckett and the Anti-Novel', *London Magazine* 5, 12 (December 1958), p. 38.

Note

Modern discussion of 'fictionality' has taken various forms: the reader is referred to Robert Scholes and Robert Kellogg, *The Nature of Narrative* (New York/London, 1966), Robert Scholes, *The Fabulators* (New York/London, 1967) and Roland Barthes, *S/Z* (London, 1975) in particular, as well as to Frank Kermode, *The Sense of an Ending* (London, 1967); see also the useful discussion by Victor Sage of 'Fiction' in Roger Fowler (ed.), *A Dictionary of Modern Critical Terms* (London, 1973).

I have referred to the works of the following authors (for a bibliography of B. S. Johnson, see elsewhere in this volume):

Alan Burns (b. 1929).
Europe After the Rain (1965); *Celebrations* (1967); *Babel* (1969); *Dreamerika!* (1972); *The Angry Brigade* (1973). Burns comments on his own work in Giles Gordon (ed.), *Beyond the Words* (London, 1975) and James Vinson (ed.), *Contemporary Novelists* (London/New York, 1972).

Robert Nye (b. 1939).
Doubtfire (1967); *Tales I Told My Mother* (stories) (1969); *Falstaff* (1976).

Andrew Sinclair (b. 1935).
The Breaking of Bumbo (1959); *My Friend Judas* (1959); *The Project* (1960); *The Hallelujah Bum* (1963); *The Raker* (1964); *Gog* (1967); *Magog* (1972).

Anthony Burgess (b. 1917).
Numerous novels, incl. *Time for a Tiger* (1956); *The Enemy in the Blanket* (1958); *Devil of a State* (1961); *A Clockwork Orange* (1962); *The Wanting Seed* (1962); *Honey for the Bears* (1963); *Inside Mr Enderby* (as Joseph Kell) (1963); *Enderby Outside* (1968); *MF* (1971); *Napoleon Symphony* (1974).

V

Reflections on 'Fictionality'

N. H. REEVE

I

A GOOD DEAL of criticism of the modern novel has given prominence to 'fictionality', regarded as the foregrounding, by a novelist, of the fictive nature of his work. Robert Scholes, for example, calls this 'fabulation', and insists that an avowedly fictional narrative is the most plausible novelistic method a contemporary author can adopt.[1] Elsewhere, in his collaborated analysis of the history of narrative, written with Robert Kellogg, Scholes distinguishes between 'empirical' and 'fictional' modes—understanding the former to include historical and mimetic realism, and the latter those romantic and didactic modes which are essentially devoted to the ideal rather than the real, are concerned with truth in an 'artistic' (Scholes's term) rather than representational sense. The empirical and fictional modes, we are told, are in perpetual if postponed conflict, and

> There are signs that in the twentieth century the grand dialectic is about to begin again, and that the novel must yield its place to new forms just as the epic did in ancient times, for it is an unstable compound, inclining always to break down into its constituent elements.[2]

A major reason for this imminent collapse is the uncertain relationship between language and its referents, as for Scholes the fabric of the empirical narrative depends to a large extent upon an agreed stability in this matter, which he believes is no longer tenable. Narrative realism is to be regarded as outmoded insofar as the conventions of its expression are outmoded; and new form, modern writing, must hence align itself with the 'fictional' mode.

[1] Robert Scholes, *The Fabulators* (London/New York, 1967).
[2] Robert Scholes and Robert Kellogg, *The Nature of Narrative* (London/New York, 1966), p. 15.

This approach consorts with much formalist and structuralist opinion, about which Scholes has also written,[3] and 'fabulation' clearly partakes of the now widely evident vogue for extending such theories into prescriptive principles. Many French and American writers have clearly subscribed to it. In Scholes's case, as I shall have occasion to remark later, the principles seem to concern methods rather than results, and take little account of the reading experience, the reader's response to narrative. My approach here will be rather to consider 'fictionality' as the degree to which fiction is recognizably present in any narrative, and so to reflect on some of the implications there might be for the reader who becomes aware that he is confronting a fiction. I have chosen some modern, indeed 'experimental', English novels which constitute, as it were, a spectrum ranging across Scholes's categories of narrative—from the differing 'documentary' styles of Alan Burns and B. S. Johnson, through approaches to 'fabulation' in Robert Nye and Andrew Sinclair, to a novel of Antony Burgess which might be, for Scholes, a pure 'fiction'.

II

The documentary novel has won much interest lately, perhaps because it aims for a heightened and more objective realism in the face of this strong contemporary unease as to realism's viability. Burns might be called a writer of documentary novels; the subtitle of his *The Angry Brigade* (1973) explicitly claims as much. He certainly calls into play the ambiguous mystique surrounding that word—an aura which probably derives as much from the influence of television as from literary sources. We might thereby tentatively identify an area in which documentary has supplanted 'realistic fiction', at least in its lay usage, in terms of the desire on the part of an audience or readership for some kind of guarantee of authority for what is being said. The case for the authority of documentary would appeal to the 'unadorned facts'. If they are presented pictorially, they rest their appeal upon the least doubtful of our senses, and both thrive on and encourage the habit of assimilating material in condensed and readily identifiable units. Their impact on the senses might sharpen the response of the imagination, and indeed affect it with a new moral charge, as we are invited to reflect on the material presented, not in terms of its being possible, but in terms of its being true. When the picture 'speaks

3 See Robert Scholes, *Structuralism in Literature* (New Haven, Conn., 1974).

for itself', an over-expansive commentary only impedes its directness. Within these limits, and covering this area of subject-matter, fiction might be relegated to a secondary status, regarded as something frivolous and distracting, ultimately imperfect. B. S. Johnson asserted as much, when he claimed that fiction was 'lying':

> A useful distinction between literature and other writing for me is that the former teaches one something true about life; and how can you convey truth in a vehicle of fiction? The two terms, *truth* and *fiction*, are opposites ...[4]

I have heard a similar complaint raised when, for example, the television screens a play about the daily life of a police officer. Why not film a real police officer, and make it a documentary?

If we extend our documentarist's position, we find directness of impact consorting with objectivity. The 'voice' of the documentary discourse supplants that of its compiler, and it acquires an impartial status through the compelling objectivity of the offered facts themselves. The compiler need not employ devices of irony or ambiguity to bring them to our attention; moreover, any selectiveness which time, space or ideological bias might demand cannot of itself deny those facts their autonomous value. He aspires to an authorial humility, whereby the audience should know exactly its relation to the 'voice' of his discourse and be free to confront it directly.

Clearly this case is hypothetical, and probably no compiler would claim such extreme control, but the more he excises overt techniques of selection, the less vulnerable, perhaps, he becomes to the questioning of his right to control. The 'documentary novel' might claim that status as well; it might argue, against the conventional novel, that it offers fewer mechanical solicitations of our sympathy. It does not hustle the reader into suspensions of disbelief; or it uses a plainer language, less prone to compromise the credibility of its referents. But we are not so easily persuaded that 'reality' in the novel is unqualified and unimpeachable. Once the documentary novel engages in the discourse of narrative prose, it is necessarily removed, by that discourse, from the events, which are now fixed in a particular continuum. It is true that the formal procedures enacted between the reader and the material do not immediately affect the value of facts, as they themselves supply the urgency and immediacy with which the event strikes, even irrespective of the novelist's decision about how they are to be set down. It becomes

[4] B. S. Johnson, 'Introduction' to *Aren't You Rather Young to Be Writing Your Memoirs?* (London, 1973).

a matter of the novel's language. We might be offered an impression-
istic record of how the event manifested itself, or the deliberate and
coherent reconstruction of the police-type statement. But there already
we have *two* accounts. If the appeal is to 'truth', then the account is
being asked to replace the event it describes—actually to *become* the
event. This appeal seeks in narrative for one set of statements to be
granted a status above that of another set, so that one is true and the
other fictitious; but this cannot be good enough, for documentary
record deals with what is observable, and thus accessible to more than
one pair of eyes and more than one type of language. Johnson, for
one, was slow to acknowledge this. I might, in passing, draw the
reader's attention to Charles Tomlinson's poem, 'How it Happened',
where we see a language struggling to identify subjective sensation
with an objective 'truth' which, finally, can only subsist at the level of
the language used to describe it.[5] The lapse into rhyme at the poem's
end suggests that linguistic manoeuvres can enforce connections here,
although 'no absolute of eye can tell / the utmost'. The poem reminds
me forcibly of Burns's work, where a similiar hesitancy as to 'how it
happened' is resolved, if at all, by technical means.

Celebrations (1967), Alan Burns's second novel, shows this clearly. It
concerns the languages of ritual, marshalled to form a system of
pressure. The 'style', as such, is constructed from an uninterrupted
sequence of clauses which aim to fix and control their content
directly, without resort to devices which might mitigate their charged
and assertive impact. Adverbs of qualification, for example, are un-
common, and when they do occur, as in the passage I select here,
they rarely suggest a limitation to the control a purely descriptive
language might exert:

> A speech was read from a piece of paper, the speaker drank cold
> water, he was a government official, he scratched his head and
> wasted time, he spoke vaguely, he had 'come to learn', Williams
> did not hear a word, his eyes concealed his thoughts, the brief
> applause ended in silence

Such monotonous impassivity tells us only that an event took place.
There is no attempt to emphasize distinctions in an experience, to
dress one kind of remark differently from any other. The prose has the
character of a relentless pursuit; just so, for it deals with the impersonal
power of remote institutions, and the pressures they exert upon thought

[5] Charles Tomlinson, 'How it Happened' in *A Peopled Landscape* (1963).

and action. Form first mirrors, then determines content, as the remoteness of the impedances between thought and action, and the processes by which the one might be successfully translated into the other, are present, ultimately, in the single sentence, constantly paradigmatic of the novel's whole condition:

> Williams changed his mind about visiting his son, he drove alone towards Michael's house, he had to turn right, his shirt was sweating under the armpits, it was too early, he would call in for drinks at ten, perhaps he would walk, walking was better for the health, but it would be foolish not to drive

This is recognizably political literature, analogous to the more overt biases of documentary. Just as, in the novel, predetermined systems bear ineffably down upon the captive consciousness in the Williams family, so the system of stylistic pressure which constitutes the book bears down upon its reader.

While this novel is heavy going, *Babel* (1969), his next book, is clearly out to get us. Burns abandons linear narrative altogether in favour of the wholly paradigmatic linguistic unit. The clause of *Celebrations* is expanded into a paragraph, whose model is the newsitem, complete with eye-catching headline:

DOWN IN THE GARDEN THE BISHOP IS FEEDING THE RADICAL THINKING EMANATING FROM HIS FANTAIL DOVES

The paragraphs 'deal with' their subject-matter almost to saturation point, such that the confused tongues of the tower of Babel merge into a blanket language of assertion. Burns offers a description of his technique in an essay for Giles Gordon's anthology, *Beyond the Words* (1975): 'Not only the narrative but also the sentences were fragmented. I used the cut-up method to join the subject from one sentence to the object from another, with the verb hovering uncertainly between. . . . The content was clear; it was about the power of the State . . . not the obvious apparatus of dictatorship but the hints nudges nods assents implications agreements and conspiracies (sic), the network of manipulations that envelopes the citizens and makes them unaware accomplices in the theft of their liberty.'[6] In the representative passage he selects, the simple fusion of separate reports is easy to follow, but it only serves to set in motion a logical process of syntax capable of

[6] Alan Burns, in Giles Gordon (ed.), *Beyond the Words* (London, 1975), pp. 66–7.

infinite self-propagation. Sometimes we seem to be reading a synthesis of different languages which, alone, might claim an unambiguous status, but fused, produce distortions; other passages appear to be pure invention, but are set beside the more accessible material in the same condensed jumble. Again, there is no attempt to differentiate stylistically between the true and the untrue; the issue is not presented as one to be settled by linguistic distinction. It is perhaps Burns attacking the State with its own resources:

THE PREGNANT THREE-YEAR-OLD IS HURLED AGAINST THE WALL, a baboon is strapped in a bus, the corpse of a small child shows restraint

Babel's cumulative effect is rather overpowering, as the extreme disjunctions are relentlessly declaimed throughout. I feel this kind of power is rather too intense, as the reader's capacity for imaginative response to the (often brilliant) marshalling of effects is eventually numbed. And perhaps thereby his own liberty is stolen? Burns claims that his deliberate fragmentation is in response to a desire to break out of the 'tyranny' of syntax, the prison of language—but it might be pertinent to ask here, who is the prisoner? One might regard the author as having been carried away by a series of manouevres designed to expose the 'power of the state' to the extent that he himself becomes implicated in the power structure; he never offers a pretence of impartiality, but he is at times sufficiently deeply immersed in the discourse for its own 'voice' to speak, and the way it speaks often seems curiously analogous to that 'network of manipulations' he seeks to expose. So much so that we are in danger of overlooking the quieter touches:

NO ONE KNOWS TIME like a street girl, she goes by nothing much more than a bell ... From the outskirts, going to the West End, what they have to offer passes slowly, studied coldly under the clock

Dreamerika! (1972), his next novel, thus comes as quite a relief, Burns having clearly profited from the lessons of overmuch austerity. This piece is more restful, while hardly less intense. Here Burns uses a sequential narrative made up of his own commentary interspersed with press-cuttings reproduced facsimile. The narrative tells the 'story' of the Kennedy family; the cuttings provide highly ambiguous signposts for it. Ambiguous, because just as the newspaper 'style' is to adapt cliché to particular use, for reasons of economy and ultimately of instant recognition, so here the cuttings can be easily transformed to apply to events for which they may not have been originally designed. For example, Jackie Kennedy is made the subject of an anonymous cutting: 'She has encountered sorrow with the same irrepressible and personal style which she displayed in happier times.' In this way, subjects are depersonalized and abstracted towards that mythical status which Burns evidently sees them acquiring and which he himself intends for them. The cuttings become the reverse of reports of the events, for they are organized into assuming arbitrary meanings dependent not on the specific, but on the general resonances they set up —what Barthes might call the 'cultural code'. The vehicles of 'fact' are twisted into supports for a fantastic narrative. A decontextualized headline, or a passage of journalese, can be a dangerous weapon:

Family

show

The family discussed ways of reporting the funeral feelings. They had the biggest issue in America, but decaying flowers would not make a happy scene. TV had the negroes sprayed with a fire hose to make them gleam. Trying to find fresh lilies would delay the funeral film.

Mother at funeral

'I've lasted well, a mother must have stamina.' Rose, in her eightieth year, smoothed down her fashionable dress . . .

Modes of reportage are easily welded into an unpleasant satirical picture. The kinds of statement which *ought* to be unambiguous are made objects of innuendo, reinforced by sly description ('TV had the negroes sprayed') or by plays on words such as 'issue'. Just prior to this passage, Burns had employed a technical trick, separating the type into two lines flanking a black slab representing Kennedy's coffin, thus forcing us to read the narrative as disjunct. Our attention is caught, just as it might be by a bold headline; and, as so often in Burns, the physical discomfort of reading stands as a metaphor for the discomforts apparent in the subject-matter—disruptions in the narrative manifest the distortions taking place at the level of 'truthful' statements. As we go on, we encounter particular effects being created in single blocks, reminiscent of the paragraphs of *Babel*, but with a subtler impact:

> Crowds attack
> At the graveside Bobby ate salmon sandwiches and made a speech about pollution. This caused so much unrest among the funeral crowds that army patrols in the cemetery were compelled to create conditions for peace, with long lines of troops flanking the grave. The subsequent few hundred protests were associated with ignorance and attributed to anarchists.
>
> > The last thing the young
> > > think about is death

Similarly, Burns's version of the Chappaquidick story takes its place alongside the newspaper versions, all mingling coyness and sensationalism in roughly equal portions. Burns's gains a disquieting acerbity by being mixed up with book-club-style advertisements purporting to reveal the 'facts' of life in the water: ' "Why is it easier to swim in the sea than in fresh water?" "Does a living cuttlefish resemble the stuff budgerigars gnaw on?" "When they saw bubbles floating on the surface of the water, Teddy grew suddenly angry . . ." ' Eventually the cuttings are drawn into the narrative and placed in the mouths of the subjects themselves:

> Onassis was determined to marry her in the first hour, he had never been so completely in love, as he explained to her:
>
> > Know how
> > > makes
> > > > all the difference
> > > > > between
> > > > > > success and
> > > > > > > failure

The novel effectively mimes the degradation of human dignity so readily achieved by facile recourse to a media-language, which *produces* stories, depersonalizing human beings and creating a system or mythology out of them—a mythology maintained at will by such language endlessly duplicating itself. For Burns: 'I . . . made crazy distortions of the alleged truth, in order to get some humour out of it, and also to raise questions about the nature of documentary realism.'[7] I

[7] Alan Burns, *ibid.*

find this book more thoughtful and more disturbing than his previous novels, as its author is clearly less confident about his own status in respect of his material.

As I suggested, the reader might find the satirical aspect of such a narrative discomforting, as there remains a gulf between the intractable nature of such events and our very limited and tentative knowledge of them; a gulf which ought to be approached respectfully, and which the techniques Burns employs make us more aware of. The uncertain quality of our response operates with even more venom for *The Angry Brigade* (1973), which is an extremely unpleasant and distressing book to read. I think this distress is occasioned by a mixture of the contents themselves, and the embarrassment we feel about our attitude to them; I hope to suggest this to be one of the peculiar and striking effects of the 'documentary novel'.

The author claims to have transcribed tape-recorded interviews with the various members of the Angry Brigade, relating the story of their activities and relationship. This offers us on the one hand a composite picture of the described events; on the other the opportunity to consider each individual in relation to the composite picture, thus probing each character by way of its account. The history of the group is one of ever-mounting tension and frustration, since its organization cannot escape the conditions of the social institutions it purports to oppose. Instead of becoming an alternative system, offering a chance to express previously repressed aspects of personality, it is controlled by an increasingly oppressive analogous hierarchy of its own: 'At first because I was the girl I did most of the typing and cooking and things like that.' The consequences of the group's actions affect each member in a different way, but none can entirely escape them, as their system cannot defy maturity and mutation among individuals. *Their* defiance is still latent:

It was pretty futile, but we had to do something and that was all there was left for us to do. ... It may seem irrational to take that trouble and risk for a useless act. Before the child got hurt, it seemed romantic, really. ... I was feeling pretty militant and I did it.

But although they might claim as much, they are not granted anything like an objective vision. Violent action, far from constituting a release, only aggravates their sense of helplessness and futility, which increasingly subsides into fantasy and outright nervous collapse.

The essential failure at issue here seems to me the failure to articulate a vision, perhaps the impossibility of communicating a vision. This issue's metaphor, and also its real governor, is the narrative itself. Firstly, the relation of the separate accounts to the composite picture shows how unaware each individual is of anything like the whole event. Secondly, the part played by 'fictional reconstruction' is disturbing. We *suspect* the presence of fiction throughout the book, but again we cannot distinguish it stylistically from any other form of writing; the true and the false remain a matter of degree rather than principle. In the case of 'Barry' we learn towards the end that he has, 'in fact,' been committed to a psychiatric institution; this being so, it is perhaps unlikely that his subsequent account of life with the group would be as coherent and purposeful as Burns makes it. But our capacity for definition here is limited; our helplessness and frustration in the face of the text, in the face of the discomfort it causes, may be analogous to theirs in the face of the world. The reviewer in *The Listener* was extremely angry that Burns had not explicitly declared his attitude to urban guerrilla politics, but such a narrative is not empowered to offer interpolated judgement. That reviewer's charge, and maybe that of others, would be that Burns had deliberately and provocatively written an 'uncontrolled' narrative where one more forthright and judgemental would be both feasible and in many ways preferable. This is no easy charge to answer, but I will essay a few remarks. I think we undergo pressure on our sympathy in proportion to pressure on our credulity, so that once a narrative has persuaded us that its characters are human beings, however unpleasant, we are inclined to feel they merit a hearing. If documentary has any moral effectiveness, it is gained by confronting us with real people, allowing nothing of that safety-valve afforded by the fictional 'character' in the matter of our judgement of him. The blurred divide between the real and the fictional forms leaves us uneasy about our response. To a greater or lesser extent, this might always be the case for the realistic novel; these gradations and their measurement are a whole subject in themselves, but the voice of the narrative is clearly heavily involved in them. A narrative of the Angry Brigade aiming to control our judgement would perforce exclude many of the features which make Burns's such an unsettling and mysterious book, and would hence paradoxically limit again the power of narrative itself. The problem of its authority is not to be so readily settled.

A gloss on this question is provided by the latter pages of the book, which treat of the bombing of the Post Office Tower and other acts of violence. The extracts from the accounts are shorter, more urgent; the immediacy of the situation is dramatically presented. We slip in and out of the present tense. Even despite ourselves, the excitement generated is compelling and seductive, and seems to arise so easily and confidently out of the earlier manner that it colours the whole book with its vague, dreamy quality. So we leave the book with a powerful impression of the minds of its characters, and their involvement in an action the authority of which cannot be guaranteed by the narrative. Documentary has succumbed to its innate problem, and, in so doing, has produced a novel.

Burns's work seems to require this kind of technical analysis, and his declared intentions do support it. His experiments aspire to make technique the servant rather than the master of effect—not always successfully, I must add. Our response to 'fictionality' is as to a *problem* in his work, and, as our suspicions increase about what we are told, we might come to further suspicion of the assumptions we tend to make about 'telling' itself.

III

Johnson's work is better known (he is referred to elsewhere in this book) and no less germane to my enquiry. He offers a quite radically opposed view to that we extract from Burns: that one can come to a 'telling' which is autonomous; and the conditions for its carriage of 'truth' concern the willpower of the author over his medium:

> The novel is a form in the same sense that the sonnet is a form; within that form, one may write truth or fiction.[8]

Johnson's remarks on literary theory are not sophisticated, and critics have easily debunked his claim to 'all truth' by reference to the inevitable selectiveness of his accounts, as one very simple way in which form can influence content. I think for Johnson that the matter of language is more problematical. He was clearly convinced not only that he knew the truth, but that the 'experimental' techniques and styles he used were assisting his telling of it; in this way his formal devices aspired to break down the conventional formal barrier between the reader and the material, until, as Johnson hoped and believed, he would be reading a novel but not a fiction. The concern then is whether

[8] B. S. Johnson, *op. cit.*

his language could ever be adequate to the truth-condition with which he burdened it.

I think Johnson was really seeking an unambiguous language of autonomous status and value. This search is the one Frege abandoned when he concluded that language was incoherent in principle, thus inadequate to the expression of mathematical proof, and the idea of truth with which Johnson deals is clearly closer to proof than to any concept of creative perception. Moreover, Frege's conditions for the precise formulation of proof-statements are akin to the conditions of the Kantian moral law; an abstract perfection unimpeded by the empirical and the particular. Just as, for Johnson, the search for the expression of truth is an ethical duty, so the abstract, unambiguous 'true statement' would carry a moral imperative insofar as it was quite divorced from any concept of psychology or the empirical make-up of the mind which produced it. If this search is as unfulfilled for Johnson as it was for Frege, Johnson's appeal is then to his own good faith in trying, to the good will as the only quality carrying this autonomous value. So *Albert Angelo* (1964), for example, closes with a rhetorical appeal to the reader's trust that, despite his many difficulties and failures, the author remains importantly in control of his operations. Given such aspirations, the place of fiction in his work would seem distinct and unproblematical, but in *Trawl* (1966) I find some interesting effects. There are certain passages in the book where Johnson seems to allow himself the luxury of *composition*, those lyrical confidences which occasionally surface through the dogged and insistent autobiography:

> Here, my knees jammed against the bunkside, my back braced against the sternside, rolled and pitched, dropped and bottomed, flung and held in three dimensions by the nomadic sea's subtle kinesis.

Certain pressures on the reader are graciously relieved. The effect of what is created, what partakes of 'fictionality', perhaps disposes us to grant concessions to that good faith, place more trust in the integrity of Johnson's writing—and this with a writer who never hesitates to instruct us about what is true and what is fictional in his novels. By the time of *See The Old Lady Decently* (1975) he was making further allowances for the kinds of truth which might be accessible through fiction, which is perhaps why Virrels the Chef is so much more memorable in that book than the elaborate description of the doctor's house where Johnson's mother worked in service.

Naturally there are many paths by which the fictional might lead back to the real, and Robert Nye, author of *Doubtfire* (1967), *Falstaff* (1976), and a handful of stories, while citing the same tradition of writing as interested Johnson, adopts very different procedures. That tradition, of Rabelais, Nashe and Sterne, is too easily reduced, by the time of the disappointing and tedious *Falstaff*, to one of wine, good company and a cosy fireside, but Nye's earlier works have real power. The premise for his writing is described in another essay for Gordon's anthology:

> If you take a few related details and look at them hard enough, you are likely to end up with a myth... [9]

—where 'looking hard enough' involves a free rein for the imagination utilizing a language of energy. We can see this principle at work in 'The Same Old Story' (*Penguin Modern Stories 6*, 1970). Like Johnson, Nye begins with the facts of his immediate creative environment, but these facts suffer no ethical pressures; they are merely 'related details'. The narrator is ostensibly describing a cathedral and its denizens as the view from his study window, when he as it were finds himself telling fantastic tales about the place and the people, tales which are impatiently interrupted by the return of descriptive language. But this only serves to provoke further tales, which occur just as the materials come to hand. What sustains this piece is the inventive energy, the headlong rushes of fantasy, constantly and startlingly arrested. These arrests remind us of the context for the fictional or mythopoeic activity, a context almost lost by the writing's breathlessness.

The same principle operates on a larger scale in *Doubtfire*. The novel deals with a few recurring scenes in a day of the life of a Southend teenager, who waits by a cinema, meets his friends at a cafe, and returns to be beaten by his father. These scenes are made significant by the various ways in which the boy's imagination approaches them—the scrutiny of related details—for at one point the scene with the father is treated as a wild baroque comedy, at another as a melodramatic screenplay. One effect of such stylistic variety is to allow the 'actual' scenes gradually to become clear from the rhetorical haze surrounding them, and this 'coming clear' has implications for my enquiry. The mythopoeia used here, which aims to invest random experience with a significant pattern, is itself an attempt to represent reality, and come

---

[9] Robert Nye, in Giles Gordon (ed.), *Beyond the Words*, p. 204.

E

to terms with what finally appears as the 'menacing indifference' of his environment. The boy's prolix exuberance is dependent for its life on the attentions of his observation, and, shorn of the necessary referents, he is helpless:

> Now he is left . . . impossibly to inhabit the menacing indifference of the street. He pokes at the screwed-up bus tickets with the point of his shoe and wonders whether the dwarfs will come back, but he knows they will not. And he has to wait outside the picture-house . . . where there is nothing to lean against, nowhere to lose his face, no room to breathe, no mask which will fit without itching or making him sweat beneath it, nothing other to do than be himself in a badly-cast part.

This passage, too, suggests the triumph of style over circumstance, the consolation of a fine ringing phrase. If this is the 'coming clear' of the real, then the language is not merely a fictional pattern, but a product of the psychology of obsessed states; thus suspicions about 'fictionality' here can be redeemed by its alignment to standard humanistic procedures. This is perhaps analogous to Morrissette's reading of the early Robbe-Grillet, for example.[10]

A similar effect of the looming presence of fiction operates in Andrew Sinclair's novel *Gog* (1967), a work I find seriously flawed but extremely interesting. Its approach to myth is to discovery rather than creation. The action of *Gog* is the progress of its eponymous hero to a degree of self-realization, which is couched in mythic terms; but the mythical intertwines with the 'real' in an effective way. Suffering amnesia, Gog can journey through England and confront places and events spontaneously, and his receptive mood is as much open to the mystical, mythic properties of that confrontation as to the historical and geographical. His experience is often tendentious allegorically, hence the flaws, but more often plausible personally; thus his vision of the Five Sisters window at York remains affecting despite the confused nature of the symbolism employed. Interest is gained from the idea that his experiences are invested with mythical significance simultaneously as they provide historical and geographical loci which, literally, help him to remember who he is. The fictional pattern stands as a contingent possibility within personal experience. So although we may be very doubtful about some of the episodes in the novel, this concept of the 'fictional' does leave us free to choose whether such episodes are

[10] Bruce Morrissette, *Les Romans de Robbe-Grillet* (Paris, 1963).

substantive in themselves, or only insofar as they are aspects of Gog's mental reconstitution through the medium of mythic fantasy. As such, the facts of history now exert a tentative but ungovernable influence upon the individual awareness, and mythopoeia is again redeemed from the merely ornamental by being regarded as a fundamental psychological impulse. With this reading, we are no longer confronting a fiction which is violating the facts, but one helping to distinguish and clarify them, much as a dreamer might gradually awake to find the sounds in his dream are taking place around him.

IV

Both *Doubtfire* and *Gog* might be regarded as 'fabulation', in that they both involve a self-referential artistic design, mediated through the central consciousness, which Scholes might identify as a 'structure'.[11] But a major problem with Scholes' critical method is that the principles he discerns at work in the various novels he analyses often seem to loom far larger than the novels themselves. His description of Iris Murdoch's *The Unicorn*, for example, almost suggests that an exegetical experience which 'accounts for' the novel's existence could replace the experience of actually reading the novel. (Incidentally, this is perhaps what makes serious criticism of B. S. Johnson such a risky business.) The Scholesian approach, as I will call it, although it is by no means confined to a single exponent, does not appear to regard fictionality as problematical, for explanation of its operations is taken to include an explanation of its effects. A novel by Anthony Burgess, *MF* (1971), makes play with this issue, I think, in a manner at once refreshingly witty and intellectually strenuous. Burgess is an odd figure, a writer of great variety, reminiscent of the amateur man of letters, turning his hand to this or that topical issue, even sometimes instigating one, often with surprising results, as witness the *Clockwork Orange* and *Clockwork Testament*. I shall concentrate on the one novel for the purpose of this enquiry only, not as representative of his career.

The most adequate synopsis of *MF*, perhaps his most 'difficult' book, that I know is by Frank Kermode, in the course of his review of the novel in the *Listener*.[12] He traces assiduously the narrative's allusions to an Algonquin Indian myth, appropriately enough cited by Levi-Strauss himself, thus direct from the annals of structuralism. Suffice it

---

[11] See Robert Scholes, *The Fabulators*, pp. 106–32.
[12] Frank Kermode, review of *MF*, *The Listener*, 17 June, 1971, pp. 790–91.

here to say that the central character. Miles Faber, encounters all the elements of this myth as he makes his circuitous journey from the Algonquin Hotel through Latin America towards marriage with his sister. We note how the text *invites* exegesis, even suggesting that no other reading could be complete. Miles himself is an obsessive solver of puzzles, while his father Zoon Fonanta (who appears to have been plotting his son's journey) offers as a clearly central axiom: 'it is a man's job to impose manifest order on the universe'; so the book takes its place here, insofar as it, too, constitutes a puzzle, and the reader's tracing of the references is the imposition of order which provides the solution. But this reading is firmly challenged. The book acquires the character of a puzzle in proportion to its burgeoning fictionality; ultimately we are in the presence of a pure fiction, whose context is a pure reading, whereby so much of the pressure on our judgement and on our emotions is relieved. By this stage, the search for 'order' is synonymous with a search for a comfortable mode of reading, one that does not allow the novel to affect us, for the narrative appears to occur quite by chance, in accordance with a whim which might easily have taken another turn. Such fiction might be regarded as an escape when the narrative's momentum is generated from outside rather than within itself. So the rigorous exegesis which I can certainly imagine Scholes practising doesn't offer much reward, and Zoon Fonanta is prepared to be ironical at its expense:

> May I say how glad I am to see you looking for connections, tightening bolts that aren't there, soldiering on despite your manifest weariness, hammering away at structures.

This rebuke is made to Miles, who earns it from his remarks about a painting of a burning trombone:

> I saw clearly how that old surrealism really truckled to the world of cause and effect; a trombone proclaimed, by being burnt, that it could not be. Here was the ultimate liberation of the spirit.

The complaint seems to be against a created 'randomness' which brings to its elements a superficial intelligibility—for Miles, the 'ultimate liberation of the spirit'. The same thing happens with the exegetical reading of *MF*. Working out the clues, innuendoes and allusions may be interesting and satisfying, but to the same extent as for a crossword puzzle.

However, I think the novel does offer us something deeper. The 'related details', as for Nye's myths, appear as discovered coincidences, in language as in phenomena. So certain words in different languages are found to carry the same meaning. Moreover, the theme of the narrative, and the myth which it follows, is incest: as Kermode says, the bringing together of elements which ought to stay separate. This, perhaps, is where the comfortable reading is rebuked, and where a kind of negative capability is to replace the yearning for an ordered meaning. For example, when Miles discovers that his sister has been raped by his double, Llew, the 'evil twin brother' of the myth, he writes:

> When I saw that it was Llew, my first attempts to explain to myself how he had managed to get here and do what he was doing were held back, like the beginning of a queue, by a portly commissionaire who gave precedence to an awed acceptance of the appropriateness of Llew as minister of pain or pleasure to my sister.

This simile seems fanciful, but is not merely so, as Miles comes to accept a passivity in the face of the 'queue' of anxious enquirers after a truth which is reduced to intelligibility. In just such a way, our reading is invited to create order from the apparently random; but as fictions are piled upon fictions we begin to suspect that the kind of 'truth' which might be found here is not the one we are looking for. Consider with what consternation the exegetical reader must view the information, mischievously presented on the last page of the book, that Miles is a Negro! I think Burgess is quite deliberately leaving us unsatisfied here; indeed, if he is saying that truth is to be discovered rather than created, he is effectively rejecting the structuralist principles on which his narrative seems to be based, and making it clear that this kind of reading cannot fully answer the riddle which it itself uncovers.

MF is, I grant, slight and playful; again the implications are perhaps more substantial than the text. But they ought not to be dismissed. There are suggestions here of how the intellectual imagination might lean on as it were *excess* fictionality, in order to approach an uncompromised 'telling' of the real. Clearly, Burgess believes that the right response to such a discovery is awe and wonder rather than an impatient and superficial questioning. Perhaps the province for such an art would be to allow glimpses of the real *beyond* the book rather than within it; to this end the narrative would be a pure, not a self-conscious, artefact. If the language we read cannot tell us directly of the real, then perhaps our conventional procedures of reading might be frustrated to the extent that our attention is shifted away from questions about the accountable material towards questions about what it might indicate beyond itself. So fictionality in the narrative disturbs our response, much as it does in such apparently dissimilar novels as *The Angry Brigade* and *Trawl*, by acting simultaneously as an impedance and a signpost to the aspirations of the language—to bring us into contact with a heightened and more urgent sense of the real. Perhaps, then, instead of a generic collapse into the Scholesian categories, which I feel can only emasculate the *power* of the novel, these English experiments might open up a path towards a new synthesis.

Note

A good introduction to questions of originality, influence and parody is the section on 'influence and imitation' in Ulrich Weisstein, *Comparative Literature and Literary Theory* (Bloomington, Ind/London, 1973). For distinctions between parody, satire and pastiche, see entries in Roger Fowler (ed.), *A Dictionary of Modern Critical Terms* (London, 1974). Jonathan Culler has some valuable if limited comments on parody, both 'local' and as a mode of play with generic conventions, in *Structuralist Poetics* (London, 1975), Chap. 7. For a broad historical view of self-consciousness in fiction, see Robert Alter, *Partial Magic: The Novel as a Self-Conscious Genre* (Berkeley, 1975). Also see Harold Bloom, *The Anxiety of Influence* (New York, 1975).

David Lodge was born in 1935, studied at University College, London, and is now Professor of English at the University of Birmingham. His novels are *The Picturegoers* (1960), *Ginger, You're Barmy* (1962), *The British Museum Is Falling Down* (1965), *Out of the Shelter* (1967) and *Changing Places* (1975). His criticism includes *Language of Fiction* (1966), *The Novelist at the Crossroads* (1971) and *The Modes of Modern Writing* (1977).

Angus Wilson was born in 1913, worked in the Reading Room of the British Museum, and since 1963 has been Professor of English at the University of East Anglia. His novels are *Hemlock and After* (1952), *Anglo-Saxon Attitudes* (1956), *The Middle Age of Mrs Eliot* (1958), *The Old Men at the Zoo* (1961), *Late Call* (1964), *No Laughing Matter* (1967) and *As If by Magic* (1973). He has written important critical books on Zola, Dickens and Kipling. There are useful interviews with Wilson in Kay Dick (ed.), *Writers at Work* (London, 1972), and in *New Review* I, 1 (April 1974) (with Jonathan Raban). Critical studies include: Jay Halio, *Angus Wilson* (Edinburgh, 1964); K. W. Gransden, *Angus Wilson* (London, 1969); C. B. Cox, *The Free Spirit* (London, 1963).

John Fowles was born in 1926, studied French at Oxford, served in the Royal Marines, and now lives in Dorset. His novels are *The Collector* (1963), *The Magus* (1966: revised version, 1977), *The French Lieutenant's Woman* (1969) and *Daniel Martin* (1977). *The Ebony Tower* (1975) collects five stories. Fowles interestingly comments on *FLW* in 'Notes on an Unfinished Novel', repr. in M. Bradbury (ed.), *The Novel Today* (Manchester/London, 1977); also see Lorna Sage's interview in *New Review* I, 7 (October 1974). Useful critical studies are: William J. Palmer, *The Fiction of John Fowles* (Columbia, Mo./London, 1974); D. Eddins, 'John Fowles: Existence as Authorship', *Contemporary Literature* XVII (Spring 1976); Ronald Binns, 'John Fowles: Radical Romancer', *Critical Quarterly* XVI, 4 (Winter 1973).

VI

The Novel Interrogates Itself: Parody as Self-Consciousness In Contemporary English Fiction

ROBERT BURDEN

I

THE LITERARY historian tells us that new forms always derive from past traditions. In this sense, a new work is always the product both of a pre-existing pattern (a genre) and a transformation of that pattern in a new creative and historical circumstance. The meaning of a work is thus often grounded in a self-conscious relationship to past forms; and the transformation and implicit questioning of these often becomes both the basis of a work's structure and of its contemporary historical character. As Claudio Guillen puts it:

> A cluster of conventions determines the medium of a literary generation—the repertoire of possibilities that a writer has in common with his living rivals. Traditions involve the competition of writers with their ancestors. These collective coordinates do not merely permit or regulate the writing of a work. They enter the reading experience and affect its meaning. The new work is both a deviant from the norm (as crime is based on an attitude toward accepted social custom) and a process of communication referring to that norm.[1]

Thus in order to account for the contemporary historical character of fiction, the critic must understand the traditions from which any work must derive, however much the work is critical of that tradition. It is thus important to avoid imposing assumptions which derive from different traditions, complicated as that is in an era like ours, when literature is increasingly internationalized.

Today, it is being argued, there are strong signs of a revival of the

[1] Claudio Guillen, *Literature as System: Essays towards the Theory of Literature History* (Princeton, NJ, 1971), p. 61.

'critical' novel in England, and comparisons have been made between it and other reflexive or post-modernist writing in other countries, notably in the United States and France.[2] It is, however, important in making such comparisons to recognize the essential differences in the fictional traditions behind such experiments. There can be little doubt that contemporary American fiction needs to be related to a literary tradition in which romance has played a much larger part than has ever been the case in England. Likewise the attempt to clarify the emergence of self-consciousness in recent English novels will run serious risks of distortion if the norms of experiment we set for such novels are derived from the French *nouveau roman*. If there is a new 'critical' novel emerging in England, then its critique is not conducted at the level of language, as it is in France, where contemporary experiment evidently owes much to a tradition influenced first by the poetry of Mallarmé. The fact is that the aesthetics of representation are simply not problematized in contemporary English fiction in the way they are in the novels of a Robbe-Grillet or, differently, a Claude Simon. There are comparisons, but they can usefully start only when we have understood national traditions in their own right as influencing and constricting factors. In what follows, I want to look at three English novels, all of which evince degrees of self-consciousness in one very specific sense: they are constructed, in part, in terms of an inbuilt aesthetic discourse with the literary tradition which defines and constricts them. Other examples might have been chosen: the fiction of B. S. Johnson or Christine Brooke-Rose, for instance. But these are also novels in which this relationship with past literature and established conventions is represented in terms of parody and pastiche—modes which function as a means of self-conscious interrogation of the English novel convention, that convention being especially understood as being one of realism. Realism, indeed, seems in these novels a crucial hypothesis—it represents the necessary stable model of fiction, through which a parody of it becomes intelligible.

Today, in times when there is much interest in inter-textuality and the relation of writings to other writings, there has been a revival of fascination with parody and pastiche. However, we still lack strong and clear definitions; and it is useful to begin by considering some of

[2] One important attempt at such comparative study is John Fletcher, *Claude Simon and Fiction Now* (London, 1975); this considers Simon's work in cross-comparison with novels by Uwe Johnson, Solzhenitsyn, Angus Wilson, V. S. Naipaul and Lampedusa.

the functions of parody and pastiche, and the traditional notions that surround these terms. One of the fundamental purposes of parody in literature has long been that of literary criticism: that is to say, the literary technique of parody often pre-empts the activity of the would-be critic, by offering within the text degrees of self-interpretation. It focuses on the limitations, personal or historical, of past forms; it often does this by suggesting the evident obsolescence of 'previous' styles.[3] This is an orthodox view; by it, parody is distinguished as a mode of imitation in a subversive form. This distinguishes it from pastiche, which implies a non-subversive form of imitation, one which depends on systems of borrowing: a patchwork of quotations, images, motifs, mannerisms or even whole fictional episodes which may be borrowed, untransformed, from an original in recognition of the 'anxiety of influence'.[4] Pastiche may be the result of the conscious recognition of influence and of the fact that the condition of writing is in fact a condition of re-writing; it can also be 'naive', an immature pre-emption which indicates the lack of any distinctive originality in a work. However, deliberate pastiche is often a far from negative device; it may be used to stress the ironic awareness that language, literary form, themes and motifs regularly come to the writer in, so to speak, second-hand form. Pastiche becomes, of course, extremely hard to identify or define when its meaning is extended to cover unconscious influence from the literature of the past. But the main concern here is with the conscious recognition of traditions and conventions, which exist in history and stubbornly refuse to be forgotten. The anxiety of originality is further aggravated by this recurrent recognition. Moreover, it is crucial for us to acknowledge another party to the parodic bargain: the reader, too, is influenced by his knowledge of the literary conventions. Indeed his presumed expectations and understandings create the normative expectations which the successful writer of parody or pastiche, or the creator of anti-form, needs in order to achieve his critique.

A sense of the complex interrelationships that exist between past convention and present narrative form is one essential aspect, then, of

[3] A classic analysis in fiction of this question is, of course, Borges's story 'Pierre Menard, Author of the *Quixote*'. There are useful comments on Borges as parodist in John Sturrock, *Paper Tigers: The Ideal Fictions of Jorge Luis Borges* (Oxford, 1977).

[4] Harold Bloom discusses this large question in *The Anxiety of Influence* (New York, 1975).

the mode of self-awareness and self-criticism which has been apparent in a good deal of recent fictional writing. We now have a good number of novels dependent on a sophisticated combination of literature and criticism, addressing themselves to a highly 'knowing' reader who is required, in various ways, to be conscious of the anxieties involved in creating novels which are asked to be thoroughly original, yet asked to be so in a time when most of the ways of being original have themselves become established modern conventions. Indeed the entire post-romantic quest for originality is both manifested and undermined in contemporary use of parody and pastiche, as we shall see in the three novels I wish to examine. In David Lodge's third novel, *The British Museum Is Falling Down* (1965), parody becomes a mode of making sense both of the anxiety of influence and of the bizarre comic world of a central protagonist who is himself 'literary', a research student concerned to relate literature to life in his daily affairs. In Angus Wilson's sixth novel, *No Laughing Matter* (1967), an old preoccupation with mimicry and past literary structures is intensified to take parody and pastiche beyond literary allusion into the whole question of social relationships, so that the book turns on the social farce of the disintegration of a family of an older literary kind. John Fowles's third novel, *The French Lieutenant's Woman* (1969), uses parody and pastiche for less comic purposes; indeed, in this richly historical romance, the reader is asked to participate in a self-conscious investigation of the relationships between conventions of writing, social realities, and the historical process.

Parody, I am suggesting, is to be understood as a mode of aesthetic foregrounding in the novel. It defines a particular form of historical consciousness, whereby form is created to interrogate itself against significant precedents; it is a serious mode, unlike some types of playful imitation which are also identified in the same category. This kind of self-consciousness requires careful understanding because it is a traditional strategy, employed in new circumstances, in the face of the way in which forms from the past persist and structurally dominate later writing. A whole tradition of English parodistic novels has historically established many features of this enterprise. We can go back to Fielding and Sterne to find intersections of this type, where creation and critique are fused by establishing a realism that co-exists with a self-conscious narrator capable of intruding into the apparently realistic surface of his text. Thus ostentatious narrators—from Fielding and Sterne through to the flamboyant intruder-narrator of *The*

French Lieutenant's Woman—can both explore and flaunt characteristic narrative devices and so remind the reader that the representation of reality is always necessarily a stylization and a fiction. It is this particular convention that seems to have persisted strongly in the critical novel today. That is to say, the English parodic novel, from *Joseph Andrews* through *Tristram Shandy* to *Northanger Abbey* and even perhaps *Ulysses*, has almost always worked within the bounds of realism, however critical of that aesthetic it may be.

Thus, by systematically displaying and flouting the conditions of its own artifice, the parodic novel of this type makes itself able to probe into what Robert Alter calls 'the problematical relationship between real-seeming artifice and reality'. In the fully self-conscious novel, Alter cogently explains, 'there is a consistent effort to convey to us a sense of the fictional world as an authorial construct set up against a background of literary tradition and convention'.[5] In this respect, then, the notion of parody which may be extrapolated from all three of the novels I am considering here is traditional; and it functions in two distinctive ways. Firstly, a number of specific writers and works may be referred to or directly imitated; this may be called 'local' parody. Secondly, a more general use of parody is seen in certain of them— those critical of the conventions of writing, narrative techniques, modes of relationship with the reader. Here the extent of their critical intentions is contained in implicit attitudes to the status of the realist text, which is generally identified as the direct level of mediation. Lodge's parodies are generally highly specific and local; and they are made intelligible through the character and consciousness of a comic protagonist with his literary and academic aspirations. Wilson's novel, which has a more sardonic sense of the comic, plays off fragments of various forms against each other to undermine as well as mime the stable form of the realist novel; this dislocation reflects the disintegration of the social world to which that realist mode refers. Fowles's yet more masterly and controlled parodies of prominent nineteenth-century writing go even further in this direction; they form part of an overall critical appraisal of the conventions and values of nineteenth-century realism, and of the underlying beliefs and life-philosophies which generated that realism and its social and aesthetic status.

In *The Situation of the Novel* (1970), Bernard Bergonzi reminds us that 'no matter how unflinchingly the novelist may try to deal with wholly new kinds of experience, he cannot escape from being influenced

[5] Robert Alter, *Partial Magic* (Berkeley/London, 1975), pp. x, xi.

by the novels that have been written before him; to this extent writing any novel is an implicit literary-critical act'.[6] However there are widely different responses to such a situation; and many novels are clearly parasitical and thus uncritical of their heritage. There are, though, periods in which such a critical attitude appears to intensify, and many novels today show themselves markedly self-conscious. They are often created with a comic awareness of craft and convention which reminds us of the literature of the eighteenth century, when the novel form was in process of generation. Parody, as then, tends to play a special part in this awareness; it founds a certain type of 'critical' novel which indicates in the writer an ironic sense of the power of literary traditions, the problems of innovation, and the limits that lie with the novel as a form. Such allusiveness and comedy exists, of course, throughout the history of poetry and drama, as well as fiction. But the novel, as its name indeed suggests, has especially been committed to 'originality and the immediate unique response to individual experience'.[7] Practitioners of fiction have long been aware of the resulting tensions. But the postwar English novelist is also a post-Modernist novelist. That is to say, he can never properly ignore the lessons left behind by the Modernist novel, with its critique of past forms of writing and their implicit presuppositions and philosophies. And this problem enters the contemporary parodic novel, though Fowles more than Wilson, and Wilson more than Lodge, firmly assert an awareness of the Modernist critique.

II

In an interview he gave Bernard Bergonzi for the BBC, a few years subsequent to its publication, David Lodge offered an account of his novel *The British Museum is Falling Down* in the following terms:

> *The British Museum* . . . is partly an effort to exorcise the enormous influence that any student of literature feels, the influence of the major modern writers. It is a kind of joke on myself in a way. The basic idea which provokes the parodies in the book is that the hero is a student of modern literature who's so steeped in it that everything that happens to him comes to him moulded by some master of modern fiction, and this is suggested in the shifts of the language of

[6] Bernard Bergonzi, *The Situation of the Novel* (London, 1970); Penguin ed., pp. 25–6.
[7] Ibid, p. 29.

the book into pastiche or parodies of various novelists. Now this obviously has an analogy with the situation of the young writer somewhat intimidated, fascinated and occasionally infuriated by the sense that it's all been done before, it's been done better than you'll be able to do it; and you could see, I suppose, the parody technique in the novel as a way of meeting ironically that problem.[8]

This statement is instructive; and it needs to be examined by giving a reading of the novel, in order to determine precisely what kind of parody it contains, and the relationship of this mode of self-consciousness to the basic realism of the work.

Lodge's novel initially establishes itself as a realist text of a familiar kind. But it soon disrupts the expectations invested in that mode of writing, through a series of sudden intrusions, presented as the protagonist's imagined compositions. This technique sets in motion the strategy of parody and pastiche—which functions on the level of the realist plot as a process through which Adam Appleby attempts to make sense of, and momentarily escape from, the troubles of his married life and his work as a research student in the British Museum. The parodies, though, also cause a subversion of the realist text, through a disruption of the ongoing narrative—particularly in the early sections of the novel. What must never be overlooked is the extent to which these intrusions into the narrative are comic: a comedy that is essentially contained in the language, as well as in the farcical situations in which the central protagonist finds himself.

From the very moment that his consciousness shakes off the numbedness of sleep, Adam is plagued with a number of worries. Most prominent amongst these are his lack of progress with his studies, and his wife's possible pregnancy. The narrative at this level is a very contemporary situational comedy, located in two particular and restricted worlds of behaviour and interest: namely, the Roman Catholic faith, and Academia. The first 'world' is clearly of great interest to the novelist, a Catholic himself, and much concerned with the birth-control issue, which was important at the time. Its role in the book is considerable but the viewpoint on it is comic, and at times farcical: a variety of comic Catholic situations are invented which primarily affect Adam's family life, his 'real' world. The second world, the academic and the literary, is greatly affected by the first. Indeed, on the particular day with which the novel is concerned, it successfully prevents Adam from

[8] David Lodge interviewed for the BBC in *Writers of the Sixties*, repr. in *Alta: University of Birmingham Review* II, 7 (Winter 1968-9), pp. 15-19.

working on his thesis: he spends much of the time telephoning his wife, to find out whether their primitive precautions have failed, and whether she 'feels' pregnant. The result is a comic relation between the two worlds—the world of domestic life and the work of literary study and literary perception. All this gives a context to the self-conscious literariness of the text.

Indeed most of the novel's fundamental ironies arise from the relationship between such controversies as the Catholic attitude towards birth control and the anxieties of a man with literary and academic pretensions, who has been taught to see life in a certain way. Adam reflects that 'Literature is mostly about having sex and not much about having children; life is the other way round.' The mundane worries of domestic existence become obsessive for Adam, creating a sense of the space between life and literature. He is, for instance, much concerned with his economic plight, as a research student with three children; and throughout the day, at various moments, he attempts to provide the second line of a rhyming couplet for an advertising slogan. He needs the prize, and assumes that it is the kind of competition a literary man should be able to win. But in the end he realizes the impossibility and futility of the exercise: and his final contribution encapsulates the ironic comparison between the use of poetry in a modern commercial world and the great tradition of art, which occupies his serious interests and justifies his work in the British Museum. Significantly, it is in the Museum that he composes his verse. The tone of the following extract is thus instructive of the comic intention:

> The Reading Room was almost empty, and an official lingered impatiently near Adam, waiting for him to leave. But Adam refused to be hurried as he penned his couplet in a bold, clear script. He leaned back and regarded it with satisfaction. It had the hard-edged clarity of a good imagist lyric, the subtle reverberations of a fine *haiku*, the economy of a classic epigram.

> > I always choose a Brownlong chair,
> > Because it's stuffed with pubic hair. (p. 161)[9]

This is the one small achievement of his day of anxieties and misfortunes. Moreover, this is symptomatic of the disintegration of Adam's academic work. Similarly, the British Museum itself, the symbol of

[9] David Lodge, *The British Museum is Falling Down* (London, McGibbon & Kee, 1965). Page references in my text are all to this edition.

the great literary and academic heritage, thrives more as a tourist attraction in this novel than as a bastion of research. The irony of the novel's title reverberates on various levels. The British Museum is a symbol of the literary past, the place of books and bookishness. Being in Bloomsbury, it also represents a literary setting, as well as the decline of what that 'Bloomsbury' group of writers stood for, and achieved. If this point has not been grasped by the reader, it is firmly established in passages like this:

> From nearby Westminster, Mrs Dalloway's clock boomed the half hour. It partook, he thought, shifting his weight in the saddle, of metempsychosis, the way his humble life fell into moulds prepared by literature. Or was it, he wondered, picking his nose, the result of closely studying the sentence structure of the English novelists? One had resigned oneself to having no private language any more, but one had clung wistfully to the illusion of a personal property of events. A fond and fruitless illusion, it seemed . . . (pp. 37–8)

Indeed, Adam himself seems to suffer from the contemporary, post-Bloomsbury malaise of the novelist.

But this issue is also complicated by Adam's need to fantasize, to see life through the eyes of the novelists he studies. And this is why the fantasy episodes are grounded in parodies of 'the sentence structure of the English novelists'. Adam works not only literally but figuratively in Bloomsbury's shadow. His sardonic awareness of the influence of past literature on the very sense he makes of his life, and on the work he does, is emphasized by the comic undermining of this concern ('or was it, he wondered, picking his nose . . .'). The parodies derive from this, as well as from his particular frame of mind on the day when he feels mounting hysteria about his wife's possible pregnancy, the lack of progress he is making with his thesis, financial worry and doubt about his future; they are thus derivatives of Adam's consciousness. All this is consistent with the novel's fundamental realism; Adam's obsessive fantasizing is made plausible from the very outset. The same level of farce that creates the episodic narrative tone infuses the parodies. In a brief discussion, there is little space to analyse the parodies themselves, but they are passages in the manner of many of the great modern writers: Virginia Woolf, D. H. Lawrence, Franz Kafka, Ernest Hemingway, and other contemporary English novelists. Usually they take the form of a direct imitation of the style and language of a writer to explore a plausible but faintly absurd situation. The result is burlesque, the most orthodox form of parody, combining both comic and critical intention, simultaneously alluding to literature of the past and advancing the comic plot.

However, the most sustained and thoroughgoing of the parodies is that in the 'epilogue', where, significantly, the narrative point of view shifts from the consciousness of Adam to that of his wife. The allusion is to the last section of James Joyce's *Ulysses*, and the style moves toward that of Molly Bloom's interior monologue, with the positive 'yes' of Molly giving way to an ironic, and foreclosing 'perhaps' in Barbara's consciousness. To understand this fully, is to be aware, again, of the novel's entire oscillation between conventional realism and intrusion into it: the parody mocks Joyce's higher style with a much more basic domestic mood. Indeed the comic parodies throughout the novel dissolve into the realism of a conventional domestic tale of intrigue and sexual adventure, with an anticipated comic outcome. Most of the later sections of the book closely resemble the mood of the modern social novel crossed with that of the standard thriller. The variations are best exemplified in the funniest episode: the academic sherry-party, where the author caricatures the problems of the postwar English novel, even engaging in comic play on the names of various prominent writers (Kingsley Anus, C. P. Slow, John Bane). Here the text involves *self*-parody, important throughout the novel; it alludes to 'academic novels of manners', and considers the thought that the novel today might well have exhausted all the possible topics for stories, given 'such a fantastic number of novels written in the last couple of centuries'. The reference to both the situation of the novel and Adam's critical concern with literature is made explicit when he states 'so all of us, you see, are really enacting events that have already been written about in some novel or other' (p. 130). Indeed Adam himself feels written already, and this is apparent when his sexual pursuit of Virginia is told in terms of the dangerous quest of the Knight Errant: similarly, his subsequent farcical withdrawal is seen as 'reenacting one of the oldest roles in literature' (p. 158).

What is clear is that the novel reveals a clearly defined attitude toward the state of the contemporary English novel and its relation to its tradition; it is no accident that David Lodge has discussed this matter a good deal in his criticism, especially in his essay 'The Novelist at the Crossroads', where he talks about his taste for realism but his sense that novelists now are pushed into diverging from it. But he has also stressed his fascination with experiment, and the possibilities of originality in fiction, a central theme of the book. He has commented on this problem, indeed, with reference to Doris Lessing:

> One of the novels that's impressed me most in recent years is Doris Lessing's *The Golden Notebook*, where she seems to be using the conventions of realistic fiction while being aware of their limitations and building this awareness into the novel itself, so that you have, I think, a very interesting, fruitful sort of tension between the novelistic commitment to rendering experience through traditional forms and yet an enquiring, adventurous, very candid questioning of those conventions, ultimately raising all kinds of questions about art and reality.[10]

Lodge's mixed sympathies are very evident in this novel, as in general throughout the development of his work, some of which is strongly realistic, other parts strongly fictionalist. The effect of this in the parodies of *The British Museum Is Falling Down* is evidently to encourage 'local' parody, which becomes a way of indicating the anxiety of the contemporary writer in search of personal signature. Lodge's parody is obviously serious and self-questioning; he comes back to a reflexive spirit in his later novel *Changing Places* (1975). Here, too, though, there is a taste for salvaging realism. For this reason one may question the rationale behind the parodies. For they do tend generally to serve the realistic intent: they are, that is, caused by plot-situations, and are part of the protagonist's plausible response to life—hence they are contained. Parody hence does not subvert the novel's realism; it becomes a function of its comic impact. This is different in spirit to Wilson and Fowles, who both produce much more far-reaching critiques of realism. For each of them, parody is not intelligible so much as a feature of the story itself (though in Wilson there are 'mimetic' reasons for many of his parodies) but as a critical discourse with the novel's tradition and an exploration of its contemporary linguistic situation.

III

Angus Wilson's *No Laughing Matter* also exploits the comic elements, the burlesque, mimicry and satire that can be drawn from parody of specific writers and forms of writing; but this novel is also especially noted for its extensive use of pastiche, and the fundamentally 'unstable' level of its text. *No Laughing Matter* is a version of the social novel, the

---

[10] *Alta, loc. cit.*

dynastic novel of the family; it contains much reference to twentieth-century history, to changes in society and psychological experience, as well as to the nature of the novel, theatre, the popular and the serious arts. Part of it is made up of 'local' parodies, but the most significant feature of the book is the totally inclusive nature of its language. For the text manifests an impressive array of language-uses, exploring many forms of linguistic communication ranging from serious liter-ature to cocktail-party banter, political and historical discourse to fictional self-analysis. It is a novel of mimicry, which means that pastiche works in a markedly comic manner. But, as its title suggests, comedy is serious indeed. And the conscious mosaic of languages undermines the traditionally non-subversive uses of pastiche. This is pastiche in its sophisticated guise: the novel is decidedly subversive of literary language used as an unselfconscious instrument of mimesis.

Wilson clearly sets out to write an historical narrative of a particular type, documenting the history of a family and the fortunes and mis-fortunes of various representative individuals in it, showing their changes over an extended period of time. The milieu is clearly upper middle class, and the historical 'progress' of the family is in fact one from concealed disintegration to almost total collapse, this process being evident from the very opening pages onward. The family is first introduced to us as if out of old, faded photographs, and the image of these comic, Edwardian figures remains with us right through the novel. All the characters begin, in fact, as frozen stereotypes of themselves, and are from the first farcical figures, who continually act out roles and mock themselves, and, more deliberately, mock each other. This level of farce is sustained through the novel at the level of self-conscious artifice by the use of playlets, in which the characters play themselves, or other family members, in caricature or burlesque. At the beginning of the book, the characters are listed as dramatis personae; the cast is significantly large in minor characters; reference to the stages of contemporary history, to which is usually attached the fortunes of one or another of the members of the family, serve as backcloth to the playlets.

Indeed, *No Laughing Matter* commences by referring to the new 'Kinema', and its possible uses as a mode of documentary realism; to the Silent Movie, the Music Hall tradition, and the medium of the Exhibition or Display. Forms of art offer widely dispersed models for the representation of contemporary reality, and they also function as entertainment: their dual function is referred to persistently through the novel. The references follow an historical sequence; thus the self-conscious family playlets parody developments in the history of modern drama itself, and there are direct imitations of Ibsen, Shaw, Chekhov, Beckett. In the section on the 1930s, many references are made to Noel Coward; towards the end of the book, the family life of the Matthews is characterized, with lucid hindsight (just in case the reader is not already well aware of the fact), in terms of the 'Noel Coward World' they all grew up in. Popular arts are likewise seen in development: from Music Hall, through early cinema, to the television of the late 1960s. Some of these changes are seen as progress, others record a loss. For instance, on the personal level of the book, Rupert, at one point a successful actor, fails to keep in touch with changes in the theatre, as serious art-form. Quentin begins as a fervent socialist and ends as a cynical television personality of the late 1960s. Margaret, on the other hand, changes from being a best-selling writer of the interwar years into a 'writer's writer.' Marcus, the effete homosexual, the most 'successful' of the family, emerges finally as the new 'hero of our time.' This is presented ironically, as the last lines of the novel suggest:

Miracle Germany—Stuttgart, Dusseldorf, Frankfurt—all that he [Marcus] admired most in the modern world, even his favourite journal *Time* urged high wages, but also seemly ambition, high profits, and determined management. (p. 479)[11]

It is really the characters in the novel who create the parodies—especially in the forms of theatre, mime and farce. Moreover they see society as a theatre, a rather bitter one, and they play themselves in a fashion of self-mimicry, so offering a continuous pastiche of social language. The artifice of the playlets thus creates a level of theatricality which is itself symptomatic of their entire mode of social behaviour. The roles that all these actors play in the theatre of society are no less ritualistic or preplanned than those inside the playlets where they mocked themselves or are mocked by their author. Thus a high degree of stylized social mimicry is self-consciously played out in the novel. Indeed history itself is available to the reader only through the self-mocking conversations and dialogues, and it becomes an anecdotal backcloth to the social farce of the Matthews' lives. To some degree, the Matthews' satirize history, as serious political issues are played off against trite personal preoccupations. On

[11] Angus Wilson, *No Laughing Matter* (Harmondsworth, Penguin, 1967). All page references in text to this edition.

the one hand, then Angus Wilson creates a novel of very dense social and historical substance, a kind of novel well within his past capacities. But, because of the way his characters and he himself as novelist use mimicry, self-mockery and distortion, because society is seen as a theatre and hence as a place of inter-reflecting images and roles, of parts and performances and scripts and prompts, the text persistently interrogates and displaces this kind of novel. As Malcolm Bradbury puts it in his essay on the novel, 'The Fiction of Pastiche', 'the great gift of the Matthewses is for caricature, for self-caricature and the caricature of others. And they in their turn are caricatured by an author who proves . . . very active, very creative, and also decidedly protean, a figure notable for extraordinary disappearances, rhetorical disguises, mixed registers, and much pastiche and parody on his own account.'[12]

No Laughing Matter is a social novel, and questions are raised in it about the forms of social behaviour and the languages of social inter-course. But these issues, which are comically enacted by the linguistic pluralism of the text, are inextricably related to questions that reach into the novel's realism, and disrupt it. Given the development of a whole new set of discourses, arising in history, in the modern arts—in theatre, painting, popular media—how do we create the modern novel? Wilson seems determined to collect as a basic field of text as many modes of presentation as possible, and the intrusions of these modes—the modes of other forms of prose beside his own, and the modes of theatre, superimposed onto those of fiction—disturb the conventional high style of the modern well-written novel. All this seems to break up the expectations established by the traditional convention of realism, and Wilson is evidently trying to exorcise the ghost of Galsworthy's *The Forsyte Saga* by doing the police in as many voices as possible. Yet the disruptive elements never completely subvert the realist text: history and social reality, character and intrigue, are fully sustained aspects of *No Laughing Matter*. In the book, Angus Wilson parodies a wide variety of modes for the representation of reality, while apparently endorsing the appropriateness of an aesthetics of realism. He is evidently aware of a crisis in realism in postwar English fiction, and a quotation from the novel, when placed alongside a statement from the author, puts explicit emphasis on this crucial dilemma. One of the characters in the book, Herr Birnbaum, comments that: '. . . the

[12] Malcolm Bradbury, 'The Fiction of Pastiche: The Comic Mode of Angus Wilson', repr. in his *Possibilities: Essays on the State of the Novel* (New York/London, 1973), p. 223. This book also contains an essay on John Fowles.

English novel is not an aesthetic novel, it is a social novel. *The Forsyte Saga* has great importance as a mirror of the British high bourgeoisie.' Wilson, with whatever self-mockery, evidently recognizes the truth of this. But he has also commented that 'the traditional form has inhibited me from saying all that I wanted to say. I tried to move out of it.'[13] *No Laughing Matter* is evidently Wilson's most determined attempt to move out of it; it both asserts and negates a classical socio-realist structure.

Thus the novelist as pasticheur, parodist and player of literary and social games builds his concern with traditional fictional form firmly into the text of *No Laughing Matter*. The play on the conventions of novelistic form both subverts, and is contained within, the realist text. Within the spectrum of his realism, Wilson allows aesthetic questions to coexist with the act of representing history and social change. *No Laughing Matter* is a truly comic novel, but the implications for the debate about the form of the novel may well be 'no laughing matter' at all. As Bradbury states: 'One could deduce that something that is happening to realism is happening in Wilson too. This, I think, would be true, especially if we discern in a number of contemporary writers not the attempt to transcend realism by fiction but the attempt to make realism and fictiveness coexist.'[14] Wilson's especial resource is the weight of the old novel that he carries, the backward reach of his fiction to George Eliot and Dickens. But he is evidently anxious about how to locate that inheritance within the world of contemporary form and contemporary social experience. And the book itself offers an historical explanation of why parody and pastiche become appropriate modern answers.

IV

It is apparent that in writing *The French Lieutenant's Woman* John Fowles faced some of the same problems experienced by Angus Wilson, and found like answers in the use of pastiche and parody. But he uses them for much less comic purposes. Fowles, like Wilson, has the classical gifts of the good story-teller, the resources of sophisticated narrative art. Like Wilson, he tends to identify those gifts with an historical form that has now come under question. *The French Lieutenant's Woman* is a remarkable dispositon of these elements: the skilful

13 Quoted in Bradbury, *loc. cit.*, p. 219.
14 Bradbury, *loc. cit.*, p. 229.

manipulation of the devices of writing that are historically germane to the Victorian period, to 1867 and its ideological and aesthetic sub-structure, devices of which Fowles has great mastery, provide the basis for an enquiry into the complex connections between history and writing. And his exploitation of the space between two world views, that of 1867 and 1967, becomes the foundation for an elaborate critique both of the novel as history and the novel as aesthetic species.

The essential questions Fowles raises for us are those which focus on the aesthetics of the novel in the nineteenth century, and those con-temporary elements of parody and pastiche which allow us to enter into dialogue with those aesthetics. In fact—and this is a consistent feature of everything that Fowles has written—the problem of distinguishing between aesthetic and historical conditions governing the production of text is always raised but never clearly solved. Fowles recognizes that art-forms contain dominant ideologies which are historically bounded and may never be separated from the production and the social understanding of works of art. Yet he is himself capable of crossing these boundaries, and of interfusing aesthetic concerns with life con-cerns. If, for Fowles, the Victorian novel, and the literary styles and strategies associated with it, are intricately related to the dominant ideology of its age (and this is part of the theme of *The French Lieu-tenant's Woman*, where these strategies are both exploited for their narrative fascination and then varied for purposes of contemporary comprehension), then the world of contemporary experience demands a quite different ethical and aesthetic fusion in fiction. Yet in the novel he is capable, as a practitioner of fiction, of giving us both forms of writing, of creating both a liberal nineteenth-century and an existential twentieth-century story which then must exist each with the other.

Fowles's historical recreation of the mid-nineteenth century in *The French Lieutenant's Woman* is a complex exercise in documentation: thought and literature, science and social document provide sources which gloss and footnote the making of his world. Quotations from the key figures of the age function in the first instance as epigraphs to head the chapters. These references, as well as enabling the evocation of a real historical period, signpost the principal thematic concerns running through his portrait of the age. For instance, references to Marx and Darwin raise questions about the human condition and the Victorian interpretation of an answer, and they define, also, a view of the historical process seen as a deterministic force, a view on which Fowles depends. Another dominant set of references are those made to the poetry of the Victorian age—Tennyson, Clough, Matthew Arnold, Hardy—and which evoke the anxious tensions of faith and of relation between individual and society crucial to the age: they enforce the introspective self-analysis demanded by love, and the persistent conflicts between individual sensibilities and instincts and the claim of public morality and social convention. The epigraphs, of course, propose many of the dominant motifs of the novel and its central action, and are crucial to the crisis-filled relationship between Sarah and Charles, and the relationship of each to their age. But of more significance here is the point that Fowles not only is evoking an historical period; he is also concerned with interfusing these modes of discourse and sensibility with his adopted pose as a Victorian novelist. The epigraphs serve to heighten the illusion of reading a type of novel, a novel arising in a clearly defined historical period, and this is an important part of the effect of the book.

Thus fashion, descriptions of place (and especially the Dickensian scenes, set in London), the presentation and de-sentimentalization of Dickensian stereotypes, like Sam and Mrs Poulteney, the web of references to the fiction of Dickens, Hardy and Jane Austen (especially *Persuasion*), and the representation of the crippling behavioural prescriptions of a stifling society: all of these things contribute to a narrative system which establishes the mosaic of a world and its culture authenticated by various reality-effects, and by a prose style which imitates the literature of that period and elaborates its view of historical and social reality. This system of well-delineated representation and organization explains much of the fascination of the novel, but it does not account for its meaning as a whole. For Fowles has other concerns: a glance at the first few pages of the book is sufficient for the reader to see a certain obliquity and game-like activity on the part of the narrator, who, ariel-like, is apparently able to adopt the guise of a particular kind of novelist at one point, only to break the illusion at will. Moreover, in so doing, he is evidently concerned to establish another historical dimension. Not only does the narrator want to play at being a Victorian novelist, and explore the ambient society; he also wants to be an historian calling on his powers of insight, to judge one age in terms of another.

In *The French Lieutenant's Woman*, Fowles's use of an ambivalent historical perspective is, initially, perplexing. One key section is chapter 35, where the modality undergoes a significant change: there is now a clear shift from the mode of confidence and certainty in gnomic statements, the mode which occurs when the pose of the Victorian novelist is in operation, to the more quizzical modalities of the self-questioning modern writer. It is evident from the text that one of the central issues in the writing of history is seen to be that of interpretation; and interpretation implies bias. Fowles foregrounds this question of perspective, while leaving us with various choices. For his own approach varies between a complete criticism and rejection of the constrictions and hypocrisies of Victorian society, and a sympathetic account of many of its resources in sensitivity and emotional depth, which have since been lost. Hardy's situation as both romantic poet and frustrated lover in conflict with his age is thus cited as a powerful, ambiguous referent (pp. 235–37).[15] In the historical continuum, there is loss as well as gain: the romantic power of poetry and its evocation of the mysteries of love are shown to have given way to a much more scientific, clinical, and Freudian view. Yet at the same time the novel seems to eulogize the enlightened post-Marx, post-existential, contemporary world view; and the development of the book is such that the two central characters, in their search for a fully authenticated self, move out of their period and emerge as post-nineteenth-century figures. To understand the apparently ambiguous historical perspective of the novel is in fact to appreciate the inherent narrative logic involved in interweaving what might be called the modality of 1867 and the modality of 1967. As chapter 35 intimates, the whole narrative is grounded in a complex set of interrelated confrontations between two historical periods, two ideologies, two possible literary styles, two distinct novelistic conventions. Thus the change of style from a Victorian literary convention of narration to that of the post-Freudian contemporary narrator involves a wide confrontation.

Fowles's theme of historical freedom and determinism is matched in the novel by another scheme of pattern and determinism more directly related to questions of fictional form. For Fowles also wants to say something about the novelist's power over his material and his characters, and above all about his capacity to overdetermine them. He is especially concerned with the convention commonly accepted in nineteenth-century fiction 'that the novelist stands next to God'. Charles, the protagonist of the novel, reaches, at the end, a point of understanding whereby he is able to perceive, through Sarah's example, a non-determined view of behaviour. Thus action becomes for him

15 John Fowles, *The French Lieutenant's Woman* (London, Panther, 1969). All page references in text to this edition.

existential, a matter of personal choice. The choices, however, are many, and the task of choosing filled with the modern anxiety. Fowles postulates a growing independence in his characters, and it is partly an independence from the controlling hand of the novelist himself. The novelist's choice of possible endings is thus dramatized in the plot for the reader too. But the lessons learned by Charles are also supposed to have been learned by the reader, which is why, though Fowles leaves the options as apparently equivalent, the second of the two endings fulfils the logic of the narrative at a deeper level. On one level, the convention of readerly choice or textual indeterminacy destabilizes the text at the level of controlled narrative logic. At another, it reinforces nineteenth-century aesthetic ideas, about the need for maturation and independence in characters: it is an ending coherent both in terms of the nineteenth and the twentieth-century plot.

Fowles thus, so to speak, carries two narrative modes all the way through the book. But a close reading of chapter 13 reveals the extent of the novel's implicit acknowledgement of the post-Modernist wisdom, its degree of dialogue with the conventions it seems both to exploit and to pastiche. Until this point, the novel has been a more or less conventional historical novel, written in the leisurely grand style of the authoritative Victorian novelist. But now the work is suddenly transformed into a metacommentary on the theory of the novel, from a modern perspective. The challenge is offered directly to the reader, who is to be involved in the assembly of a novel that wishes to be more than a Victorian work that was never written. The desire is to create a thoroughly conventional novel of a certain era, but also to exploit those conventions in both the aesthetic and the ethical realm, with the aim of analysing, self-consciously, the convention of mid-nineteenth-century realism and the society to which it refers and by the existence of which it is supported. The brief intrusion of authorial hindsight in chapters previous to this one will have already raised in the reader the sense that a certain critical task was in progress, and that a mode of naive pastiche was not the central intention. But now, with chapter 13, the knowing reader is addressed, and manipulation of past convention is established as much more widespread and deep-seated than has earlier been apparent. Chapter 13 is the first major defamiliarization of the conventional realist text: that is to say, it disrupts the illusion of history at the level of style. As well as declaring his intention not to overdetermine his characters, the twentieth-century author informs his reader that his expectations of passivity and uninvolved observation, appropriate as they are to the leisurely prose and the anecdotal, detailed descriptive processes of a typical nineteenth-century novel of realism, will now be undermined. The reader is to be as committed to the conditions of meaning, and the problems of interconnecting the various levels of the telling, as the central characters will be to their existential crisis.

This self-consciousness is the most un-Victorian element in the style of *The French Lieutenant's Woman*. Auerbach tells us that the major characteristic of realism in the Victorian novel is 'a serious representation of contemporary social reality against the background of a constant historical movement.'[16] The type of novel written in the mid-nineteenth-century is marked by an acute sense of the deterministic force of history, a commitment to the individual as a cherished entity in the coming commercialization of life, and a zero degree of self-consciousness in the presentation of realism. Fowles endorses the elements of this realist mode, and yet he introduces self-consciousness, as an indication of the work's critical intention. Thus the novel is an attempt to dramatize the need for the active transcendence of the 'ironic certainties and rigid conventions' (p. 315) of the Victorian age, as these shape both its social reality and its art. The type of novel of which *The French Lieutenant's Woman* is both a skilful imitation *and* a thoroughgoing critique is seen as limited both in its fundamental aesthetics and in its image of man, especially in terms of possible relationships with others (most notably between men and women). Thus in addition to detailed local pastiche (scenes of characters done in the manner of Dickens, or Thackeray) Fowles postulates the entire type of a literature and then challenges it, establishing the massive gulf between then and now at every instance in the text. The defamiliarization of such an historically defined convention of writing is thus located somewhere between parody and pastiche. And it is made intelligible by Fowles through the instrument of his own existential philosophy, which he wishes to dramatize for the reader, as well as for his characters.

The French Lieutenant's Woman is a book that concentrates many of the problems of the contemporary English novel. It recognizes the substantiality of realism and its historical place, both as an ethic and an aesthetic. The novel thus richly documents the world of 1867: the Victorian world picture is intensely realized by detailed physical descriptions, characterization, and references to dominant intellectual

16 Erich Auerbach, *Mimesis: The Representation of Reality in Western Literature* (trans. W. Trask) (Princeton, NJ, 1953; repr. 1968), p. 518.

and literary practices which create both a sense of historical authenticity and a lore of realism. I have suggested the extent to which the book is a patchwork of allusions and pastiches, drawing not only on specific character stereotypes and situations, but on an entire specific style of writing. However, I have also suggested that the novel is a critique of the conventions, especially as these have to do with constriction, both social and literary. Parody was defined earlier as enabling a mode of literary criticism to enter a text, a mode that focuses on the inherent limitations of past forms, and serves to underline the inbuilt historical character of modes of writing. *In The French Lieutenant's Woman*, parody, manipulating the expectations of the reader, exploiting the resources of pastiche, transcends the comic playfulness of burlesque, and asserts serious intentions. In the book, we may locate the parody of a past convention in the disruption of expectations exemplified in all the various intrusions of a modern hindsight, in the direct addresses to the reader about the confrontation that exists between tradition and recent versions of the novel, and in the intentional violation of all expected endings, Victorian or modern. The parody in this self-conscious book is thus located in the oscillations in it between implicit and explicit critiques of a literary convention and its founding world-view. A critique of the view of life articulated in the forms of a past art, it is also a critique of that art. It is significant that the novel ends in the company of the Pre-Raphaelites, who intended their own art to raise the question of the relation between form and life, and who sought to establish the enigma of form: the enigma of story and the danger of old narrative sequences is one of Fowles's abiding concerns.

V

Today the self-conscious novel has been predominantly concerned with responses to realism and to the modernist critique of that realism in the earlier part of this century. In the United States, there has been a tendency in fiction toward an extravagant, highly imaginative writing, often hovering on the limits of psychological understanding, and concerned with the enactment of extreme states of mind and bizarre experiences. Alternatively, the 'non-fictional' novel has sought to find new instrumentalities for replacing the displaced claim for authoritative knowledge that was central to the old realist text. The works of Thomas Pynchon and John Hawkes are different examples of the first

kind of writing; those of Truman Capote and Oscar Lewis of the
second kind. In France, a deliberate, programmatic form of experimentation has been extending the boundaries of fiction by questioning
our basic conventions of reading, as well as the aesthetic, epistemological, and linguistic implications of realism. The postwar English
novel has shown some parallelism in these matters, and since the mid-
sixties especially has evinced a markedly speculative bias. Examples are
many and varied, but a list of such critical novels would include the
work of Muriel Spark, Doris Lessing, B. S. Johnson, Lawrence
Durrell, William Golding and Anthony Burgess, as well as those
works by Lodge, Wilson and Fowles discussed here. That is not to
say that all novels by these writers are speculative, or that this is the
only tradition in contemporary English fiction. The literary critic must
not fail to acknowledge the force of an ongoing aesthetics of realism in
contemporary English fiction.

It is in this milieu that the question of parody—which has engaged a
good number of writers, including Johnson, Burgess, and Malcolm
Bradbury—has a strong importance. Functioning, as we have seen
above, in various ways, it has nonetheless added an enquiring dimension to the evolution of the current novel. Both Lodge and Wilson
seem essentially to employ parodic and pastiche strategies for comic
purposes; however, their burlesque and mimicry include serious
concerns about the form of the novel. John Fowles's novel is characterized by a flamboyant display of stylistic mastery in a text which plays
the documentary bias of a certain kind of realism against a modern
critique of its fictive status, his serious concern is quite evident. But in
all these writers the power of the realist mode is granted a crucial
recognition. Today the merger between a realist convention and a
quizzical post-Modernist awareness of the bounds of the convention
seems common. David Lodge has called this an 'aesthetics of compromise,' whereby 'the pressures of scepticism on the aesthetic and
epistemological premises of literary realism' is strongly felt, yet does
not deter, in England, the production of realist novels.[17] This being
the case, the persistence of that realist tradition indicates the controlling
boundary on experiment in contemporary English fiction. Parody
serves to meet this situation by permitting an intertextual level of
writing to evolve, in which previous writers, forms and conventions
can be both reinstated and criticized. In Lodge, the joke is that literary
conventions and perceptions may dominate us; Fowles, working

[17] Lodge, quoted in Bradbury, *loc. cit.*, p. 174.

with an historical continuum, suggests that there may be philosophical-aesthetic grounds for the systematic subverting of realism (though the form of his other writings suggests that he is prepared to take this view only so far). Casting around for appropriate foreign comparisons, we might cite *The Lime Twig* (1961), by the American novelist John Hawkes, where the soporific plot of the conventional detective story is disrupted in order to emphasize the apparent inadequacies of realism, and the need is to find a form which would enable the dramatization of the hidden psychological motivations of man's most disturbing actions. A different example of the radical use of general parody would be the French novelist Claude Simon's *nouveau roman*, *Le Vent* (*The Wind:* 1957), which undermines the status of the realist text through questioning its claims to knowledge. The bounds of the traditions of realism may be best understood, then, by comparing instances of the contemporary critique through diverse international examples. But that requires another study. Here the important issue is to recognize that contemporary parody and pastiche arises as a feature of the evolving English tradition; for, as the more traditional aspects of the parodic and pastiche modes in the novels above indicate, the claims of realism continue to operate in the English novel even while it interrogates itself.

Note

Life.

Born in 1918 and educated in Edinburgh, Muriel Spark went to live in Central
Africa in 1937. She married there, but returned in 1944, to work in the political
Intelligence Dept. of the Foreign Office. She became secretary of the Poetry
Society and edited *Poetry Review*; later, a 'constitutional exile', she has lived in
the USA and Rome. She holds the OBE. Originally a poet, her early work
includes radio plays, literary journalism, criticism (studies of Mary Shelley and
John Masefield), and editions of writings by the Brontës, Mary Shelley and
John Henry Newman—sometimes with Derek Stanford, who gives reminiscences in his *Muriel Spark* (London, 1963; including a useful bibliography by
Bernard Stone) and *Inside the Forties* (London, 1977). Mrs Spark provides autobiographical information in 'Edinburgh-Born', *New Statesman* LXIV (10
August, 1962), 'My Conversion', *Twentieth Century* CLXX (Autumn 1961)
and 'How I Became a Novelist', *John O'London's* III, 61 (1 December, 1960).

Writings.

Novels: *The Comforters* (1957); *Robinson* (1958); *Memento Mori* (1959); *The
Ballad of Peckham Rye* (1960); *The Bachelors* (1960); *The Prime of Miss Jean
Brodie* (1961); *The Girls of Slender Means* (1963); *The Mandelbaum Gate* (1965);
The Public Image (1968); *The Driver's Seat* (1970); *Not to Disturb* (1971); *The
Hothouse by the East River* (1973); *The Abbess of Crewe* (1974); *The Takeover*
(1976); *Territorial Rights* (1979).
Stories: *The Go-Away Bird and Other Stories* (1958); *Collected Stories I* (1967).
Poetry: *The Fanfarlo and Other Verses* (Hand and Flower Press, 1952); *Collected
Poems I* (1967). (All publ. in London by Macmillan unless otherwise indicated.)
Also a children's book, two vols. of plays, etc.
Criticism: Two valuable interviews with Mrs Spark are Frank Kermode, 'The
House of Fiction', repr. in M. Bradbury (ed.), *The Novel Today* (London/
Manchester, 1977) and Ian Gillham, 'Keeping It Short', *The Listener*, 24 Sept,
1970. Kermode is one of her most perceptive critics; see reviews collected in his
Modern Essays (London, 1971). Useful studies are Peter Kemp, *Muriel Spark*
(London, 1974) and Karl Malkoff, *Muriel Spark* (New York/London, 1968).
Important articles are: W. Berthoff, 'Fortunes of the Novel: Muriel Spark and
Iris Murdoch', *Massachusetts Review* VIII (Spring 1967); George Greene, 'A
Reading of Muriel Spark', *Thought* XLIII (1968); D. Lodge, 'The Uses and
Abuses of Omniscience: Method and Meaning in Muriel Spark's *The Prime of
Miss Jean Brodie*', repr. in his *The Novelist at the Crossroads* (London, 1971);
M. Bradbury, 'Muriel Spark's Fingernails', repr. in his *Possibilities: Essays on the
State of the Novel* (London/New York, 1973).

VII

'Angels Dining at the Ritz': The Faith and Fiction of Muriel Spark

RUTH WHITTAKER

I

MURIEL SPARK is widely recognized as one of the most important of contemporary English novelists, but her distinctive novels have caused critics much uneasiness in their attempts to classify her work. Where Frederick Karl calls her 'light to the point of froth', Frank Kermode describes her as 'obsessed with her medium', a 'difficult and important artist'.[1] The problem of reconciling the frothy and serious aspects of her work is directly related to the paradox she seeks to convey—that, in spite of the humour and manifest absurdity of human behaviour and events, there is nevertheless 'a supernatural process going on under the surface and within the substance of all things' (*The Mandelbaum Gate*, p. 199).[2] This belief she clearly demonstrated in her first published fiction, a short story called 'The Seraph and the Zambesi' (1951), of which she said: 'I do not know what gave me the idea for the story, but certainly I believe in angels, and I had been up the Zambesi on a boat.'[3] Her assurance in acknowledging as inspiration both angels and boat-trips (to each their due) is characteristic; indeed, it is the disclosure of the relationship between the profane and the divine that is the moti-vation, and ultimately the abiding theme, of almost all her work. Such anachronistic moral confidence might well tempt a twentieth-century novelist to make a stylistic withdrawal to earlier forms of fiction, quietly asserting faith in the departed order by reverting to the moral tone of certain nineteenth-century novels. However, Muriel

[1] Frederick R. Karl, *A Reader's Guide to the Contemporary English Novel* (London, rev. ed., 1963), p. 280; Frank Kermode, 'Sheerer Spark', *The Listener* (24 September, 1970), pp. 425, 426.
[2] Page references are to the Penguin editions, with the exception of *Collected Stories I*, which is to the Macmillan, London, edition.
[3] Muriel Spark, 'How I Became a Novelist', *John O'London's Weekly* III, 61 (1 December, 1960), p. 683.

Spark does not do this. Her novels have an ethical and a realistic bias, but of a strange kind. They also have a feel of moral obliquity and a distinctly contemporary hardness; indeed, they have a sharp stylistic authenticity brought about through techniques which are peculiarly post-modern. She has adopted twentieth-century technology, as it were, to deal with eternal truths; and, having suited the weapons to the fray, she persuades us that angels and demons are neither metaphoric nor outdated conceits, but exist here and now in convents, classrooms, and on the factory floor. In doing this, she has not reverted to old forms of fantasy, nor utterly succumbed to the current pressures against realism. But she has acknowledged them, felt them in her work; and it is worth looking briefly at what these pressures are to see that to maintain this balance is a very considerable achievement.

One source for the doubt that many post-modernist writers feel about the contemporary appropriateness of the realistic novel is that, in recent decades, reality has been judged as increasingly 'fictive'. A reason sometimes suggested is that reality is more bizarre than it ever was; alternatively, that in a plural world a consensual reality is hard to establish. Yet another reason given is that life comes to us already fictionalized, by what might be called the lay fiction-makers of our times: the media men, the public-relations network, the press secretaries. In the proliferated information and dramatization fed to us by the technological media, in the pre-organized structures of modes of thought like psychology and sociology, we have an ordering of experience, a structure of representation, which already rivals the fictional act. We live, in short, in what Nathalie Sarraute calls 'the era of suspicion', where pre-mediated reality makes us anxious, and where the attempt of the realistic novelist to give an authoritative version of what is so has been seriously challenged. Hence many contemporary novelists have tried to create a fiction that is without authorial domination. Some have abandoned the attempt to compete with reality by offering simply to cooperate with it: thus the techniques of the New Journalism merge with the new fictionality, so that the author abdicates his responsibility of creating characters, as Truman Capote does in *In Cold Blood*, accepting the happy fortune of people and events granted him by the seemingly absurd world outside. Others have emphasized the fictionalist element by working with fabulous and autonomous worlds that are deceptively free of the contraints, conventions and probabilities of realistic writing. Some novelists, unable to reject realism with such panache, have turned their unease into a credo of self-doubt, by querying within their novels the possibility of realism, or the rightness of it. This fictional introspection, though not entirely new in fiction, is one of the familiar features of post-modernist sensibility, and it frequently takes the form of an assertion of vulnerability. The novelist, instead of asserting his power over the real, takes his quest for it as sufficient task: As Robbe-Grillet puts it: 'L'écrivain, par définition, ne sait où il va, et il écrit pour chercher, à comprendre pourquoi il écrit.'[4]

One of Muriel Spark's great strengths as a writer is that she does not share this routelessness, even though she is perfectly aware of its prevalence, and the reasons for it. She is a writer who firmly knows her own authority and powers, though she speculates about them and qualifies them. She is a writer who has a sense of the reality of the world she creates, and yet she is capable of showing us flamboyantly how unreal the realistic can be. She creates characters who can protest against their creators, and reveals facts which are infiltrated with strange and unimagined potential. Critical judgement of her work has thus been divided. There are those who see her as a Catholic writer of a moderately realistic kind, dealing with issues of faith in a contingent and substantial world. There are also those, however, who see her as concerned with form—increasingly so, as her fiction develops. Her faith then becomes a useful felicity which enables her to view the world as a divine fiction, with her own writing as a textual analogue; thus her interest in teleology can be accounted for almost entirely in formal terms. In fact, the strangeness of her work, which lies in a recognizable Catholic tradition of speculative fiction, is that it depends on the interconnection of these viewpoints. In this essay, then, I want to show that, in spite of an increasing emphasis in novels on the theory of fiction, they are also highly concerned with the fact of God. Form itself is shown to make a theological statement, and God's design to be analogous to that of the artist. Endings have eschatological as well as structural implications; the problem is to see both these aspects simultaneously, and so to share her vision of how things irreducibly are, to recognize the absolute fact of divine order and its fittingness.

[4] Quoted by Stephen Heath from *Esprit* (July 1964) in his *The Nouveau Roman* (London, 1972), p. 31.

II

Biography is an essential starting point. Muriel Sarah Camberg was born in Edinburgh of parents both part Jewish; in 'My Conversion' she said that her childhood environment 'had a kind of Jewish tinge but without any formal instruction'. When asked in an interview how important to her it was that she was half Jewish, she replied: 'I don't particularly associate myself with Jewish causes. But I defend them sharply if they're attacked.'[5] But *The Mandelbaum Gate* (1965) and a story like 'The Gentile Jewess' reveal that her mixed blood much influences her thinking, making her aware of disparate elements in her make-up, and the need to reconcile and come to terms with them. *The Mandelbaum Gate* suggests that she sees no contradiction between her Jewish background and her Catholic faith. Indeed in an interview with Malcolm Muggeridge she said that, to her, 'the Catholic church is a continuation of the Jewish church'[6]; the heroine of *The Mandelbau— Gate* says that

> the Scriptures were specially important to the half-Jew turned Catholic. The Old Testament and the New, she said, were to her—as near as she could apply to her own experience the phrase of Dante's vision—'bound by love into one volume'. (p. 26)

At her school in Edinburgh, she was, she says, 'the school's Poet and Dreamer, with appropriate perquisites and concessions';[7] the Edinburgh schooling duly takes its place in *The Prime of Miss Jean Brodie* (1961). In 1937, straight from school, she went to live in Central Africa, where she married and had a son. She has never published a novel about Africa, but some of her best and most evocative short stories are set there, and the experience clearly made an indelible impression on her. On her return, in 1944, she worked as a typist in a branch of the Intelligence Service concerned with writing anti-Nazi propaganda; it was useful grounding for her keen interest in the process of creating fictions, and the atmosphere is described in *The Hothouse by the East River* (1973), as 'black propaganda and psychological warfare ... involv[ing] a tangled mixture of damaging lies, flattering and plausible truths' (p. 52). Since she had continued writing poetry since she left school, her

[5] Muriel Spark, interview with Philip Toynbee, *Observer Colour Magazine* (7 November, 1971), p. 74.

[6] Muriel Spark, interview with Malcolm Muggeridge: unpublished transcript of a Granada television interview.

[7] Muriel Spark, 'What Images Return', in Karl Miller (ed.), *Memoirs of a Modern Scotland* (London, 1970), p. 152.

work with the Poetry Society after the war was fitting. But it was when she left that she began writing various critical works, some in collaboration with Derek Stanford, on Wordsworth, Emily Brontë, John Masefield; editions of collections of letters, of the Brontës, Mary Shelley and, later most significantly, John Henry Newman.

Newman's writings were a very important influence on her decision to become a Roman Catholic. She admired the clarity of his style, and the thoroughness with which he had considered his own conversion. For her, as for Newman, Catholicism was not something which required strenuous intellectual adaptation; for both of them it seems to have been the religion with which their beliefs instinctively accorded, and it was the authenticity of this instinctive attraction both had to test, rather than the Church's dogma itself. Mrs Spark said in the interview with Muggeridge: 'The reason I became a Roman Catholic was because it explained me'; in the same interview she calls herself a 'Catholic animal'. Like Newman, she took time over her conversion. Her education was Presbyterian; by 1952 she was an Anglican, and in 1953 was Anglo-Catholic for nine months. After instruction from a monk at St Benedict's Abbey, Ealing, she was received into the Roman Catholic church in 1954. The conversion greatly affected her writing. She had started publishing fiction in 1951, winning an *Observer* short story competition with 'The Seraph and the Zambesi'. But poetry was still dominant; in 1952 *The Fanfarlo and Other Verse* appeared. It was in the year of her conversion, 1954, that she began her first novel. Alan Maclean at Macmillan, looking for new authors, had approached her; and supported by an advance, and a monthly allowance from Graham Greene (whom she had never met), she retired from London to a religious community in Kent, there beginning *The Comforters* (1957).

Newman had described 'Catholic literature' not as that which deals specifically with Catholic matters, but as writing including 'all subjects of literature whatever, treated as only a Catholic would treat them'.[8] The sureness of what, to the non-Catholic, seems a vague proposal is founded on the conviction that what Catholic writers hold in common is not a single standpoint but an immutable frame of reference arising from the dogma of the Church. This certain belief was Muriel Spark's liberation as a writer; it is no coincidence that she was able to start a first novel after becoming a Catholic. She remarked that, after her conversion, 'I began to see life as a whole rather than as a series of

[8] J. H. Newman, *The Idea of a University* (Image Books Edition: New York, 1959), p. 285.

disconnected happenings';[9] this view intersects with that of the novelist, seeking imaginative sense out of apparent randomness. For Mrs Spark, her sense of coherence means that she sees the external visible world not as distinct from the spiritual world, but as a manifestation of it; not as two worlds, but one, utilized to the utmost to express the extraordinary through the ordinary. In this way, nothing is arbitrary. Each event or action has its use, which may not, however, be evident until the life is completed. This awareness produces in her work both an acceptance of and a reverence for the ordinary; what she calls in *The Prime of Miss Jean Brodie* 'a sense of the hidden possibilities in all things' (p. 81). Even sin is not wasted. In *The Bachelors* (1960) one of the characters says 'The Christian economy seems to me to be so ordered that original sin is necessary to salvation' (p. 85). In Mrs Spark's novels, one might say, sin particularly is not wasted, since her evil characters invariably sin grandly and to great purpose. This paradox, whereby we realize that the most unlikely people and incidents can be a means of grace, recurs in her work. As in the novels of Graham Greene, we are shown that the way to God is not always through conventional channels, and that there is a kind of divine satire being practised when God mocks the rational expectations of those committed to piety. For example, in *The Girls of Slender Means* (1963) we keep our spiritual expectations on the pure Joanna, and our secular ones, as it were, on the sexy Selina. But ultimately it is the recognition of the existence of evil in Selina that is to Nicholas a means of grace; a nice economy ironically adapted from Ecclesiasticus, quoted in a later novel: 'As well may foul thing cleanse, as false thing give thee a true warning.'

A further economy joyfully and thriftily utilized by Mrs Spark is the analogy between God and the novelist. As a Christian, she sees nothing anachronistic in this, and indeed, time and again draws our attention to certain immutable parallels, as if by reiterating them she makes a point about their inescapability. Both God and the novelist create a world which they then people with characters simultaneously free and limited. Sometimes in novels, as in real life, characters resent and fight back at authorial or divine omniscience, and the dynamic relationship between creator and character is integral to Mrs Spark's plots. Not surprisingly, her novels very often end with death, because, having seized on the connection between mortality and the novel form, she fuses the eschatological interests of the Roman Catholic with the aesthetic teleology of the novel. Indeed, death and ending is the retro-

[9] Muriel Spark, 'How I Became a Novelist', cited above.

spective subject of her novels—in so far as the life of a Christian is a preparation for death, and the plot of a novel an extended preparation for its ending. This is not to say that she denies the beauty and validity of contingency, particularly in her early work. But both the religious and the novelist, being concerned with endings, are consequently aware of the continual relationship between the contingent and the absolute. So, while recognizing and even rejoicing in the arbitrary appearance of random happenings, Mrs Spark makes the reader aware of their potential in an ultimate design. Newman, refuting the argument from design, said in one of his letters, 'I believe in design because I believe in God; not in a God because I see design,'[10] and for both the Catholic and the novelist, truth is arrived at through what is originally an act of faith, the fusion of contingency into pattern.

For someone so committed, it is initially surprising that the hallmark of Mrs Spark's work is coolness and detachment. In most postmodern novels, authorial detachment is an attitude taken as a submission to chaos, a denial of omniscience, or a reverence for the quiddity of the ephemeral world. However, for Mrs Spark it is a way of revealing God's truth. Instead of interpreting events, she stands aside and shows them, unadorned. Describing the way she writes, she said in the 'House of Fiction' interview with Frank Kermode: 'Things just happen, and one records what has happened a few seconds later.' This is an odd description of the creative process, and it is in fact a denial of it, since in her terms it would be a kind of blasphemy. Instead, it is rather like being the Recording Angel: 'one records what has happened', leaving God to pass judgement on it. God, like the novelist, knows the beginning and the end, and the struggles of his characters to evade their destinies, that is, the process of most people's lives, are watched by Mrs Spark with cool, ironic amusement. And since she writes about inevitability, she abandons the element of suspense as irrelevant, often revealing the end at the beginning, or at least very early on in the novel. Reading her books is a bit like watching a football match on television when you already know the result; the interest lies not so much in the outcome, but in the ways in which it is achieved.

Mrs Spark practises a stylistic thrift by which situations are given through action and dialogue, with little or no attempt to explain or reveal the internal, psychological motivation of her characters. This

[10] J. H. Newman, quoted by Muriel Spark in her introduction 'Newman as Catholic' in Derek Stanford and Muriel Spark (eds.), *The Letters of John Henry Newman* (London, 1957), p. 147.

makes reading her work a demanding process ('Readers' she once remarked coolly, 'are a very meagre species'[11]) since the lack of authorial comment is a means of forcing the reader to engage in his own ethical evaluations. In *The Prime of Miss Jean Brodie* (1961) a girl runs away from school to fight in the Spanish Civil War and gets killed. We are told that 'the school held an abbreviated form of remembrance service for her' (p. 118). By shortening her remembrance service the school is shown to question the value of the girl's action. But, on reflection, the reader may question the implicitly censorious attitude of the school. The impetus to this reflection arises very economically from the word 'abbreviated' and not from a detailed analysis of the pros and cons of the situation, nor from a particularly sympathetic build-up of the girl's personality.

Her style reflects the austerity of her vision. For Mrs Spark there is none of the doubt or muddle which makes most of us hedge our bets in ambiguity or imprecision. Her prose is suited absolutely to the expression of a clear belief in the existence of order. It is, indeed, an enactment of it, since no word is redundant or insignificant, each evidently having a function within the grand design. She uses words with poetic economy, and in her later novels avoids figurative speech in favour of particular and minute description. This resembles the hard, specific world of the *nouveau roman*, and Mrs Spark has expressed interest in the techniques of Robbe-Grillet. However, for her the commonplace and the contingent are not totally significant in themselves, but signposts to an authenticity beyond them. Thus, when she describes things in clinical, neutral manner, as in *The Driver's Seat* (1970), this method is used to alert us to the neurosis of a character, or the mood of a situation, rather than as a celebration of objects for their own sake.

Nevertheless, the effect is one of coolness. The most striking omission in Mrs Spark's work is that of emotional expression. It is as if she cannot accommodate the imprecision of passion. In situations where novelists usually expend most effort to involve their readers' feelings, Mrs Spark conspicuously abstains. Violent deaths occur frequently in her work, but are always related with extreme detachment. For example:

He looked as if he would murder me and he did. ('The Portobello Road', *Collected Stories I* p. 29)

---

11 Muriel Spark interview with Ian Gillham, 'Keeping it Short', *The Listener*, (24 September, 1970), p. 411. Quotation taken from an unabridged transcript.

He wrenched the stick from the old woman's hand, and, with the blunt end of it, battered her to death. It was her eighty-first year. (*Memento Mori*, p. 179)

He came towards her with the corkscrew and stabbed it into her long neck nine times, and killed her. Then he took his hat and went home to his wife. (*The Ballad of Peckham Rye*, p. 136)

This objectivity serves a purpose. It reminds us, above all, that, for a Christian, death in itself is not important, but only a means to an end. It also forces us to think instead of feel. Devoid of the expressions of shock, horror or moralizing that usually attend death in novels, we as readers have to exercise our own moral intelligence in each case, without explicit authorial guidance. But in spite of the evident use Mrs Spark makes of her detached technique, a sense of omission, a feeling of holding back remains, particularly in *The Abbess of Crewe* and *The Takeover*. It is as if, instead of working from sensibility, and subduing emotion into style, she cuts short the process, by using style for its own dazzling effect, rather than as an evolution of feeling. In an address delivered to the American Academy of Arts and Letters in 1971, she condemns what she calls 'the literature of sentiment and emotion', because it enables us to substitute feeling for action. She goes on:

I would like to see ... a more deliberate cunning, a more derisive undermining of what is wrong. I would like to see less emotion and more intelligence in these efforts to impress our hearts and minds.

Certainly, 'less emotion and more intelligence' is increasingly the formula for her novels, but I think her justification of it is less altruistic than she makes out. Various critics have noticed this. Henk Romijn Meijer, talking about her comedy says: 'It isn't difficult to assume great shyness behind this humour, some embarrassment to show her feelings.'[12] Writing in 1971, Douglas Reed puts it more forcibly:

What persists most strongly in the memory after putting aside Miss Spark's books is the constant pitch of controlled tension pervading them. ... Miss Spark is taut, inhibited from fully tapping the primitive and romantic passions within herself, perhaps because they are too clearly related to the unknown terror ricochetting through her tales ... not susceptible to calm reason. ...[13]

---

[12] Henk Romijn Meijer, 'Het Satirische Talent van Muriel Spark', *Tirade*, VI (1962), unpublished translation by Tony de Vletter.

[13] Douglas Reed, 'Taking Cocktails with Life', *Books and Bookmen* (11 August, 1971), pp. 10–14.

And reviewing *The Hothouse by the East River* (1973) Michael Ratcliffe concludes: 'The sense of a desperate evasion persists.'[14]

III

This sense of evasion can in part be explained by Mrs Sparks' refusal to fulfil the reader's expectations of a traditional English novel. The Catholic novel is motivated by, and works from, a different set of assumptions and values from its more liberal, humanist counterpart. By a 'liberal, humanist' novel I mean the kind of work which is distinguished by its commitment to realism, combined with a deep concern for the individual character: his creation and motivation, his interaction with the forces of society and the environment in which he is placed, the consequent tensions and the resulting changes both to the individual and to society. What I have just described is, of course, a plot, and a further concomitant of this kind of novel is the implication of a belief in the human, rather than the divine or the authorial, capacity for effecting change. This is not to say that the emphasis is necessarily on individually determined growth or regression, but that the possibility of an individual being in charge of his own destiny is not ruled out, as it is in novels where he is shown to be part of a pre-ordained structure (as in Catholic novels) or patently a construct and plaything of the novelist (as in reflexive novels). Thus the concept and presentation of character in the liberal novel are associated, above all, with what John Bayley calls 'the supremacy of personality'—that is, the creation and interaction of individuals not merely as embodiments of ideology, but as characters for whom the author feels love. Bayley goes on:

> What I understand by an author's love for his characters is a delight in their independent existence as *other people* . . . an intense interest in their personalities combined with a sort of detached solicitude, a respect for their freedom.[15]

Clearly 'the supremacy of personality' is precisely what Mrs Spark's novels are *not* about, and this emphasis on freedom and independence of character is far from the Catholic view of a being bound by the ordi-

---

14 Michael Ratcliffe, Review of *The Hothouse by the East River*, *The Times* (1 March, 1973).

15 John Bayley, *The Characters of Love* (London, 1960; paperback edition 1968), pp. 7, 8.

nances of God, and by analogy, bound as rigorously by the restrictions imposed by the novelist. It is a definition conceded by Graham Greene in *The End of the Affair* (1951) where he writes:

> ... we are inextricably bound to the plot, and wearily God forces us, here and there, according to his intention, characters without poetry, without free will.... (p. 182)[16]

It is explored by Muriel Spark in *The Comforters*, where the difficulties experienced by the heroine on her conversion to Roman Catholicism are paralleled by the resentment she feels at being a character in a novel. Both roles entail a loss of freedom, or rather, a redefinition of freedom as part of a divine and structural coherence.

This makes Catholic writers—I am thinking particularly of Firbank and Waugh—seem somewhat bleak towards their characters; this is notably true of Mrs Spark. In an interview with Lorna Sage, she describes her attitude to human failing as 'a lack of expectancy', and this exactly sums up the tone of her later novels.[17] There is none of the loving curiosity of, say, Henry James for Isabel Archer: 'Well, what will she *do*?' Mrs Spark knows only too well what her characters will do. She views them, not exactly with cynicism, but with the lack of intensity and involvement with which one watches a situation when the outcome is already known. For all their liveliness and verve, her characters are finally denied a humanistic individuality; we, and usually they, are made aware that they function as components inescapably subordinate to an overall design. And because their roles are predetermined, it is part of Mrs Spark's economy not to give us interior views of her characters, their thoughts and motives, since this might elicit irrelevant sympathy for their personalities at the expense of our attention to their role within the overall plot. This tendency greatly increases in her later work, to the point of changing its spirit and foregrounding its technique. For here, especially, Mrs Spark seldom gives us sufficient background to her characters for us to iden-tify with them. They rarely have families or a sense of belonging, and it is as if, by isolating them, discarding the distractions of environment, the half-truths of heredity, she can immediately get down to essentials. There is a feeling of urgency in her dealings with her characters; not just an insistence that the end is what matters, but the conviction that

---

[16] Graham Greene, *The End of the Affair* (London, 1951; Penguin edition, 1968), p. 182.

[17] Muriel Spark, interview with Lorna Sage, *The Observer* (30 May, 1976).

the careful nurturing of sympathy for the foibles and nuances of personality is an indulgence when the state of the soul is what needs to be
considered.

Muriel Spark combines a thorough knowledge of worldly wheeling
and dealing with a belief in divine stability; in her novels she makes the
satiric juxtaposition of this knowledge with this belief. Thus the
people she writes about most frequently are those who best illustrate
the irony of worldly preoccupations, the shifting surface of plot-
makers who (with authorially implied blasphemy) take upon themselves the roles of creators. These are usually manipulators of various
kinds: blackmailers, teachers, film-makers, poseurs and con men. Their
interest to the reader lies mainly in the dynamic of their actions as these
lay fiction-makers organize people and events into their own patterns.
This world is increasingly dominant in the later novels, and takes on
an internationalist, a modern European character. A further plot, a
super-plot, emerges from the way their patterning may conflict or
collude with God's divine pattern, so that in Mrs Spark's novels the
individual is always kept within a divine perspective, losing thereby
some intrinsic importance which would be retained and enlarged on in
a humanist novel.

A further deviation from the realist tradition can be accounted for by
the Catholic view of the phenomenal world. This is summed up by
Cardinal Newman's motto, *ex umbris et imaginibus in veritatem* (from
shadows and types to the reality). The 'reality' is not the apprehensible
world, but the divine one, and this means that, in Muriel Spark's
work, realism is not the main objective. She has an impatience with
mimesis since her real concern is with the inimitable. Thus, whenever
our attention is drawn to the familiar and the commonplace within her
novels, it is invariably to show us that they contain elements of the
extraordinary; that is, they function in her work not to establish a
recognizable world, but demonstrably as part of a divine and unfamiliar pattern. Reality is used for didactic purposes: one can almost
see Mrs Spark sizing up a situation with a sophisticated and professional
eye as to its divine or satanic potential, like a priest in a new parish.
And although some of her novels are very evocative of the period
they describe (Edinburgh in the thirties, London in the forties) realistic
events are always subordinated to the demands of the plot, and not
vice versa. For example, in *The Girls of Slender Means* the Second
World War is used to provide a bomb which in turn provides the
hero with the opportunity for a revelation of grace, and we are left in

no doubt as to which event is considered by Mrs Spark the more important.

The subversion of realism in Mrs Spark's novels is assisted by the introduction of a supernatural element in almost all of them. This device is presented without authorial explanation, and is initially as puzzling to the reader as it is to the characters, who seldom share their creator's awareness of the supernatural as part of everyday reality. The ways in which they cope with the intrusion of the irrational are, however, a measure of their insight and moral growth. Those who recognize and accept the existence of a world not explicable in human terms find the experience liberating. Their idea of reality is enlarged to include heaven and hell. In *Memento Mori*, for example, death is originally seen in terms of old age, nursing homes, funeral wreaths and obituaries. However, the perceptions offered to the characters within the novel are also available to the reader, who gradually realizes that these realistic, accountable aspects of death are totally peripheral to the main theme, which is the state of the soul of each individual as he or she comes near to dying. The novel becomes, very seriously, a meditation on the Four Last Things, Death, Judgement, Hell and Heaven; and a genuine *memento mori*.

Yet another departure from the humane world of the traditional, realist novel is Mrs Spark's uncomfortable and distinctive humour. It seems somewhat odd, initially, that the highly committed religious novel so often generates comedy when, as Bergson points out, indifference is the primary condition for laughter. However, for many Catholic writers in particular, a passionate caring for the spiritual leads to an indifference to the commonly accepted values and mores of the secular world. These, viewed objectively, can be comic, while to those without such spiritual perspectives, they can be highly serious. A religious writer can also use comedy as an escape from his painful vision of the gap between humanity and perfection, as in the work of Evelyn Waugh. This escapism verges on 'black humour'—the macabre kind of comedy which arises from suspending the appropriate emotional response to a situation which usually elicits shock or horror or compassion. Muriel Spark's wit and sharpness are often compared with those of Waugh. But whereas his comedy is cyclic, arising from pessimism and returning to it, Mrs Spark uses laughter as a dynamic moral weapon. Her comic impetus arises not so much disgust with contemporary society as from a comparison of secular with divine values. This means that incidents and situations, which, judged by worldly standards, are weighty and significant, are shown by her to be very trivial indeed in comparison with God and eternity. Her characters are constantly getting worked up about the wrong things and, if she is not sympathetic to them, it is because that would be to collude with their folly, rather than to reveal it. Thus the humour comes from our awareness that the characters' estimates of their own importance are often misdirected and wildly out of proportion, and they undergo, in the course of her novels, a humorous but instructive realignment of priorities.

A fruitful source of comedy in Mrs Spark's novels is her choice of eccentric and bizarre characters: a grandmother who leads a gang of diamond smugglers, a princess who hatches silkworms in the warmth between her breasts, an Abbess who bugs her own convent. She is also attracted to the absurdity of extreme cults and charismatic movements, whose leaders take themselves immensely earnestly, and whose pomposity she sharply deflates. While the sheer enormity of such characters is comic, they often emerge as unrealistic. Flayed by Mrs Spark of the comfortable, conventional layers of *politesse*, her later protagonists appear as grotesque embodiments of the ills to which she is drawing attention. She is also capable of setting up lesser characters with a stylistic grandeur reflecting their own self-importance, and then puncturing with sudden bathos the expectations she has aroused in the reader. Here is the description of Sir Edwin Manders (of Manders' Figs in Syrup) from *The Comforters*:

> It is possible for a man matured in religion by half a century of punctilious observance, having advanced himself in devotion the slow and exquisite way, trustfully ascending his winding stair, and, to make assurance doubly sure, supplementing his meditations by deep-breathing exercises twice-daily, to go into a flat spin when faced with some trouble which does not come within a familiar category. (p. 113)

Mrs Spark utilizes the deceptive, poetic power of language to reveal, with an apt ironic awareness of her own ability, the fact of its deception. The slow, dignified prose at the beginning of that extract initiates lofty expectations about the nature of the man it describes. Its stately, spiralling clauses, its metaphor and literary allusion, its careful, contemplative diction seriously establishes itself, before being subtly undermined by the inclusion of 'deep-breathing' exercises in the same reverential tone. This incongruity, this misplaced earnestness, calls into doubt the spiritual maturity of its subject, a doubt confirmed almost as soon as we are aware of it by the down-to-earth, no-nonsense language which completes the sentence. As the high-flown prose crashes deliberately down into the colloquialism of a 'flat-spin', it reflects the inadequacy of Sir Edwin's religiosity when faced with an embarrassing family crisis. This stylistic precision is motivated by Mrs Spark's acute sense of the difference between façade and reality. The result is comic; it is also a warning that the truth is easily disguised. Sir Edwin's pretensions are revealed, and then revealed as insubstantial—mere words, the author implies, an audacious reminder within the novel of the power of words to create fictions.

Mrs Spark has never had any compunction about undermining realism by drawing attention within her novels to their fictive nature. In *The Comforters*, the narrator points out that 'the characters in this novel are all fictitious', and in subsequent novels the protagonists often demonstrate such a blatant expertise with fictional technique that the reader cannot but apply this knowledge to the novels themselves. However, these assertions of fictionality are not made (in contrast with many post-modernist writers) to proclaim the inadequacy of the novel in relation to the truth. Mrs Spark is highly confident about the function of the novel in this respect. In the 'House of Fiction' interview with Frank Kermode she said:

> I don't claim that my novels are truth—I claim that they are fiction, out of which a kind of truth emerges. And I keep in my mind specifically that what I am writing is fiction because I am interested in truth—absolute truth. . . .

Just as she is concerned that worldly phenomena are not mistaken for reality, so she is intent that we, as readers, do not confuse the surface of her fiction, which is parabolical, with the truth to which it directs us. In her early novels, this truth was unambiguous; the emphasis of her work was deeply moral and each chronicle of events was unified by a clear expression of her faith in God. However, since *The Public Image* (1968) her work has taken on an increasing ambivalence which is to do with a more explicit interest in the aesthetics of the novel form. This interest was indeed apparent in her first novel, but whereas in *The Comforters* it was subordinated to moral issues, in the later novels this priority is reversed. In *The Abbess of Crewe* (1974), for example, the heroine perverts her spiritual vocation, the right end of which is immortal life, to the lesser demands of artistic immortality. Finally, she announces in triumph (appropriately near the end of the novel), 'I am become an object of art.' In *The Takeover* (1976), 'style' is the redeeming feature of existence, the survival-kit of the nineteen-seventies:

> You must understand that with a woman like the Marchesa everything must be done in style. If your style wavers she takes immediate advantage of it and walks all over you. (p. 126)

Not surprisingly, the later novels have been viewed predominantly as 'objects of art' rather than works with a moral impetus. This shift of emphasis becomes clear if we compare the way reflexiveness is used in *The Comforters* with its use in later novels.

The overt plot of *The Comforters*, bearing fleeting but distinct resemblances to True Romance and Dennis Wheatley, lives up to its heroine's description of it as a 'cheap mystery piece'. Flaunting its debt to popular fiction, its fictiveness, Mrs Spark subjects this novel to a stringent test of its own validity; that is, whether or not it can say something truthful. The intricacy of the plot, and the abundance of 'novelistic' coincidences, are used as realism and simultaneously as a perpetual reminder that behind seemingly random and bizarre events we may always find a controlling creator. Within the novel, the omniscient narrator manipulates his characters whilst giving them the illusion of freedom. But the heroine, Caroline, resists submission to 'someone else's necessity'. She herself is writing a book called 'Form in the Modern Novel', and is 'having difficulty with the chapter on realism'. She knows the passive role that she as a fictional character would be expected to assume, but as a Catholic convert she applies her interest in absolute truth to her role in the novel:

> I won't be involved in this fictional plot if I can help it. In fact, I'd like to spoil it . . . I intend to stand aside and see if the novel has any real form apart from this artificial plot. I happen to be a Christian. (p. 105)

Caroline's Christianity is granted considerable narratorial attention. The reader is involved not only with her awareness of herself as a fictional construct, but also with her religious convictions, since her new role as a Catholic convert has frequent and distressing parallels with her role as a character in a novel. The balance in *The Comforters* is maintained between realism and reflexiveness. Contingency is given free rein before the ultimate revelation of the true, non-contingent nature of events. This means that Caroline as a realistic character, with spiritual and emotional dimensions, is carefully presented. Later protagonists, in contrast, are shown to usurp the narratorial role, making the aesthetic patterning of plot their sole preoccupation. This concentration on form leaves Muriel Spark no room to engage our sympathy with individual characters. Whereas for Caroline, or even Lise (in *The Driver's Seat*), we feel concern, Lister (in *Not to Disturb*) and the Abbess of Crewe are automatons—plot-making machines with nothing but the end in view.

In *The Comforters*, reflexiveness is used to jolt the reader into moral alertness. Mrs Spark breaks novelistic conventions for a didactic purpose. For example, having been introduced to a character in a novel, we usually assume his quiescent fictive existence somewhere in the background, until he reappears at the precise invocation of the author. Mrs Spark reminds us of this convention by disturbing it. A repulsive character, Georgina Hogg, is made to disappear, that is, attention is drawn to her non-existence, whenever she is not actively in the plot: 'as soon as Mrs Hogg stepped into her room she disappeared, she simply disappeared. She had no private life whatsoever.' (p. 156) With significant thrift, this joke about generally accepted fictional conventions also acts as a moral evaluation of Mrs Hogg, who has no inner spiritual resources, and who battens off other people's insecurity to boost her own religious complacency. Another character says of her, with unconscious double-entendre: 'I am beginning to think that Georgina is not all there.' (p. 154) Character assassination takes place in later novels, but solely through the exigencies of plot, and not in order to make a moral point. In *Not to Disturb*, the protagonist Lister is organizing the plot of his employers' deaths. Two people arrive at the house unexpectedly, but Lister is an expert at dealing with such contingencies. 'They don't come into the story,' he says briskly. And later someone says 'Forget them . . . they're only extras.' And so they are. So superfluous that Mrs Spark eliminates them in a subordinate clause:

> Meanwhile the lightning, which strikes the clump of elms so that the two friends huddled there are killed instantly without pain, zig-zags across the lawns, illuminating the lily-pond and the sunken rose garden . . . (p. 86)

This callousness is of course a joke, a literary game, but it remains callous for all that. What is left out through Mrs Spark's increased interest in the mechanics of plot in this novel is the buoyant sense of moral concern which pervades her earlier work. Mrs Spark was able, totally without sentiment, to draw attention to the need for faith and love. Often this was done obliquely by describing the consequences of their absence, by evoking the reader's sense of loss so vividly that the omission of these qualities became a deliberate and eloquent reminder of their necessity. However, in her most recent novels, particularly from *Not to Disturb* onwards, these omissions do not give the sense of a satiric or didactic withdrawal, designed to arouse concern; they are just omissions. Attention is no longer drawn to the absence of love and human pity; they are simply not there, and the dynamic of the plots is such that it becomes convenient, indeed necessary, to forget about them. Thus, in *Not to Disturb*, the only redeeming feature, in a very literal sense, is Mrs Spark's ironic title. However, it is too simplistic to assume that this lessening of moral emphasis is a necessary and inevitable consequence of her increasing interest in teleology. Mrs Spark is perfectly capable of writing a superb piece of reflexive fiction which is simultaneously a sharp comment on a sad and godless society, and she achieves this in *The Driver's Seat*. It is worth examining the versatility of this novel to demonstrate that, as in *The Comforters*, moral values as well as fictional theory are expounded within its end-directed plot.

IV

In *The Comforters*, Caroline resents being in a plot, and tries to sabotage the author's intentions for her. In *The Driver's Seat*, however, the heroine Lise (whose name means God-like) tries to take over the plot-making, to become one with the creator of the story by manipulating her own destiny. Seeking her death, Lise fuses it with the end of the novel, and turns her fate into the plot. She gradually takes over the driver's seat figuratively, by assuming control of the novel, and realistically, in that she drives herself to her final destination, where she plans to be killed. The vehicle for Lise's aspirations, the narrative, is gruesomely simple. She flies from a northern country, possibly Denmark, to a southern city, possibly Naples, at the start of a holiday. She is seeking a man, not for a sexual encounter, but to be murdered by him. She is a potential murderee with an obsessive quest. She finds her man, and achieves, in every sense, her end.

What is unique and striking about this novel is the fusion of the causal and the contingent. Usually in a novel only the ending reveals the relation between the two, but in *The Driver's Seat* Mrs Spark tells us the ending fairly early on, so that what appears arbitrary is understood by the reader to be absolutely significant. So, as we read the novel, we are offered not only the narrative, but an integral demonstration on how narrative is constructed. The author, after giving away the ending with calculated panache, allows us to see the process of selectivity which leads to it. And as we learn that Lise is to be murdered, random incidents become significant. For instance, she buys a dress, and then angrily refuses it when the salesgirl points out that it is made of stain-proof material. Why does she need a dress that stains? Why does she buy such unforgettably vivid clothes? Why does she make a conspicuous scene at the airport? We are soon told why, in a series of flash-forwards which is one of the hall-marks of Mrs Spark's technique. We are told how, in the determined future tense, 'She will be found tomorrow morning dead from multiple stab-wounds . . . in a park of the foreign city to which she is travelling . . .' So, because she seeks to be murdered, her dress must, in a novelistic sense, be found to have been blood-stained, i.e. in novels the victims of stabbing have blood-stained clothing, so she must buy the appropriate dress. In this way, the novel becomes an elaborate double-entendre where incidents, innocent in themselves, are made absolutely ironic according to the reader's awareness of Lise's plan. For example, when she tries to finish off her work at the office in the compulsive way one does before going on holiday, someone says 'It can wait until you get back,' and she breaks into hysterical laughter, because she knows she will not be coming back. Later Lise meets a woman who talks about her nephew, and imagines a romance between them: 'you and my nephew are meant for each other', she says. The nephew is indeed meant for Lise, being created especially to be her chosen murderer. The ambiguity of these knife-edge sentences is a delight to read—a delight composed perhaps of a certain sense of gratified intellectual curiosity, that we as readers are allowed to see how a novel is made, instead of being kept in ignorance, slaves of suspense.

However, no amount of sophisticated fascination with reflexiveness can disguise the fact that *The Driver's Seat* is a very sad and nasty story; an arid, motiveless, unloving world, where a lonely woman seeks her suicide by finding someone to murder her. Because there is almost no authorial comment within the novel, Lise's insane view of the world stands unqualified, even endorsed. Evil predominates: maniacs of one kind or another moving under the impetus of their own obsessions, a riot, traffic jams, the impersonal twentieth-century dreariness of plane journeys and hotel rooms, and above all, the terrible lack of communication between people talking at each other. Lise, impelled by the necessity of her own narrative, dominated by the inevitability of her violent ending, renounces all distractions irrelevant to her death. So the novel, both initiating and reflecting her action, denies us any deviation in the form of explanation or commentary from the inevitability of *its* ending. *The Driver's Seat* thus becomes both a study and an enactment of what Henry James, writing about literary form, calls the 'mutilation' necessitated by the artistic process.

Lise is self-mutilating. From the beginning of the novel she is shown to be obsessive about her self-imposed role, which is one of submission to form. She is surrounded with symmetry, and, as a neurotic, suffers the demands of compulsive patterning. But occasionally we are given glimpses of a vitality, untidy and unconfined, which reminds us, and sometimes Lise herself, of her wasted potential for living. In her office she has hysterics, as she has done before, against the dull precision of accountancy, where even the staff are arranged in orderly figures around her: 'she has five girls under her and two men. Over her are two women and five men' (p. 9). Her apartment is no less rigid. It is described with a precision which emulates its functional nature:

> She has added very little to the room; very little is needed, for the furniture is all fixed, adaptable to various uses, and stackable. Stacked into a panel are six folding chairs, should the tenant decide to entertain six for dinner. The writing desk extends to a dining table, and when the desk is not in use it, too, disappears into the pinewood wall, its bracket-lamp hingeing outward and upward to form a wall-lamp. The bed is by day a narrow seat with overhanging bookcases; by night it swivels out to accommodate the sleeper. . . . A small pantry-kitchen adjoins this room. Here, too, everything is contrived to fold away into the dignity of unvarnished pinewood. And in the bathroom as well, nothing need be seen, nothing need be left lying about. . . . Lise keeps her flat as clean-lined and clear to return to after her work as if it were uninhabited. The swaying tall pines among the litter of cones have been subdued into silence and into obedient bulks. (pp. 14, 15)

There is a sense here of inflexibility, of over-tidiness, of pointless ingenuity, which extends, by association, to Lise herself, and reflects her fatal self-sufficiency—she would never borrow cups of sugar from a neighbour. Lise keeps her life, like her flat, 'clean-lined and clear', and we are offered a comment on this in the final sentence, where there is the only figure of speech in the passage; metaphoric, and thus guilty, in Robbe-Grillet's terms, of establishing a relationship between the world and the individual. The sudden lyricism of 'the tall swaying pines' and the weighted sadness of the verb 'subdued' contrasts the trees with what they were and what they have become, dull 'obedient bulks'. From a world defined by order within four walls, we are shown something other, the beautiful but defeated possibilities of grace and freedom.

For Lise, emotion is a distraction from the inexorable progression of her plot, and is therefore to be avoided. But she is friendly to the elderly lady she meets outside her hotel: 'It was very kind of you to come along with me,' says Mrs Fiedke, 'as it's so confusing in a strange place. Very kind indeed.' 'Why shouldn't I be kind?' Lise says, smiling at her with a sudden gentleness (p. 55). For a moment we see warmth and softness, apparently altruistic, alternatives to the hard plotted world Lise creates for herself. But immediately this kindness is made to seem a lapse, an aberration, and is swiftly made a purposeful part of the plot. 'One should always be kind', Lise says, 'in case it might be the last chance. One might be killed crossing the road, or even on the pavement, any time, you never know' (p. 55). The plot is relentless, and Lise denies herself spontaneity or disinterested action in order to comply with it. She also denies herself grief, and, horribly, she is aware of her loss. At one point she says: 'I want to go home . . . I want to go back home and feel all that lonely grief again. I miss it so much already' (p. 96). But again, the dynamic of the plot does not allow the irrelevancy of emotion, and it is only after Lise's death that it can be mentioned in all seriousness.

The last few lines of the novel are very significant. It is as though Lise's murder, the completion of her plot, now allows the narrator to assume control, and to name explicitly the feelings that have been evoked all through the novel, but ruthlessly suppressed by Lise herself. After he kills Lise, her murderer 'sees already the gleaming buttons of the policemen's uniforms, hears the cold and the confiding, the hot and the barking voices, sees already the holsters and epaulettes and all those trappings devised to protect them from the indecent exposure of fear and pity, pity and fear' (p. 107). The Aristotelian formula reminds us, if we need reminding, that the novel is a tragedy of a woman who dies a violent death. Devoid of parents, lovers, husband, children, friends, in fact of any relationship which furnishes constant drama and interest for most of us more fortunate, Lise is reduced to making drama out of the most elemental plot of all, the knowledge that her life will end. Having no other purpose for her poor life, she makes her design the ending of it, and, curiously, the energy and zest with which she goes about it are not completely negated by their being self-destructive. But it is only at the end of *The Driver's Seat* when 'pity and fear' are finally spoken aloud, as it were, that we realize, retrospectively, their relevance, and thus their nagging omission from the whole story. Cunningly, Mrs Spark has implicated us in the callousness of Lise's world, a world of outward appearances, where people hear words but do not listen to what is being said. The novel says a lot about 'trappings' of one kind or another; books are sought because their covers match a colour scheme, people are judged by their appearances, and the 'trappings' of the policemen, their uniforms which endorse their public image as upholders of form, are worn to help them to seem aloof from human feelings. Thus the 'trappings' of this novel—the reflexiveness, the flash-forwards, the revelation of the intricate apparatus of the fictional process—are all devices to insulate us, the readers, from emotional reaction to Lise's tragedy. But, having exposed her readers to the same temptation as she exposes Lise, that is, of accepting evil without protest for the sake of a satisfactory pattern, Mrs Spark allows us, at least, a means of salvation. And that is to realize with what painful irony she calls the expression of emotion 'indecent exposure', and how 'fear and pity, pity and fear' are most appositely the final words of the novel.

V

Muriel Spark has published fourteen novels in twenty years, and during this time her work has shown a distinct shift in emphasis from the religious to the secular. This is not to say that she is now irreligious, but that the later novels express a greater satiric revelry at the expense of contemporary society, highly sophisticated in tone and deriving from a thorough knowledge of it. Mrs Spark moves with the times, and refocuses her sights accordingly. Current international themes— the counter-culture, political unrest, inflation—are now endowed with her imaginative attention. However, these trends do not disturb the smooth surface of her work with undue realism, since they are treated as if she sees them in an eternal context, whereby they become merely another series of aberrations. The Watergate scandal, which threatened some writers with literary impotence in the face of such plotted, such fictive reality, was viewed by Mrs Spark with complacent recognition; the manufacture of worldly fictions has always been the subject of her novels. She swiftly incorporated Watergate within one, revealing beneath the little mutations of history the timelessness of myth. The heroine of *The Abbess of Crewe* connives at this:

> . . . as far as I'm concerned, history doesn't work. Here, in the Abbey of Crewe, we have discarded history. We have entered the sphere, dear Sisters, of mythology. (p. 16)

Working on this premise, and self-assured of her immortality as a mythic figure and an object of art, the Abbess transcends reality. Mrs Spark no longer details in her work the wearisome, day-to-day struggles of an individual with a soul to lose or save. Her recent protagonists have taken on a metaphoric dimension, which is less to do with good or evil than with sheer survival in a godless world. It is as if in inflationary times, survivors take the place of martyrs, and instead of bemoaning this, Mrs Spark's characters energetically make a virtue of necessity. Maggie, the heroine of *The Takeover*, copes buoyantly with the collapse of values and of fortunes. Anarchy is countered by adaptability, both by the heroine and by Mrs Spark, who, in a novel about inflation, significantly abandons her former stylistic thrift for a dazzling loquacity. But it is unmistakably Sparkian; the hallmark of her novels being a steadfast refusal to take too solemnly the vicissitudes of this world, since her impetus is constantly towards the world to come. In *The Girls of Slender Means* a popular song of the forties wafts through the novel:

> There were angels dining at the Ritz,
> And a nightingale sang in Berkeley Square.

Mrs Spark knows all about the Ritz; but, unusually, she believes in angels too. Her novels are an intense combination of that knowledge and that belief.

Note

This essay enlarges some observations of mine in two essays in *Encounter*, entitled 'A Dog Engulfed by Sand'. For valuable comments by a stylistic historian on the 'analogical comparison' of style in painting and literature, see the introduction to Wylie Sypher's *Four Stages of Renaissance Style* (New York, 1956). Sypher's fascinating approach continues into three more books directly relevant to my theme, to which I am indebted: *Rococo to Cubism in Art and Literature* (New York, 1960); *Loss of the Self in Modern Art and Literature* (New York, 1962) and *Literature and Technology: The Alien Vision* (New York, 1968). E. H. Gombrich, *Art and Illusion* (Princeton, 1961) also has crucial comments. Fuller background to my discussion of modernism is in Malcolm Bradbury and James McFarlane (eds.), *Modernism* (Harmondsworth, 1976) 'Pelican Guides to European Literature' series), especially the introduction.

For modern discussion of the relation between realism and character, see especially John Bayley, *The Characters of Love* (London, 1960) and 'Character and Consciousness', *New Literary History* V, 2 (Winter 1974), 225–35; Iris Murdoch, 'Against Dryness', *Encounter* XXVI, 1 (January 1961), repr. in M. Bradbury (ed.), *The Novel Today* (London/Manchester, 1977); and W. J. Harvey, *Character and the Novel* (London, 1965). For an argument systematically disputing the 'liberal concepts of character' expressed in these, see Robert Scholes, 'The Illiberal Imagination', *New Literary History* IV, 3 (Spring 1973), 521–40. Also see Jonathan Culler, *Structuralist Poetics* (London, 1975), espec. pp. 230–38, and Roger Fowler, *Linguistics and the Novel* (London, 1977). Other useful discussions occur in Roland Barthes, *S/Z* (Paris, 1970; London, 1975) and his *Image-Myth-Text*, ed. Stephen Heath (London, 1977). Also see Alain Robbe-Grillet, *Towards a New Novel* (Paris, 1963; London, 1970).

On the *nouveau roman*, see Vivian Mercier, *A Reader's Guide to the New Novel* (New York, 1971), John Sturrock, *The French New Novel* (London, 1969) and Stephen Heath, *The Nouveau Roman* (London, 1972). On 'post-modernism', see Robert Scholes, 'Metafiction', *Iowa Review* I, 4 (Fall 1970), 109–15; Tony Tanner, *City of Words* (London 1971); Leslie Fiedler, 'Come the Border—Close that Gap', in *Sphere History of Literature in the English Language Vol. 9: American Literature Since 1900* (ed. M. Cunliffe) (London, 1975); Ihab Hassan, *Paracriticisms: Seven Speculations of the Times* (Chicago, 1975). Also Raymond Federman (ed.), *Surfiction* (Chicago, 1975); Joe David Bellamy (ed.), *The New Fiction: Interviews with American Writers* (Urbana/London, 1974); and Jerome Klinowitz (ed.), *The Life of Fiction* (Urbana/London, 1977), which starts on 'post-post-modernism'.

I have used the term *abstraction* with some freedom, but have had in mind Wilhelm Worringer, *Abstraction and Empathy* (London, 1953) (originally *Abstraktion und Einfühlung*, Munich, 1908); Vicktor Shklovsky's essays on 'Art and Technique' and 'Sterne's *Tristram Shandy*', reprinted in L. T. Lemon and M. J. Reis (eds.), *Russian Formalist Criticism: Four Essays* (Lincoln, Nebr., 1965), and, especially, Jose Ortega y Gasset, *The Dehumanization of Art and Other Writings on Art and Culture* (London, 1972).

VIII

Putting in the Person:
Character and Abstraction in
Current Writing and Painting

MALCOLM BRADBURY

I

I WANT HERE to offer some thoughts on the way a novelist writing now
—in England or in any other country, for today the serious novel is
an international and an inter-related affair—might feel under pressure
to diverge from the spirit of realism in the novel, to have problems in
the representation of character and the supposedly substantive world,
and so incline in the direction of what we might conveniently call
'abstraction'. 'Abstraction' is a word we use more familiarly in talking
about painting than writing, but part of my point is that the analogy
between writing and painting is significant. I wish to look at the matter
from the standpoint of the practising novelist, rather than that of the
critic, for many current critical theories on the matter seem to me to
diverge from a direct recognition of the nature of contemporary
artistic experience. And I write as a novelist who began writing in the
postwar season of realism, with a decided attachment to that empirical
moral, liberal tendency, but who has since felt—one might say for
reasons of personal aesthetic development, but, since this is not a
solitary matter, also under the exterior weight of reasons that have
affected many modern writers—that the mode of realism is filled with
implicit understandings and assumptions that it grows harder to
accept. And in particular I want to reflect on the question of how to
create and pose a human figure in a world, a landscape, that no longer
can be regarded as comfortably 'realistic'. Painters, and film-makers,
and television writers and directors, evidently have the same anxiety;
the serious modern canvas or camera frequently insists on it. 'I began
to write fiction on the assumption that the true enemies of the novel
were plot, character, setting and theme,' one novelist, John Hawkes,

has observed, 'and having once abandoned these familiar ways of thinking about fiction, totality of vision or structure was really all that remained.'[1] These are familiar judgements to have now, the sort of things to say now; though of course the underlying propositions are not new. Realism has been a matter of anxiety right through our anxious century, for all sorts of reasons. But what is interesting is the extent to which, in reading fiction, or writing it, we still worry about it. And it is worth beginning by considering why.

In a television programme not long ago, Iris Murdoch offered some interesting thoughts on why it is that divergences from realism still manage to create in us a certain unease. Art, she suggested, speaks to our desire to have a common-sense reality, and it becomes a repository for our sense of the real and the true. And in this matter, the novel has a special place, being of all the artistic forms the one most associated with our conviction that there is an empirically given world, and our moral wish that the contingencies of life be ordered and assessed. In short, we desire that world of rounded persons and solid society which we associate with the novel, and divergence from this—in fictions that become predominantly textual, or which pattern or deface the person —disturbs us humanly.[2] Yet we well know that in the arts the sense of the real has never been a single, stable thing. Art is a mode of espistemo-logical speculation; that is one reason why styles and forms change. And if the empirical and representational aspects of art, visual or written, have always been crucial to its power and meaning, so have the Platonic anxieties about the nature of imitation. In painters and writers of seriousness, realism has never been innocent, or of a fixed nature. What complicates our present response is the way in which it

---

[1] John Hawkes interviewed by J. J. Enck, *Wisconsin Studies in Contemporary Literature* VI, 2 (Summer 1964). The interview is reprinted in L. S. Dembo and C. Pondrom (eds.), *The Contemporary Writer* (Madison, 1972).

[2] Iris Murdoch's comments on the matter may be found more fully in 'Against Dryness', where she also raises the problem of 'the now unfashionable naturalistic idea of character':

> Reality is not a given whole. An understanding of this, a respect for the contingent, is essential for imagination, as opposed to fantasy. Our sense of form, which is an aspect of our desire for consolation, can be a danger to our sense of reality as a rich receding background. Against the crystalline work, the simplified fantasy myth, we must pit the destructive power of the now unfashionable naturalistic idea of character.

> Real people are destructive of myth, contingency is destructive of fantasy and opens the way for imagination . . .

has become involved with an historical conviction about the relationship between man and his world. Modern complexities of form are webbed in with our dark, contemporary sense of broken connections between man and nature, individual and society, the fictions of the subjective imagination and the fictions that pass for ideology or consensual significance. In the course of our century, we have become increasingly anxious about the path from the motions of the imagination to the facts of the world. This is often expressed as a sense of loss, both aesthetic and social. The old language of art has gone because the old language of truth has gone; thus that old, mimetic poetics of fiction—that discourse of character, plot, setting and description, with which, in school, we were taught to read novels and narrative poems and plays—seems old fashioned. 'The contemporary writer who is acutely in touch with the life of which he is a part—is forced to start from scratch: Reality doesn't exist, time doesn't exist, personality doesn't exist...', says one American writer conventionally called a 'postmodernist', Ronald Sukenick.[3] This was probably always true as an account of the claims of creation; still, Sukenick is emphasizing the contemporary case. For, to traditional artistic problems, there has come to be attached the modern one that the critics, especially, have much pressed on us: we have, it seems, passed through an essential evolution of consciousness and society, from the nineteenth to the twentieth century, which has taken us across some essential divide in the matter of reality.

And so, Roland Barthes argues,[4] we have moved from that high bourgeois age when the novel could have a name, proclaim itself, escape from the terror of an expression without laws, wherein 'reality becomes slighter and more familiar, it fits within a style, it does not outrun language'. For we have passed beyond the age of the *lisible* into an age of the *scriptible* only, and lost the epistemological right to such realism. This cannot be quite true, since clearly a realism and representationalism of a direct and familiar sort is still available to perfectly serious and good writers, while many of the laws of realism still pervade texts that appear to question them. Still, there is a new provisionality in art, a loss of the sure narrative preterite; imagination in modern art insistently questions fact and its capacity to pretend to be fact, and the text that insists on its nature as text, the fiction that foregrounds its

---

[3] Ronald Sukenick, *The Death of the Novel and Other Stories* (Chicago, 1969).
[4] Roland Barthes, *Writing Degree Zero* (Paris, 1953; London, 1967), and *S/Z* (Paris, 1970; London, 1975).

own fictionality, has become a commonplace, even in ostensibly literal realms like journalism, documentary, or history-writing. Much the same is so in painting, where the colour code, the canvas, the material nature of the artistic object itself, have come into the foreground, and the object of representation has moved back, or into the distance, or into a realm of speculation. 'Men have learned' it is written, in Nabokov's *The Real Life of Sebastian Knight* (1941) 'to live with a black burden, a huge aching hump: the supposition that "reality" may be only a "dream". How much more dreadful it would be if the very awareness of your being aware of reality's dream-like nature were also a dream, a built-in hallucination.' It is a dream that both haunts and releases fiction; we have many works now that are disposed for such reasons to secrete, or play with, those elements of the real they gesture toward representing, and some that propose, in fiction always with an obvious ambiguity, that they represent nothing whatsoever. But more commonly abstraction is relative, and the move away from representation not total; the growing convention is toward a certain scepticism.

In fiction this is in fact an old ambiguity, longstanding in the novel's history: but we have come to take it as especially ours, and offer it with a new sense of necessity and authority. For this, we are encouraged to think, is the art that is possible for, and authentic to, our time, a time when language is, says Barthes, offered to the writer as a decorative and compromising instrument, 'inherited from a previous and different History'. Only by confessing our unease with realism and its narrative and its character can we give an art that is true to the present state of language, that truly, post-modernly, follows on from the perceptual and technical discoveries of art at the beginning of the century, and that recognizes the writer's historical unease. Given the referential nature of language and the history of literature, it is difficult to conceive of a totally abstract literary text, though of course we can and do have a purely abstract painting.[5] But we can have an art that aspires toward abstraction as a mode of doubt about the depiction of reality, and in many of our poems, plays and novels these uneasy dealings with mimesis are usual. The linear evolution of story, the detailed rep-

[5] On this matter, David Lodge's essay 'Samuel Beckett: Some Ping Understood', in *The Novelist at the Crossroads* (London, 1971), is interesting as an analysis of an apparently purely 'abstract' story, 'Ping', by Samuel Beckett, where he concludes that 'words do not merely demonstrate their emptiness' in the story.

resentation of milieu, the grammatical sureness of narrators, the fixed representation of personages: all these have been thrown into great doubt. In writing, in painting, the object, the scene, the figure have grown clouded. We are asked to look beyond them, to some larger notion of concept or compositional process, itself not fixed but provisional. And nowhere is this clearer, and perhaps nowhere more disturbing, than in the field of what used to be called, in the old fictional poetics, 'character'.

Now this is of especial importance because, in much humanist art, it is through the presentation of 'characters' that the identification between reader and text, or viewer and painting, occurs, or occurred. In most realism, characters are seen as natural inhabitants of the world of culture, just as they are natural citizens of the world of story; we sympathize with them, enter art through them, and use their company to find our sense of the significance of the work we encounter.[6] But today those elements of a work represented by the term 'character' have low philosophical credit, reflecting a decline in the social credit or credibility of the 'individual' as a discrete, self-governing and boundaried entity. One reason for this may seem to be that the arts of form and consciousness have triumphed over the old arts of representation and of story. Thus, in the *nouveau roman*, the boundaries of discrete single characters are systematically transgressed, to allow access to a world beyond identity or chronology, a world of images, tropisms, language itself. Another reason, apparently opposite, is that an art concerned with the crisis of identity, with the engulfing of the subject in the object, that art whose clearest exponent is Kafka, has become, understandably enough, important to our times. In the novels of Peter Hanke, or Italo Calvino, the relations between individual and landscape become hallucinatory; perception seems to come from a disorder of consciousness, or a mad world overwhelms the intelligent functions of psychology altogether. In other modern writers, like Thomas Pynchon, William Burroughs and William Gaddis, it is modern cybernetic and scientific world-views as such that seem to have displaced the old 'character': figures are paste-ups or cut-outs, role-players or pastiche agents moving through a world of disjunct relations tending towards absurdity or entropy. This displacement of the person may produce an intensification of form, a new pre-eminence for the text; it may produce a hyper-realism, by which the forces and

[6] For discussion of this, see especially the books by Bayley and Harvey mentioned in the prefatory note.

processes that dwarf the individual are a main object of fictional attention. But whatever the outcome, the old relationship between a reader and a person viewed as a discretely bounded individual moving through a comprehensible landscape of objects and society, and a comprehensible timescape of growth and evolution, is under challenge. 'Character' becomes a less than adequate word for such webs of relations, and we are uneasily faced with what Fredric Jameson calls the 'problem' of 'the stubbornly anthropomorphic nature of our present categories of character'.[7]

In short, modern art has been much preoccupied with the problems of putting in the person, in an age when both our historical experience and the prevailing neo-behaviourism of modern sociological, philosophical and even theological theories of man make this difficult. In the arts subject–object relations must always be a prime matter of concern; in the novel, traditionally a species much devoted to the relationship between individuals and society, the pressures will acquire a special intensity. Novelists have long known the paradox that there is a strange parallelism between their own plots and those of the world, between the teleologies and the freedoms that we discern in the outward universe and those which writers, the Gods of the universe of fiction, may or may not afford in a text. To invent and plot a life for a person is a strange matter; it touches on the entire question of the value of novels themselves. Part of that disposition toward realism that we still observe in the English novel undoubtedly arises from the desire of a number of English novelists, though novelists in other countries do share their passion, to redeem or retain the concept of character as a central function for fiction. Iris Murdoch—though her novels are highly patterned rituals—seeks a novel that will be 'a fit house for free characters to live in'. John Fowles—though he insists on the parodic nature of his text, and his contemporaneity with the world-view of Roland Barthes and Levi-Strauss—concludes *The French Lieutenant's Woman* by offering to free his characters from the trap of his own plot and imagination, in which they have been contained. Muriel Spark more exactingly and divinely insists that her characters may live only within the universe of her plot, but she offers them rights of struggle and occasional grace, permitting them once in a while to take over the driver's seat of the narrative sequence, despite its predetermined outcome. Such struggles are not only to be found in

[7] Fredric Jameson, 'The Ideology of the Text', *Salmagundi* 31–2 (Fall 1975–Winter 1976).

the English novel. Kurt Vonnegut notes in *Slaughterhouse-5* that 'There are almost no characters in this story. . . . One of the main effects of war, after all, is that people are discouraged from being characters,' but he nonetheless hungers to release his from his world of fatalism and passivity, and offers to do so at the end of *Breakfast of Champions*. Robbe-Grillet notes that there are no ' "characters", in the traditional sense of the word', in his books, but insists that man is present on every page, in every line, in every word, as a passion and a perceiver. Nonetheless the human figure in much modern writing tends often to have paradoxical status. And, in other ways, this has been true in modern painting, where representation of the figure has been surrounded with much anxiety. Indeed, to take the question further, I should like to look more at the painterly analogy.

II

Let me, though, begin with the familiar, often repeated, and common-sense reservation. Writing and painting are really not the samesorts of activity at all. Painters paint, with paint, or draw, or sketch, or nowadays do many other things, with buckets, and bricks, and bicycle-pumps, but they work in an eminently visual medium, their main instruments of expression being colour and form. They create objects of and for perception, and these explore that most crucial of human borders, that between the seer and the seen. Painters make what we may call, in the most kindly sense, unspeakable objects. Their artefacts achieve cohesion in space, and may normally be taken in as a unity; anyone who has ever seen a reviewer with a Martini at an art opening will know how quickly this may be done. What they do is not in-herently referential. Writers, on the other hand, write, and their material, their instrument of expression and analysis, is words. Words are universal currency. They are serial, referential, have structural logics (grammars), and are extremely difficult to privatize, though writers may seek to make them so. Because language is serial, writing works in sequences, more like a film than a painting, and is hence assimilated in sequences; which is why critics, over the period of apprehension, need quite a lot of Martinis, and frequently seem to have had them. There is a classic analogy between writing and painting, *ut pictura poesis*, but it is false—as Lessing tells us in *Laocoon*, distinguishing between spatial and temporal arts. It becomes proportionately more false when the objects in comparison are a novel and a painting. Poems can have an eminently visual and spatial existence, become, so to speak, a concrete abstract. Short stories, especially modern ones, by Katherine Mansfield, or Borges, or Beckett, can often manifest the pictorial analogy quite powerfully.

But the novel is seriality at its largest: a fiction committed to prose and to length, using the instrument of public discourse on a scale of extended exposition and hence of linear codes. It thus works close to familiar habits of extended narration and modes of expository report: it is kin to history, or biography, or extended argument. It comes in that complex system of infolded packaging that we call a book, and demands a long, engrossed, sequential mode of attention; it is a story, and hence a version of the stories we tell ourselves all the time when we offer to put events in an order and attach a significance to them. The underlying difference is sometimes pinned down in a simple assumption: paintings have style and form, and novels have subjects, plots, characters. Paintings are thus a window on the world where one examines the window, novels a window where one examines the world. The distinction is not totally true, but it contains a truth by which novelists are often anguished: the novel is disposed to represent, has empirical roots. Still, most novelists of seriousness have, since the form began, recognized the ambiguity of that representation. And, when they wish to emphasize it, to stress technique over subject, or urge that they have created a complex object, they have turned, with a certain envy, to the painterly analogy.

It *is* forced, but then all analogies must have discordance as well as concordance, and it has depth and resource. It goes back to the beginnings of the novel in England, in the eighteenth century, when, in a neo-classical season, a new form could only be explained as a mutant from old codes. Novelists like Fielding and Sterne, engaged in generic innovation, had three especial points of reference to turn to: history-writing, drama, and the painting. Fielding's famous preface to *The History of the Adventures of Joseph Andrews* (1742) borrows from all three sources, turning to Aristotle to give him a formula for the new mutant: it is 'the comic epic poem in prose'. But then he adds a discussion of an essentially painterly problem, that of distinguishing between character and caricature in comic portraiture. An obvious reference-point was Hogarth, who responded by illustrating the distinction in several cartoons. The sense of stylistic analogism that began then has long persisted in subsequent relations between novels and paintings: indeed the most fruitful line for comparison is through

the general history of style. It was central for the eighteenth
century:

> I will not so much as take pains to bestow the strip of a gauze
> wrapper on it [Truth], but paint situations as they actually arose to
> me in nature, careless of violating those laws of decency that were
> never made for such unreserved intimacies as ours . . .

notes the painterly writer-narrator of another eighteenth-century
novel where problems of representation posed considerable problems.
Her name is Fanny Hill, otherwise John Cleland, and among her
problems was the post facto, or post coital, problem of turning 'past'
sexual experiences into a kinetic 'picture' to transmit them to the
friend to whom she is reckoned to be writing. How, she asks, do you
depict in universal prose 'the most interesting moving picture in all
nature'? This is the erect male organ, and the problem is specialized;
nonetheless Cleland shared the era's anxiety about reconciling the gap
between linguistic and pictorial representation, the problem of mimesis
and universality.

Romanticism, emphasizing the subjectivity of perception, the inward
power of the imagination, would change the problem, but not silence
the analogy. For writer and painter were both romantic heroes, carriers
of vision, unacknowledged legislators. With Romanticism, both the
psychic energies of the imagination and the heroic rhythms of history
took on, in novels and paintings alike, a central importance. Painters
and writers changed, and almost interchanged (so Washington Irving
became 'Geoffrey Crayon, Gent.'). Painters became discursive, and
posed their figures in an historically moving world; novelists sought
stasis out of process, and in the great romantic novelists like Scott and
Cooper the tendency is to create in a sequence of poses—situations
are held, figures postured in a landscape, the texts report the scene as
if it were already a painting. The interchange of imagination and
history generated myth, and the tension between the two dimensions
of the novel—the mythical or 'romance' element, and the empirical or
realistic element—began to grow. This is the great tension of nineteenth-century writing, and we should remember how much the
painterly analogy played in it; indeed it might help us to understand
Charles Dickens's complex mixture of these elements, and the nature of
his fertile, populous, symbolist imagination, the better if we recall that
he began as a verbal illustrator, 'Boz', working alongside a visual one.

Still, it is as this stylistic season moves further, and the lore of realism

G

begins to dominate in the novel, that painting and fiction appear most to diverge. For, in the expansive stage of nineteenth-century bourgeois and liberal society, the novel could become the book of the individual in the social and historical world. It began more and more to explore its looseness, its openness, its common-sense ordinariness, its interest in fact and detail, the range of classes, the material fact and wonder of the world. By virtue of its character as narrative, it could pass beyond formalism, and become a mode of truth itself. It could do this by its devotion to the truth that underlay dream, by its sense of fact and contingency, by its humane capacity to engage us sympathetically and cumulatively with individual characters, by its freedom to work to the length of a life, to note the passing of the days. Fact thus had its weight, and story its engrained morality, and by moving into the social stuff of life and the motion of collective history was generating a modern art form. Engaged in this was a distrust of the 'aesthetic' or the imaginary, a taste for the middle ground beyond and outside form. Hawthorne's *The Marble Faun* (1860) and George Eliot's *Middlemarch* (1872) both test this issue, and finally draw their central characters away from the bohemianizing, aesthetic, but a-moral viewpoint of the artists of Rome, back into a homespun puritanism which is a moral equivalent for realism. And yet both enact the power of the reverse quest, the voyage into imaginative fullness and the unknown arts—for perhaps only in a romantic painterliness and an aesthetic immersion can the full nature of art and the artist be known.

This tension is especially important because it is sometimes forgotten —notably by contemporary critics who see realism as a naive art, and who pose it antithetically against 'experiment'—that realism was mid-nineteenth-century *avant gardeism*.[8] And, after 1848 in Paris, its cumulative achievements became formulated as a 'movement', uniting painters and writers: Degas, Courbet, Flaubert, the Goncourt brothers, Champfleury. Indeed, time and again, the validation for

[8] These issues are admirably discussed by J. P. Stern, *On Realism* (London, 1973); also see Harry Levin, *The Gates of Horn* (New York, 1963) and F. W. J. Hemmings (ed.), *The Age of Realism* (Harmondsworth, 1974). In *Writing Degree Zero*, Roland Barthes sees 1848 as the crucial axis in realism, the point where it changes from a relatively naive realism founded on the preterite and the third person, wherein 'the false is equal to the true', to 'an art which in order to escape its pangs of conscience either exaggerates conventions or frantically attempts to destroy them. Modernism begins with the search for a Literature which is no longer possible.' But less apocalyptic interpretations are possible.

fictional realism—whether of Dickens's satirical, abundant, Frith-like kind, or George Eliot's compassionate, humanist kind, or Balzac's spirit of human comedy, or Flaubert's intersection of banality and the *mot juste*—came from painting. When George Eliot sought to justify her mode of social and moral realism, she explained that she was painting not large historical canvases, nor fantastic works of imagination, but, as she put it in *Adam Bede* (1859), in the manner of the Dutch genre painters, who made 'faithful pictures of monotonous homely existence, which has been the fate of so many more among my fellow-mortals than a life of pomp or absolute indigence, of tragic suffering or of world-stirring actions'. Flaubert's novels are works from the realist studio. They embody painters, canvases, frames; they carefully enact composition and the modalites of perception; they seek a transcendent formal wholeness. Like any movement, the realists felt they wrote in a season; realism was, said Champfleury, 'only a transitional term which will last no longer than thirty years'. And indeed, though the realist compound is a central moment in the novel's history, and defines essential aspects of the novel's potential, this is more or less true. For, as the Victorian world-picture began to disintegrate, and bleaker lore arising from Darwin and positivism put the landscape into a new per-spective and shrank the image of the human figure, then the sense of social and historical possibility on which realism, with whatever ironies, depended began to give way to less sympathetic pictures of process and indifference. It was possible to extend the realist principle by insisting that the study of reality was an experimental science; this led forward to naturalism. Alternatively, as social perception divided, accounts of human consciousness altered, and the very substantiality and significance of the exterior material and historical world came into question, a new art, much concerned with modes of perception, states of mind, and aesthetic hyper-awareness moved to the centre; this led forward into impressionism.

Both of these tendencies involved the displacement of the realist notion of character. In naturalism the free-standing character is dis-placed, ironized, set against or engulfed by a dark world of system and process. He becomes less the agent of plot than a tragic case or a victim. In impressionism, Pater's art of arts, where not the moral fruits of experience but experience itself is the end, the individual becomes the anxious artist, displaced, heightening his sensations, stylizing his poses, accumulating around him disguise and chaos. He is beautiful down-stairs; his picture ages in the attic. Meanwhile consciousness dissipates reality into chaos and contingency, from which, by the magic rescue of the imagination, form is distilled. Beyond is the naturalist waste. We may see these dissolving landscapes and figures in the late paintings of Turner or Whistler, or the French Impressionists. They may take the age of steam and city; but they divest it of Frith's abundance or Courbet's narrative. The outward world of technology, city, figure is naturalistically behind or beyond the painting. But they yield to impression; the subject is veiled through insistence on the moment of perception, the motion of light, and the position of the perceiver, who is not an individual but an artist, hunting, in the contingency of reality, the instant of purified form.

It is perhaps in this double evolution out of realism, toward impressionism and naturalism, that we can see the roots of a modern abstraction. In both aesthetics, the notion of a liberal history and a social communion are diminished: process operates against man, art grows more formal, the human subject diminishes. Naturalism foregrounds the process, and impressionism the weight of perception, but the aesthetics are not discrete, and frequently they merge. In Stephen Crane's *The Red Badge of Courage* (1895), a naturalist view of the universe as hostile and indifferent to man merges with an impressionist view of consciousness as a flickering and momentary mode of apprehension at work, seeking significance and form. War and aggression are the ultimate metaphors; the army is a machine, operating collectively, for no stated cause; heroic individualism is impossible, except as an ironic quirk; the characters are barely named. Against the contingency, the mind works, taking impressions; the central character is no military hero but an artist of sorts, making pictures of consciousness, kin to the aesthete heroes of the many books with painterly titles that came around the turn of the century: *The Portrait of a Lady*, *The Picture of Dorian Gray*, *A Portrait of the Artist as a Young Man*. Perhaps, indeed, the writer who sums up the whole sequence best is Henry James, who would never have called himself a naturalist, or an impressionist, but a realist, and yet who now occupies for us a position on the beginning edge of modernism.

For James, of course, the painterly analogy was crucial and insistent, though his painters change as he does. Not only do they afford surrogates for the writer himself, seeking to find the relation between art and reality, image and truth, experience and its fruit; they also afford him a means into two of his central concerns—with the way in which the moral pursuit of the real might generate not simply story but, through an intensive creative germination, form itself; and with the ambiguous nature of perception, and the way man, seeming to see reality, in fact invents it. James's early, more realist work is greatly interested in the theme of how we shape the solid world about us, negotiate with its materiality, and acquire a sense of the real and the true; this involves the emendation of art in the direction of morality and reality, and the need to free character from confining images or patterned abstractions. But the problem of generating perception as significant knowledge becomes increasingly difficult for him, and his later work owes much of its complexity to the problem of finding a grammar accurate to perception. *The Ambassadors* (1903) is a novel about a man who learns to see: Strether, by perceptual necessity, becomes an Impressionist, and the crucial scene by the river, the meaning of which he first fails to fathom, is a painting he has yet to penetrate. As for James himself, he too became more or less an impressionist, with symbolist tastes: an increasingly *abstract* writer, caught in the complex synaesthetic problems of the end of the nineteenth century, when the world-view was so deeply changing. The opening of *The Wings of the Dove* (1902) is a hazardous walk through the world of subject–object relations:

> She waited, Kate Croy, for her father to come in, but he kept her unconscionably, and there were moments at which she showed herself, in the glass over the mantel, a face positively pale with the irritation that brought her to the point of going away without sight of him. It was at this point, however, that she remained: changing her place, moving from the shabby sofa to the armchair upholstered in a glazed cloth that gave at once—she had tried it—a sense of the slippery and of the sticky . . .

James is the anxious seer; material goods are strangely positioned with regard to his character's acts of consciousness; the person is a condition of multiplied angles of vision. On the century's turn, James, in a famous statement, argued that the novel, freed of the onerous moral controls imposed on it in the Victorian era, was now free to become more itself. But, if so, then it was doing this, if his own case is a guide, by moving in the direction of a new abstraction—and with benefit of the painterly analogy.

III

I have been suggesting that there are significant ways in which writers and painters are kin, and know it; that one of them is that they share a parallel sense of the evolution of style; that it is probably at moments of stylistic change—which is, I take it, the consequence of deep-rooted preceptual change throughout society—that the analogy is especially important. And nowhere is this more evident than in that profound shift of artistic sensibility and in underlying assumptions about man, society and experience that occurred around the beginning of this century, and which we call for convenience 'modernism'. This was a tendency that included all the arts (though painting was central), and many cultures, including the English. Its radicalism is apparent (in painting, according to Herbert Read, 'the aim of five centuries of European effort is openly abandoned'[9]) and in the sequence of the novel it can be identified as a crucial point of transformation—though this, of course, depends on your devotion and standpoint, for what happened in the novel was not a total displacement of realism, and the clear-cut coming of a new age of style, but a bifurcation, between an *avant garde* and experimental lineage on the one hand, a much more adaptable continuity from moral realism and from naturalism on the other. And it was, in general, for those writers who identified their task as an *avant garde* one, those who made the Dedalus voyage into the unknown arts, that the painting analogy was to be especially important, though we should not forget that it mattered to many others: to Arnold Bennett, to Somerset Maugham, to Joyce Cary, and so on. Joseph Frank's proposal that we might identify as the great characteristic of modernist writing the emergence of ideas of 'spatial form' is a useful starting point[10], for if you wish to move away from narrative causality, away from a sense that there are primary social relations between outer time and inner, and into the tropes of consciousness and the logics of epiphanic revelation, then the painterly analogy has a special importance. For painting, especially modern painting, from post-Impressionism on, seemed to be dissolving not only representational sequences but chronicity itself—pointing toward that 'luminous stasis' with which Joyce seeks to redeem the contingency of the novel.

[9] Herbert Read, *Art Now* (London, 1933; rev. ed., 1960).

[10] Joseph Frank, 'Spatial Form in Modern Literature', repr. in his *The Widening Gyre: Crisis and Mastery in Modern Literature* (New Brunswick, NJ, 1963).

In the movements of modernism, novelist and painter met and remet, in different phases, through different movements. But from the many crucial contacts, let me select one.

In 1903 two people crossed the Atlantic from America to Europe on the now old quest from 'reality' to 'art'. They were Gertrude and Leo Stein, from a rich, artistic Baltimore background. Gertrude, who 'meant to be historical, from almost a baby on', came with a particularly high sense of destiny. She thought first of settling in London, but rejected it on inspection: 'Gertrude Stein was not very much amused,' she said. For the Steins wanted an artistic milieu and, as readers of *Trilby* well knew, bohemia was Paris and the Left Bank; the Steins eventually settled at 27 rue de Fleurus, close to the painting quarter. They had two activities in mind: one was art-collecting, especially pursued by Leo, an art-historian and a friend of Bernard Berenson; the other, Gertrude's speciality, was prose-writing. Though not entirely well-trained in contemporary art, the Steins had good instincts, and could take advice. They first became involved with post-Impressionists, notably Cezanne, and then with the Fauves and the movement toward Cubism; they became personally close to Matisse and Picasso. In 1905, they bought Cezanne's portrait of his wife; the following spring, Gertrude began sitting for her portrait by Picasso. Soon after, she saw in his studio 'Les Demoiselles d'Avignon', the painting usually taken as the turning point into Cubism. It was not, of course, pure abstract; rather it was abstractified, as her own writing was to become. Around this time she put aside the novel she had come with, a portrait of a lesbian relationship posthumously published as *Things as They are* (1951), and began—under the Cezanne portrait, which gave her, she said, 'a new feeling about composition'—a translation of Flaubert's late *Trois Contes*, which gradually amended itself into an original work, *Three Lives* (1909). This was, she later said, the 'first definite step away from the nineteenth century and into the twentieth century in literature'. She came to see it as a form of verbal post-Impression, and especially important to it was Cezanne's growing abstraction, his way both of creating and decreating a portrait, so that it conveyed both the inner energy of the sitter and the outward energy of the creative act, so spatializing form and aestheticizing content. 'Nothing changes from generation to generation except the thing seen and that makes a composition,' she said, adding 'The composition in which we live makes the art we see or hear.'

Stein's mode of 'new composition' is most evident in the middle one of her three prose portraits, 'Melanctha', about a black servant girl in Baltimore: this is present tense, post-causal, and largely made from the repetition of rhythmic tropes. But if Cezanne lies behind *Three Lives*, it is cubism, Matisse and Picasso that lie behind her next major venture, *The Making of Americans*, mostly written between 1906 to 1908—though it was not published until the 1920s, when the revolution of the word reigned, and modernist blockbusters became common. It is a massive text of some 1,000 pages, her one full novel, based on the proposition that Americans themselves were cubists, inhabitants of the new space–time continuum. What that continuum required was an 'abstract' novel, depending on the defeat of the realist noun, the elimination of remembering as a source of causality, and, especially, a principle of collective characterization, the principle being that the history of one American is the history of all. 'I was sure that in a kind of way the enigma of the universe could in this way be solved,' Miss Stein said. The result is spatial form: a reaction against narrative, causality, creation via the single character. It is work that hungers for the synchronicity of a painting; and, for all its slowness and even its boredom, it in many ways bears out her claim that it is the first twentieth-century novel. The problem Miss Stein now found, however, was that there was no way of stopping it ('it went on and on') and she began to deduce that the novel itself was no longer a relevant modern form (a suspicion held by other modernists, including Joyce). So she turned to short prose pieces, exactly dependent on the painterly analogy; they were portraits, collages, abstracts, and to read them we have to think of them as paintings, equivalent to the post-impressionist and cubist canvases on display at the Armory Show in the United States in 1913, which not only established experimental abstraction in America, but also the reputation of Gertrude Stein.

Stein's perceptions on most of these matters seemed eccentric at the time, but she was, in her way, aesthetically shrewd. Like Joyce or Proust, who also began their postwar modernist classics in the prewar atmosphere, she was a product of that synaesthesia of the years before 1914 when all the arts seemed to be drawing marvellously together and acquiring a totally new stylistic identity. Other writers, too, felt the need for this new push toward abstraction in the novel, and acknowledged the pressure of painting. Arnold Bennett looked at the post-Impressionist exhibition at the Grafton Galleries in 1910 and judged that if he were a young novelist he would have to start again. Virginia Woolf probably had the same exhibition in mind when she said that

in 1910 human character changed, and with it the whole nature of the
modern arts, which would need to become less material, more responsive to the atoms as they fell. Stein's kind of novel thus became a
protypical version of fictional modernism, which led forward to
Joyce, Woolf, Faulkner and the other writers who offered to defeat
seriality and produce a revolution of the word, who amended the
novel's liberal causality, its tendency to follow the logic of a life, the
rhythm of the plot, or the temporal regimen of the clock and of history. Gertrude Stein, in her *atelier*, under her Cezanne and Picasso,
is an admirable image of that toward consciousness and aesthetics,
toward composition and painting-like sequences, which was one
essential part of modernism. 'The primal artistic impulse has nothing
to do with the rendering of nature,' wrote Wilhelm Worringer, in
Abstraction and Empathy (1908), a book that coincided almost exactly
with cubism, and *The Making of Americans*, and offered an essential
terminology for the new developments, 'It seeks after pure abstraction
as the only possibility of repose within the confusion and obscurity of
the world-picture. . .'[11] This meant, as Virginia Woolf indicated in her
essay 'Mr Bennett and Mrs Brown', a new conception of the human
figure and its place in the world, one in which the self was not
defined by historical action or material possession or naturalist detail,
but was released into an atomized universe which dispelled time and
conventional identity. Mrs Ramsay may be a focus in *To the Lighthouse*,
but much of the book is about her absence, and the book's completion
is in more than one sense the completion of a less than representational
painting. Lily Briscoe finishes her canvas, and Virginia Woolf her own,
a triptych, three canvases, one virtually bare of human figures, set in
time, but reaching out of it, as an aesthetic object should.

   Yet in this evolution we may see a paradox. For Stein and Woolf,
abstraction might mean an increased power of penetration, of comprehension of the human being, seen not as social agent or liberal
actor but as a reservoir of consciousness. This, however, remains
uncertain and ambiguous. What is clear, though, is that other writers
were also decentralizing the human figure with a different aim in
mind. Conrad's *The Secret Agent* may be called a novel without a hero
—there is Stevie, who draws our sympathy, but ambiguously, for he is
an idiot—for all human action is overwhelmed by the context of
social anarchy, and the devastating, depersonalizing, insistent irony of
the novelist, perceiving an incoherent word. In Wyndham Lewis's

   [11] Wilhelm Worringer, *Abstraction and Empathy* (London, 1953).

Tarr, the characters are automata, human machines seen in absurd performance through Lewis's Bergsonian method of 'the Great Without'. Tarr's mind is full of 'sinister piston-rods, organ-like shapes, heavy drills'; he is a figure in a Vorticist painting, a comic machine man. Lewis rejects 'fiction from the inside', the interiorized novel, on the grounds that it romanticizes and falsifies consciousness. His deliberate displacement of the human figure is a statement about the modern condition in a world where the landscape is assailant, man a motor in an environment, and not a controlling agent. 'As far as one can see, the new "tendency toward abstraction", will culminate, not so much in the simple geometrical forms found in archaic art, but in more complicated ones associated in our minds with the idea of machinery,' T. E. Hulme observed in his 1914 lecture on 'Modern Art', evidently directed in Lewis's functionalist-futurist-vorticist direction.[12] It was an argument far less sympathetic to humanism than Stein's or Woolf's; a new art of hard form was needed. This view was much canvassed in the futurist-vorticist climate of the immediately prewar years; it is this sort of lore that, to different effect, D. H. Lawrence's famous statement about character in the novel comes from: 'It is the inhuman will, call it physiology, or like Marinetti—physiology of matter, that fascinates me. I don't so much care about what the woman *feels* . . . I only care about what the woman *is* . . . You mustn't look in my novel for the old stable *ego*—of the character . . .'[13] This form of abstractionism was both formal innovation *and* a response to an historical circumstance —a commentary on an historical process of mechanization which displaced the human being, and perhaps too the humanist lore that had supported him, from the centre of the world.

There were, then, two justifications for modernist abstraction that were beginning to emerge in the prewar climate. One, espoused by Gertrude Stein, and later Virginia Woolf, saw the new forms as an opportunity for the deeper penetration of the human subject, the path to a new art of consciousness and the unconscious which penetrated beneath the material surface and let the arts grow more intense. This was largely the lore from impressionism. The other was a much bleaker argument, a lore from naturalism; history itself was a depersonalizing force. By the 1920s, after a calamitous war which destroyed

[12] T. E. Hulme, 'Modern Art and Its Philosophy' (1914), reprinted in T. E. Hulme, *Speculations* (ed. Herbert Read) (London, 1924; repr. 1960).

[13] D. H. Lawrence, letter to Edward Garnett, 5 June, 1914: in Harry T. Moore (ed.), *The Collected Letters of D. H. Lawrence* (London, 1962).

much of the content of traditional culture, disoriented morality, displaced older social usages and languages, questioned all rhetoric, and challenged the view that the individual could transact profitably with society or with history, the exterior causalities enforcing abstraction and irony in the arts became that much more apparent. The dread of nothingness, the sense of the landscape as assailant, the conviction of the abstract hostility of the social system, and the belief that modern existence was dominated by processes concerned with the mechanistic destruction of organic life—all these elements of modern awareness, which Frederick J. Hoffman very excellently explores in his book *The Mortal No: Death and the Modern Imagination*, generated, as Hoffman stresses, a new modern concept of form, which became a tense and unstable instrument for expressing disorientation and displacement.[14] There is a disfiguration of character that comes from exterior cause: thus the damaged or wounded human figure—Tietjens, Jake Barnes, Clifford Chatterley—became familiar in the fiction of the 1920s, and we find it too in painting. There were other kinds of exposed character to explore: Musil's man without qualities, Kafka's identityless heroes, Waugh's Bergsonian dancers, on the treadmill of an empty and anarchic social round. Man became a weak actor on a dangerous stage: writers like Rex Warner and Edward Upward explored psychologically unstable figures moving through mechanized, meaningless landscapes; dehumanization was thus incorporated into texts or paintings not as a means toward the intensification of art, but

[14] Frederick J. Hoffman, *The Mortal No: Death and the Modern Imagination* (Princeton, 1964). This interesting study is concerned with the impact of 'the modern manoeuvring of force'—especially war, but also in the massive modern state—on the representation of relations between man, object and nature in literature, which amounts to a total redefinition of the landscape and the place of life and death in it. Hoffman notes:

> One important description of violence is that it serves to threaten the balance of forms. Since forms are a result of the mental and imaginative functions, violence frequently comes from a distortion of one or the other, which throws the formal economy into imbalance. . . . One may explain modern culture by saying that the relationship between the two functions responsible for forms has broken down, that as a result of this failure of balance it has become extremely difficult to comprehend life and death formally. The forms no longer contain the force; the force is unleashed; it is perhaps at the disposal of the intellect, but not reliably of the imagination.

Hoffman thus rightly emphasizes the importance of the war novel in the making of modern literature.

as a mode of response to a disfiguring history, which generated a loss of the self, an alienation, a necessary sense of human absurdity. Thus we might trace two different lineages for modern abstraction—the contrast, say, between Virginia Woolf's aestheticized portraits of consciousness and Waugh's mechanized, modern comic performers. Abstraction thus could manifest not only new content, but a loss of content; it could be assimilated within the work, and become a modern realism. And a very significant proportion of modern style and form has arisen somewhere between these two poles.

IV

Today, of course, we no longer reckon ourselves to be within the age of modernism. During the 1930s through to the 1960s there came a revival of realism, a modification of, indeed in some respects a reaction against the modernist impulse. During the 1950s, the 'angry' writers in England, the neo-existential novelists in France, and the moralistic writers of Jewish-American fiction all sought to bring fiction back toward a humanist and communicative function; so Sartre, in *What Is Literature?* (1949) could actually distinguish prose as the one committedly referential form of expression. More recently, though, there have been many signs of a move toward a neo-modernist or at any rate a decidedly more experimental stance, and so a new phase of enhanced stylistic anxiety. Realist or referential versions of art have been attacked; 'In the fictions of the future,' one critic, Raymond Federman, tells us, 'all distinctions between the real and the imaginary, between the conscious and the unconscious, between the past and the present, between truth and untruth, will be abolished';[15] sceptical and formally self-aware texts and paintings have become dominant again. There are signs, then, of a return to formalism, but this is a formalism negotiated on new terms, so that it is discontinuous with or even hostile to certain kinds of modernist formalism— especially to the modernist tendency to see the social and historical world as chaotic but art itself as redemptive or whole. At the same time, as often happens in experimental seasons, painting and the novel have grown closer together again. Indeed we have seen a whole new cult of synaesthesia, in the happening, the multi-media event, in street theatre

[15] Raymond Federman, 'Surfictions: Four Propositions in the Form of an Introduction', in R. Federman (ed.), *Surfiction: Fiction Now and Tomorrow* (Chicago, 1975)

or performance theatre, which has aimed to break down the fixed generic boundaries of art. Perhaps one essential area of common ground to be found in much contemporary art is indeed that the very idea of art as solid, self-subsistent and hermetically whole has become ironized. Nonetheless there is in much of that new art a determinedly post-realist or abstract dimension. It is very apparent in painting, but it has found its equivalents in all the other media, including the verbal ones: drama, poetry, fiction.

It has been said, by A. Alvarez, that we live today in an era of No Style, an era, that is, where there is such stylistic profusion that it is not possible to identify a significant centre.[16] Certainly in art since 1945 we have seen both an extraordinary creativity and a marked stylistic prolixity. Isms and movements have, as Edward Lucie-Smith aptly notes in his useful survey of painting,[17] succeeded each other with an ever more rapid tempo, and in consequence an historical provisionality has become a marked feature of contemporary artistic production. There is a high rate of stylistic consumption, of style about style, of fashion as form and form as fashion; this has occurred in a late modern situation where the very functions of fashion and style seem to have changed culturally, so that there has been a new symbiosis between *avant garde* derivatives from modernism and especially surrealism and the spirit of the popular and counter culture. Evidently we live, in our late technological world, in a complex transformation of social, sexual, epistemological and political relationships, in which stylistic negotiations have significant social functions. There are bohemians on every street corner, self-parodists in every boutique, neo-artists in every discotheque, and style and narcissism have become global commodities. This new foregrounding of style has led, in discussion of art and writing, to much talk of meta-art, sur-fiction, even para-criticism. Indeed one feature of the scene is that criticism is as active in the matter as creation. Modernist writers did not call themselves modernists, though they employed more local labels for corporate identification and publicity; critics affixed the terms afterwards. But nowadays critics and writers consort together, though often in acts of mutual incomprehension: terms like *nouveau roman*, *surfiction* and *post-modernism* have become both creative and critical currency, to identify creative options for artists and afford overall stylistic postulates for critics.

16 A. Alvarez, *Beyond All This Fiddle: Essays, 1955–1967* (London, 1968).
17 Edward Lucie-Smith, *Movements in Art Since 1945* (London, rev. ed., 1975).

There may indeed be some aesthetic or stylistic wholeness that links together such varied phenomena as theatre of the absurd, the American new journalism, the French new novel, aleatory art and music, and a wide variety of tendencies in painting, ranging from photo-realism to abstract expressionism, from pop art to op art to conceptual art, and takes in, too, new-wave and experimental cinema and the street happening. One element, certainly, is a tendency to question established structures of reality, either by intensifying and probing them to the point of stylization and mockery—as in photo-realist painting, or the work of artists like Hockney or Caulfield, or in documentary or non-fiction novels—or by attempting elaborate acts of scepticism and re-construction, as in the decomposed canvases of Pollock, or the fiction of Borges or Claude Simon. We have seen both a new baroque, in many of the extravagances of pop music and science fiction, and a new minimalism, in the blackness of conceptual art, or the textual silences of a Beckett. The traditional canvas has been penetrated, violated, reconstructed; the writerly text has been reformed, mocked, subdivided; art has aspired to the condition of provisionality and irony, indeed the condition of parody. As painters have focused on the conditions of the medium, so writers have come, often, to concentrate on the lexical surface of their text, presenting something that exists only relatively, dominated not by sympathetic characters, designed formal perspectives (like point-of-view) or ordered systems of value and coherence, but by chance rhythms arising from the free-running opportunities of composition set against the inherited lore of structure and form. The work of art tends to become a game-like construct with which numerous permutations can be played. And the traditional content, based on a clear alliance of writer, character, plot and reader, itself often becomes the subject of the work.

Thus art becomes the instrument by which the contingency of experience can be playfully ordered, given or not given significance, defined or not defined as reality. As for reality, the tendency is to incorporate it on a basis of variable distrust. The dehumanized text or the dehumanized painting are our modern commonplaces; and they also—in the concrete poem, or the pictorialized story of Donald Barthelme—tend to meet and merge. Indeed the foregrounding of text makes the book a visual object, open to various material poses; the format may shift, the text can be treated as phenomenon, the events and episodes can become painterly sequences, and characters can be variant poses in hard space. Meanwhile the author is posed himself, a performer shifting his performance, changing his angle of perception. Sequential narration wanes; the page becomes hard; things are seen as inert or unconnected with human beings, who may themselves become caricatures or fictional objects; text does not yield to sympathy or anthropomorphic identification. Systems and codes dominate: the plots of the social order contend with the plots of language. The author foregoes his or her firm preterite and the discourse of narration; the human other is a figure at the further end of a labyrinth, or a victim of the world's plot, or the word's. Subjective consciousness may expand, or stories may grow hard and ironic, but a direct humanist quest for person and personality grows difficult and perplexed. In paintings, too, the same issues arise; forms are notably soft or notably hard; represent-ation, if offered, is elusive. Systematically then, if for good and under-standable reasons, given the nature of our view of man, the nature of our experience of the world, we are discouraged away from a direct contact with the work, the forging of the nexus of sympathy. Of the consequences we may give two accounts. One is that this is an art that assaults contemporary dehumanization, and calls on our sense of what is missing. The other is that we have acquired an art of detached fic-tional technology in parallel with the world. Indeed much of the work is, on this axis, ambiguous—the paintings of Lichtenstein, the films of Warhol, the 'cybernetic' novels of Pynchon, Burroughs and Gaddis, the hard-style fictions of Handke and Calvino. What does seem evident is that the model of a cybernetic world has led to an art in which the human figure exists itself as a parody—as a role-player, a formless performer, a cardboard cut-out. From this we may draw a dark con-clusion: that many modern writers feel they can yield to us only a post-humanist model of man. Or the lesson may lie in the displacement, so that, as Gabriel Josipovici has argued, negation implies its own opposite.[18]

V

Thinking about these matters as I wrote my novel *The History Man*, I found myself recalling a painting by Goya, called 'A Dog Engulfed by Sand'; this is a museum title, not his own, for it is one of the 'Black Paintings', done from private need on the walls of his own country house somewhere between 1814 and 1819, and then later removed

[18] See Gabriel Josipovici, *The World and the Book: A Study of Modern Fiction* (London, 1971), pp. 293–317.

onto canvas and into the Prado. Goya worked of course, on the turn from neo-classicism to romanticism, and his paintings show that turn in its complexity and variety: there are polite portraits and sensuous nudes, court paintings and canvases of romantic rebellion, paintings of reason and paintings of unreason, such as the earlier, dark Caprichos, with their ambiguous motto: 'The sleep of reason begets monsters.' But the monsters come, especially in the Black Paintings, fantasies done in his darkest period, over a time of political disenchantment and withdrawal, deafness and serious illness, despair and growing nihilism. Anguish, horror, the sleep of reason are unmistakable in them; they are grotesque, surreal works, studies in pain, portraits of suffering and cruelty, desperate images drawn from the dark depths of the imagination, though also from the bleak facts of a war-torn and violent world. The colour-range is narrow and sombre, the faces in the figure paintings contorted, the subjects horrifying—Saturn, or Time, devouring his children; a battlefield seen as a Witches' Sabbath. The paintings make a sequence, but 'A Dog Engulfed by Sand' stands out from the others, and this is mainly because of its element of abstraction.

For on first sight one is not sure whether it is a figure painting at all. There are two dominant blocks of colour, distinct but intersecting: a fainter third panel rises up on the right. In the line where the two main panels meet, low down on the painting, there is a flurried blob of grey paint. Even when we gradually identify the painting as representational—a composition of sky and sand—we have difficulty in identifying this; in fact it is one of Goya's typically anguished heads, the head of a dog, bodiless, protruding up through the point at which the two main planes join, and so oddly perspectivized. We may read this missing body as hidden from us by the contours of the sand, or we may, as the (later) title to the painting suggests, read it as being engulfed in quicksand, caught at the moment before the head, too, disappears. But by either reading the painting acquires an element both of identification and of horror. The head deconceptualizes the painting, and, like a character in a novel, encourages us into entrance, generates empathy, produces realism. The sandy colour becomes sand, the green, brown and blue above becomes pitiless sky. The abstract element remains, but not now as pure form; it is form as the field that surrounds, threatens and ironizes the figure, and hence agonizes the painting. Abstraction is a modern word, at odds with Goya's own aesthetics; in any case, the painting underwent serious restoration in the move from Goya's house to the museum, and some of its abstract effect undoubtedly comes from the loss of detail. Still, the compositional assumptions seem clear. Large blocks of colour in three big planes form the fundamentals of the painting; these emphasize the bodilessness and the smallness of the figure. The painting thus allegorizes or enacts the problem it poses. Its abstraction *enforces* its fantastic realism, because we become aware that not only the pitiless world but form itself engulfs the central figure. It both asserts and denies the idea of pure form; it both qualifies and insists on the figure; it opens up two divergent dimensions of art—one toward a greater and more intense realism, the other toward a greater abstraction.

It would seem highly likely that Picasso knew the painting, and perhaps thought of it in compounding the spirit of his Cubism. And it also seems likely that the Spanish philosopher Ortegay Gasset knew the work; certainly his interesting essay 'The Dehumanization of Art' offers many useful insights on the problems it raises.[19] Ortega's essay deals with modern art, and especially with the tendency of that art to 'dehumanize' itself by taking art away from familiar identifications and involvements into the realm of elite and *avant garde* speculations. The impulses of this art, Ortega says, are striking in that they are 'not of a generically human kind', and this is because the artist feels the need to violate normal perception in order to establish art's true subject, which is art itself. Ortega's proposals closely resemble those of the Russian formalist critic Viktor Shklovsky, whose concept of 'defamiliarization' or 'making strange' has become so important to modern aesthetics.[20] 'The technique of art is to make things "unfamiliar", to make form obscure, so as to increase the difficulty and the duration of perception,' Shklovsky says; Ortega says much the same. But where Shklovsky is more concerned with generating a theory of form and structure from this, Ortega especially emphasizes the change in attitude toward the human figure, the character. 'For the modern artist,' he says, 'aesthetic pleasure derives from . . . triumph over human matter. That is why he has to drive home his victory by presenting in each case the body of the strangled victim'—that 'strangled victim' being the vestigial remnant of the human figure, or the humanist outlook, that remains as a marker in many of the modern arts. This is, however, only an enlargement of the traditional tendency of the

[19] Jose Ortega y Gasset, 'The Dehumanization of Art', first published in English in 1948, repr. in *The Dehumanization of Art and Other Writings* . . .

[20] Viktor Shkolvsky, 'Art as Technique' (1917); repr. in L. T. Lemon and M. J. Reis (eds.), *Russian Formalist Criticism: Four Essays.*

arts: 'Before, reality was overlaid with metaphors by way of ornament: now the tendency is to eliminate the extra-poetical, or real, prop and to "realize" the metaphor, to make it the *res poetica*.' But the difference is one of degree rather than kind: 'All great periods of art have been careful not to let the work of art revolve around human contents.'

Hence, Ortega argues, we are wrong to think of realism as the *norm* of art; rather it is a divergence, 'a maximum aberration in the history of taste'. It was in the nineteenth century only that art was humanized, laid open to our identification, our feelings of direct involvement. Realism and humanism consorted, and men, houses and mountains became, in art, 'our good old friends'. However, it was in the nine-teenth century that narrative and the novel flourished, and there is a special companionship between the novel and realism. In another essay, on the novel, Ortega indeed goes on to argue that the novel is distinct in the way that in it 'imaginary personages appear like living persons,' and hence that the new arts of abstraction have significant consequences for the form, turning its direction and turning it from an art of adventures to an art of figures.[21] This, as I have said, is a familiar recognition; people, as Iris Murdoch says, have indeed long read novels in order to know the world and familiarize themselves with its people, and the novel is a classic art of humanization. And especially there is the novel's concern with what E. M. Forster once called 'roundness' of character, and defined as a kind of love: 'Since the novelist is a human being,' he tells us in *Aspects of the Novel* (1927), 'there is an affinity between him and his subject-matter which is absent in many other forms of art.' And one result of this historical companionship between the novel and realism is that the arts of dehumanization and abstraction tend to function in the form as a kind of irony. In the novel more perhaps than in any other form, we are aware of Ortega's 'strangled victim' and his appeal. Realism and abstraction tend, in many of our great modern works—*Ulysses, As I Lay Dying, The Unnamable*—to tug painfully against each other, to create an art somewhere between metonymy and metaphor, an art where what Forster calls those 'wordmasses..., [the novelist's] characters' lie in an ambiguous place somewhere in the contingent plane of existence *and* in the purified plane of art. Ortega notes this irony, and sees it largely as an aesthetic matter, though he comments on its appeal, and says that there are many modern readers who cannot

21 Ortega y Gasset, 'Notes on the Novel', in *The Dehumanization of Art and Other Writings* . . .

read a work without it. But, as I have argued, it is more than an aesthetic matter, and in many of our best works, from Camus to Kafka, it is the tragic irony of our condition in the modern world.

It is indeed because of this irony that Goya's work exerts such a powerful impression. It is not a work of pure abstraction, or of pure intent toward abstraction; indeed it rather works against abstraction, and toward an extreme or fantastic realism. Working, as he did, at a time when classical aesthetics were giving way to the claims of the romantic and the anguished imagination, Goya is prefiguring nine-teenth-century realism as much as he is twentieth century abstraction; the tension proves his force—a force that made me wish to use the painting as the image on the cover of *The History Man*. For I did not, in my novel, intend to reject realism and its works, but rather to enact the irony. *The History Man* is a novel about dehumanization; behind the book is a strong visual analogy, of a flat, hostile landscape, not our good old friend, of multi-storey car parks, block buildings, blank walls, treeless spaces, run-down city scapes, a graffiti-scarred new university which could, if events require it, be well converted into a factory, a world in which it is hard to put in the person. The characters, too, are hard objects, and there is no entry into their psychology or their con-sciousness: they manifest themselves by their speech and their actions. There is one ostensibly sympathetic character, who speaks for humanism; she is a deception to the reader. The central figure, Howard Kirk, the radical sociologist who, four years after the revolutionary season of 1968, when onerous reality seems wonderfully to lift, tries to sustain his transforming passion in an inert world. But he believes that privacy is over, and the self is no more than the sum of the roles that it plays. Howard acts, but otherwise, in a world where speech-acts and ideas cannot affix themselves to a sense of value in action or history, passivity is the norm. Accidents become important, and so do happenings, those chance events that arise when we give a party or juxtapose students in a classroom. There are no purposeful plots, except Howard's; he plots in a plotless world, hoping to serve the radical plot of history. The dominant tense is the present, diminishing the sense of historical or personal rootedness, making the world instantaneous; the text is hard, presented in long paragraph blocks which immerse the agents and their speech. The mode is irony, and neither the world nor its per-sonages are our good old friend. And realism moves toward a harsh abstraction.

Now styles are not, in the end, pure theories, acts of aesthetic devotion only. Writing does not come like that. Rather they are negotiations with the nature of current experience: modes of epistemology, grammars for apprehending connection or disconnection, explorations of our capacity to construct, or not, meaning and significance. It is a proper anxiety to wonder whether we are making, in art, a world of dehumanization that is not needed, through simple acquiescence in an aesthetic convention. There is enough lore of crisis and enough formal theory about to encourage this. Yet there seems to me every cause why it is that one intuits in the novel a significant change of emphasis: a new topography, a new displaced person, a new style. In the hardened, acryllic realism of Hockney, in the cityscapes of Antonioni, in the arbitrary, contingent psychology of Handke, we can see a tone that is ours. It is notable that the third-person narrator seems a failing figure, that the present tense is becoming the significant narrative tense of much fiction, that the art of a hard landscape and an eviscerated person is dominant, that plot is increasingly generated not from the actions of persons but by a power outside them in which they are forced to acquiesce. Abstraction seems to come into these works because it is outside them, because a sure and solid substantiality is not possible. Today we live in an abstractified, process-centred, depersonalizing world which shrinks and displaces the human figure; we also have theories of behaviourism that validate that shrinkage and displacement. We are capable of confirming the defamiliarized world by consenting to it in thought and in form. The power of Goya's painting is that it enacts abstraction as pain and unease and horror. And part of the fascination of the novel is that, standing, like Goya, somewhere between realism and abstraction, it also contains this tension, the capacity to see the pain in the strangled victim. In all the discussion of contemporary fiction that now surrounds us, obsessed as it is with the new experimentalism, we should, I believe, make a larger space to say so.

INDEX

Index

[*This index excludes footnotes, preface and information given in the notes before each chapter.*]

abstraction 181, 184, 195–8, 200, 204–8
Alter, Robert 137
Alvarez, A. 201
Amis, Kingsley 10, 12, 19
Amis, Martin 14
Antonioni, Michelangelo 208
Aristotle 188
Arnold, Matthew 55, 149
Arnold, Thomas 55
Auerbach, Erich 153
Austen, Jane 25, 149

Bailey, Paul 22
Bainbridge, Beryl 14, 85–6
Ballard, J. G. 14
Balzac, Honoré de 51, 56, 191
Barth, John 45, 111
Bartheleme, Donald 202
Barthes, Roland 27, 119, 183–4, 186
Barzun, Jacques 104
Bayley, John 20, 25, 166
Beckett, Samuel 11, 12, 14, 48, 56, 68–9, 89–102, 110–11, 145, 188, 202
Beerbohm, Max 78
Bellow, Saul 92
Bennett, Arnold 9, 23, 194, 196
Berenson, Bernard 195
Berger, John 30, 50–1, 57
Berger, Peter L. 44
Bergonzi, Bernard 8, 9, 10, 11, 20, 137–8
Bergson, Henri 169
Binns, Ronald 12
Bloom, Harold 21
Borges, Jorge Luis 48, 56, 188, 202
Bowen, Elizabeth 60
Bradbury, Malcolm 53–4, 146–7, 154
Braine, John 12
Brautigan, Richard 111
Brecht, Bertolt 48

Brontë, Emily 161
Brooke-Rose, Christine 14, 70, 110, 134
Bunyan, John 74
Burden, Robert 13, 15
Burgess, Anthony 12, 14, 114, 127–30, 154
Burns, Alan 14, 114–23
Burroughs, William 20, 185, 203
Butor, Michel 51
Byatt, A. S. 9, 13, 14, 15

Calvino, Italo 185, 203
Camus, Albert 207
Cape, Jonathan 103
Capote, Truman 56, 154, 158
Carter, Angela 14, 85–7
Cary, Joyce 194
Caulfield, Patrick 202
Caute, David 46–51
Cervantes, Miguel de 55
Cezanne, Paul 195–7
Champfleury (Jules Husson) 190–1
Charles I 46
Chekhov, Anton 23, 145
Churchill, Sir Winston 56
Cleland, John 189
Clough, Arthur Hugh 55, 149
Compton-Burnett, Ivy 11
Conrad, Joseph 8, 70, 197
Cooper, William 11, 12, 189
Coover, Robert 111
Courbet, Gustave 190–2
Coward, Noel 145
Cowley, Abraham 105
Cromwell, Oliver 46
cubism 195
Culler, Jonathan 92–3

D'Annunzio, Gabriele 61
Dante 31, 160

Darwin, Charles 55, 148, 191
Day, Douglas 90
defamiliarization 205
Degas, Edgar 190
dehumanization 199, 202–3, 205, 207–8
Dickens, Charles 9, 22, 26, 72, 147, 149, 189, 191
Dostoevski, Feodor 26–7, 31, 37, 39
Drabble, Margaret 14, 54, 74–7, 80, 85
Durrell, Lawrence 11, 14, 89, 154

Eliot, George 9, 21–3, 25–6, 30, 147, 190–1
Eliot, T. S. 32, 49, 94
Ellis, Mrs Sarah 67–8
Erskine, Albert 94
Escher, M. C. 54

Fanon, Frantz 46
Farrell, J. G. 14, 30, 57–65, 111
Faulkner, William 94, 197
Fauvism, 195
Federman, Raymond 200
Feydeau, Georges 36
Fiedler, Leslie 93
Fielding, Henry 9, 10, 55, 136, 188
Firbank, Ronald 167
Fitzgerald, Scott 105
Flaubert, Gustave 190–1, 195
Forster, E. M. 8, 25, 37–8, 58, 206
Fowles, John 13, 14, 27–9, 34, 48, 54–5, 63, 136–8, 147–54, 186
Frank, Joseph 194
Frege, G. 124
French Impressionists 192
Friedman, Alan 9
Frith, William 192

Gaddis, William 185, 203
Galsworthy, John 146
Gaskell, Mrs Elizabeth 74, 77
Gasset, Ortega y 105, 205–6
Genet, Jean 20
Gindin, James 9–10
Giroux, Robert 95
Goethe, Johann Wolfgang 22, 25, 27
Golding, William 12, 14, 89, 154
Goldmann, Lucien 50

Goncourt brothers 190
Gordon, Giles 32, 117, 125
Goya, Francisco José de 203–4, 207–8
Graff, Gerald 93
Green, Henry 60
Greene, Graham 11, 14, 161–2, 167

Handke, Peter 185, 203, 208
Hardy, Thomas 148, 150
Hawkes, John 45, 153, 155, 181
Hawthorne, Nathaniel 190
Heath, Stephen 8, 92
Heller, Joseph 20, 45
Hemingway, Ernest 141
Hinde, Thomas 49
Hockney, David 202, 208
Hoffman, Frederick J. 199
Hogarth, William 188
Hollingdale, R. J. 37
Hulme, T. E. 198

Ibsen, Henrik 23, 145
impressionism 191, 198
Irving, Washington 189

Jacobson, Dan 14, 34, 48
James, Henry 8, 10, 21, 25–6, 29, 49, 67–8, 104, 167, 176, 192–3
Jameson, Fredric 186
Jarrell, Randall 104
Johnson, B. S. 13–14, 19, 20, 30, 32–3, 39, 48, 51–3, 111, 114–16, 123–5, 134, 154
Josipovici, Gabriel 14, 30, 91–2, 110, 203
Joyce, James 7–8, 19–94, 103, 142, 194, 196–7

Kafka, Franz 100–1, 141, 185, 199, 207
Karl, Frederick R. 9–10, 24, 157
Keats, John 106–7
Keller, Gottfried 21
Kellogg, Robert 113
Kermode, Frank 9, 43, 127, 129, 157, 163, 171

Lawrence, D. H. 8, 26, 107, 141, 198
Leavis, F. R. 13, 21

Lessing, Doris 12, 14, 34, 38–41, 48, 68, 80–5, 143, 154, 187
Levi-Strauss, Claude 127, 186
Lewis, Oscar 154
Lewis, Wyndham 197–8
Lichtenstein, Roy 203
Life 105
Listener, The 127
Lodge, David 9, 14, 20, 45, 48–9, 136–43, 154
Lowry, Malcolm 11–12, 14, 89–95, 102–11
Lucie-Smith, Edward 201
Luckmann, Thomas 44
Lukacs, Georg 46–8, 50–1

Macaulay, Thomas Babington 55
McCarthy, Mary 31, 39
McEwan, Ian 14
Maclean, Alan 161
Mailer, Norman 20, 91
Mallarmé, Stephane 134
Mann, Thomas 27, 37–8
Manning, Olivia 54
Mansfield, Katherine 188
Marlowe, Christopher 32
Marx, Karl 55, 148
Masefield, John 161
Matisse, Henri 195–6
Meijer, Henk Romijn 165
Millett, Kate 84
Mitchell, Julian 33, 40, 48
Modernism 12, 25, 30, 36, 55, 70, 111, 138, 153, 192, 194–5, 197, 200–1
Moorcock, Michael 14
Morrissette, Bruce 126
Moseley, Nicholas 14
Muggeridge, Malcolm 161
Murdoch, Iris 72, 13–14, 20, 24–5, 27, 30–2, 34–6, 38–9, 60, 68–74, 127, 182, 186, 206
Musil, Robert 199

Nabokov, Vladimir 48, 56, 69, 184
Nashe, Thomas 125
naturalism 191–3, 198
New Journalism 158

Newman, John Henry 161, 163, 168
New Review, The 15
Nietzsche, Friedrich Wilhelm 27, 37
Nouveau roman 8, 13, 93, 134, 155, 164, 185, 201
Nye, Robert 14, 114, 125, 129

Oates, Joyce Carol 79, 84
Observer, The 161
Orwell, George 11–12, 46, 49

parody 13, 23–5, 27, 30, 33, 37, 40, 133–9, 142–3, 145–8, 152, 154–5, 202–3
pastiche 23, 30, 134–6, 139, 143, 145, 147–8, 151–2, 154–5
Pater, Walter 191
Peake, Mervyn 60
Picasso, Pablo 195–7
Poe, Edgar Allan 106–7
Poetry Society, The 161
Poirier, Richard 101, 110
Pollock, Jackson 202
Post-impressionism 196
Post-modernism 10, 13, 91, 93, 134, 138, 151, 158–9, 163, 171, 184, 201
Powell, Anthony 14, 41
Pre-Raphaelites 153
Proust, Marcel 70, 92, 196
Pynchon, Thomas 20, 45, 50, 111, 153, 185, 203

Quin, Ann 14

Raban, Jonathan 22–3
Rabelais, François 125
Rabinowitz, Rubin 9–10
Ratcliffe, Michael 166
Read, Herbert 194
realism 9–11, 13–15, 19–22, 24–7, 30–1, 33–4, 36, 47–8, 51, 55–8, 90, 92–4, 113–14, 134, 136–7, 141–3, 146–7, 151–2, 154–5, 158–9, 166, 168–9, 172, 178, 181–6, 189–94, 200, 205–7
Reed, Douglas 165
Richardson, Samuel 67

Robbe-Grillet, Alain 21, 27, 126, 134, 159, 164, 176, 187
Romanticism 189
Ryder, Albert Pinkham 105

Sage, Lorna 167
Sage, Victor 44
Sand, George 21
Sarraute, Nathalie 21, 51, 70, 158
Sartre, Jean-Paul 24, 30, 58, 70, 200
Scholes, Robert 13, 45, 113–14, 127–8
Scott, Paul 14, 54
Scott, Sir Walter 47, 51, 56, 189
Severn, Joseph 107
Shakespeare, William 26, 35
Shaw, Bernard 23, 145
Shelley, Mary 161
Shelley, Percy Bysshe 106
Shklovsky, Viktor 205
Sillitoe, Alan 12
Simon, Claude 134, 155, 202
Sinclair, Andrew 114, 126
Smiles, Samuel 55
Snow, C. P. 19–20, 29
Sollers, Philippe 51
Solzhenitsyn, Alexander 45, 51
Somerville and Ross 60
Spark, Muriel 12–14, 34, 48, 78–9, 84, 86, 154, 157–79, 186
Spengler, Oswald 46
Stanford, Derek 161
Stein, Gertrude 195–8
Stein, Leo 195
Steiner, George 28
Stern, J. P. 55–6, 58, 94

Sterne, Laurence 99, 125, 136, 188
Stevens, Wallace 43–4
Storey, David 12, 14, 26–7
Sturrock, John 8
Sukenick, Ronald 183
surfiction 201
surrealism 201

Tanner, Tony 8
Tennyson, Alfred, Lord 55, 149
Tolstoy, Leo 38, 50–1, 56, 70
Tomlinson, Charles 116
Trilling, Lionel 13, 25
Turner, Joseph Mallord 192

Upward, Edward 199

Vonnegut, Kurt 45, 111, 187

Wain, John 12
Warhol, Andy 203
Warner, Rex 199
Waugh, Evelyn 78, 167, 169, 199, 200
Wheatley, Dennis 172
Whistler, James McNeill 192
Wilson, Angus 12–14, 22–4, 27, 29, 34, 36–8, 53, 136–8, 143–7, 154
Winstanley, Gerrard 46
Wittgenstein, Ludwig 24, 110
Wolfe, Tom 56, 104
Woolf, Virginia 7–8, 19, 30, 68, 141, 196–8, 200
Wordsworth, William 161
Worringer, Wilhelm 197